Endorsements

"*Rooted in the Stars, Planted on the Earth* is a vital contribution to the current spiritual conversation around the tough choices we each have to make when embracing our unique human divinity. Annette's story emboldens every woman to embrace the Sacred Feminine and demonstrates that, while we seek the heavens, true power lies in the manner in which we embody spirit through our humanity. Her voice as a brilliant psychotherapist, teacher, and mystic healer shines brightly, and she writes with the profound humility of an authentic and deeply courageous holy woman. The book is a gift for us all."

—Carol Rich, MEd, Corporate Leadership Development Educator and Trainer

"For such a sensitive soul as Annette to stand in witness to the Divine Feminine as She has manifested in our lifetime, and remain conscious while doing so, is remarkable. To have done so with tenderness and humor, spinning a yarn while teaching us, is a miracle and a gift."

—Pat B. Allen, PhD, ATR, author of *Art Is a Spiritual Path, Art Is a Way of Knowing*, and *Cronation*

"Annette's story is a gift for the collective because it expresses the commonality of the feminine voice—the creative, compassionate voice—that yearns to be brought into our world. So many of us are saddled with a crippling theology, and we need a new theology of honesty before God, oneself, our families, and society. This kind of refreshing theology of knowing we are loved unconditionally is in Annette's story, and she gives us a model for living it. She has known and made peace with profound suffering in her life and carries a deep spiritual sensitivity because of her journey. Besides her wonderful human quality, she is gifted shamanically and has a rich sense of humor and a practical common-sense way of living. She is an embodied mystic, and her book shows us the path."

—Fredrick R. Gustafson Jr., DMin, Diplomate Jungian Analyst, Lutheran Minister, and author and editor of *The Moonlit Path: Reflections on the Dark Feminine, Dancing Between Two Worlds: Jung and the Native American Soul, Pierre Teilhard de Chardin and Carl Gustaf Jung: Side by Side,* and *The Black Madonna of Einsiedeln: An Ancient Image for Our Present Time*

"Annette Hulefeld has written an astounding spiritual autobiography that crackles and glows with insight and humor, tragedy and heroism, madness and mystic realization. In *Rooted in the Stars, Planted on the Earth*, Hulefeld eloquently traces her lifelong struggle to deliver a song from God—a 'song that embrace[s] the sacredness of [the] human body, a body that was one with the Divine.' Over the decades, she comes to recognize and free herself from the shackles of patriarchy that disfigure and destroy family, culture, economics, religion, and self-identity. As she strains and stumbles to move her life forward, she slowly, painfully discovers her own authentic star-born self—a fully embodied spirit.

Throughout her fascinating life, a mystical part of her being always knows she has an intense and fundamental connection to the Divine. Hulefeld experiences many encounters with Jesus but also realizes that the Divine Mother has continued to guide her in new directions in order to bring her to a fuller realization of her mission to share the story that the Divine lives in us all. We see her evolve her family's heritage and 'honor all women who believe they are crazy and do not belong because they have not embraced being mystics in everyday life.' This book is a radiant gem and will be of great interest to both women and men who are yearning to become whole and holy human beings."

—Charles Burack, PhD, author of *Leaves of Light* and *Songs to My Beloved*

"While reading this magnificent book, I experienced the heartbeat of God and heard the music of the Universe. Annette invites us on her soul's journey—a journey that expresses strength in raw vulnerability and finds the wisdom of humor in her challenges. She encapsulates the Warrior Woman of Feminine Rising. Annette's connection to the Divine is as natural as her next breath. Her narrative is powerful—her essence forever changing the landscape of our Universe. This book is for those whose spirit yearns to experience the power of transformation."

—Rev. Ruth Lesher, MDiv, MA, ELCA Pastor, Hospice Chaplain

"The longing and yearning of a spiritual life is to be touched by God, and Annette is touched. Through the telling of her own healing and spiritual journey, she reminds us that the poverty of spiritual intimacy and loneliness of our times is a yearning for spiritual connection with each other and all creation. Her words remind us to follow a spiritual path and to embrace the invitations wherever they may lead us. In writing about where she was led, Annette shows how this is where the richness of soul, the path of service, and the very mystery of life unfold."

—Myron Eshowsky, MA, Shamanism Teacher, Codirector of the Social Health Care Project for Syrian Refugee Children and Families, Founding Member of the International Consortium for the Treatment and Research in Transgenerational Trauma, and author of *Peace with Cancer: Shamanism as a Spiritual Approach to Healing*

"This is the story of someone journeying to the center of a labyrinth—now finding a way forward, now running into a dead end, but always getting closer to the center. However long and difficult the journey, what is clear is that grace is never absent, and in the end we catch a glimpse of the 'good enough'—(far more than 'good enough'!)—woman that Annette is and continues to become."

—Father Steve Bevans, SVD, author and editor of more than twenty books, including *Models of Contextual Theology, An Introduction to Theology in Global Perspective*, and (with Roger Schroeder) *Constants in Context: A Theology of Mission for Today*; the Louis J. Luzbetak, SVD, Professor of Mission and Culture at Catholic Theological Union in Chicago

"In *Rooted in the Stars, Planted on the Earth*, readers get to meet a rare person filled with healing light and love. I was first Divinely guided to Annette Hulefeld a few short months after the sudden death of my forty-three-year-old wife. Annette's wisdom and compassion changed the trajectory of my life—her shamanic gifts opened a window to a new paradigm of spirituality for me. I am forever grateful and so happy she is sharing her gifts with the world in this book."

—Tom Zuba, author of *Becoming Radiant: A New Way to Do Life Following the Death of a Beloved* and *Permission to Mourn: A New Way to Do Grief*

"Readers for many, many years to come will benefit from the transformational message of Annette's book."

—Connie Kaplan, author of *The Invisible Garment: 30 Spiritual Principles that Weave the Fabric of Human Life* and *The Woman's Book of Dreams: Dreaming as a Spiritual Practice*

"An amazing story of self-discovery and self-acceptance. As a young woman, I found this story of learning to love your whole self and the journey that life brings uplifting and inspiring."

—Anne Adams, MD

"In 1993, my oncologist notified me that my cancer had metastasized to my bone. Annette then led a healing service for me, attended by many friends of my faith community. Later in the week, the report from the CAT scans revealed there was no evidence of cancer. A friend said, 'It was a miracle, that's for sure,' and truly Annette was a Divine channel of love that evening. She continues to be an instrument and a source of inspiration for those seeking a deeper relationship with God—I'm so happy she has written a book to share this gift. I felt God's presence that day, and, through Annette's story, others can also know that God is among us."

—Carole Albores, MSW

"In this elegant book, Annette has captured the mundane, the raucous, and the profound, giving people permission to experience the whole bailiwick of spirituality through her powerful writing. Annette's path is accessible to anyone, but especially to women who juggle and try to hold the tension between ordinary life and spiritual transformation.

There is also a thread of grief in Annette's story, but grief doesn't annihilate her. Instead, she shows the way of coexisting with grief, facing levels of discomfort most of us cannot step into or put words to. She was able to move forward on intuition even when there were no clear signs. Her path is an inspiration to us all."

—Shay Harris, LCSW

*Rooted in the Stars,
Planted on the Earth*

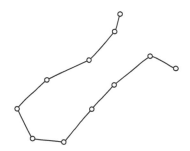

ANNETTE M. HULEFELD
DMIN, LCSW

Rooted in the Stars, Planted on the Earth

One Woman's Path to Embodied Mysticism

Printed in the United States of America

First Edition: May 2019
10 9 8 7 6 5 4 3 2 1

Library of Congress Cataloging-in-Publication Data
Hulefeld, Annette M.
Rooted in the stars, planted on the earth: one woman's path
to embodied mysticism / Annette M. Hulefeld.—1st ed. p. cm.
ISBN Paperback: 978-1-61066-075-4
ISBN Digital: 978-1-61066-076-1
Library of Congress Control Number: 2019902164

Writers of the Round Table Press and the logo
are trademarks of Writers of the Round Table, Inc.

Writers of the Round Table Press
PO Box 1603, Deerfield, IL 60015
www.roundtablecompanies.com

Publisher: **Corey Michael Blake**
President: **Kristin Westberg**
Editor: **Aleksandra Corwin**
Cover Artist: **Bridget Steed, MA, LMHC**
Cover Layout: **Sunny DiMartino**
Interior Designer: **Christy Bui**
Proofreaders: **Adam Lawrence, Carly Cohen**

To Frank—the love of my life, best friend, partner, and Earth angel. You have always seen the light of my soul and gently called it forth—keeping the flame alive, even during those times it was close to being extinguished.

To Grandma Helen, Aunt Anna, and Ma—and to all women who are diminished, labeled unworthy, and silenced as they struggle to remember their divine nature within the confines of a human body.

Contents

Introduction

Living on the Fault Line

Annette Hulefeld is one of countless women in whom, as she likes to say, "the feminine spirit has been held hostage." Like many of us who came into embodied existence as female at this particular time in history, Annette has experienced life as if living on a fault line where seismic shifts are constantly occurring between the seen and the unseen realms. The quest to live and love, raise a family, do good, and serve God in the material world, while carrying the terror of internalized self-hatred passed down through generations of misogyny, has manifested in women everywhere as a paralyzing illness both physical and emotional. Few are perhaps tasked with so much awareness of the task at hand. Annette, from her earliest days, was extraordinarily aware of the Divine—she spoke to trees and birds, felt God's seamless love in all of creation. Ordinary reality dealt her a tough hand in the form of a lineage of mental illness among her female relatives and abuse at the hands of those whose job it was to love and protect her.

As I read this work, her spiritual autobiography, I found myself envisioning Annette's story as the crest of the next wave of authentic, embodied mysticism. Annette has given voice to experiences that are not uncommon but are rarely spoken of in detail by generations of women devoted to service, family, and God. These women suffer whenever they step out of a submissive role, claim an iota of agency, or claim the divine right of holiness that resides in the female form. Society has conspired to shame each woman into imagining she is uniquely unworthy, she is meant for the background, and she has nothing valuable to add or offer. I suspect as women read Annette's story it will spark flickers of recognition and memories of being told, directly and more often silently and covertly, that we are insufficient, unworthy, and to blame for all that went wrong for others.

In the present patriarchal reality largely defined by male-directed religions, culture, and commerce, the feminine spirit has been subservient at best, persecuted and demonized at worst. Annette shares her story of following the golden thread of Spirit and pulling on that thread to unravel the lies that keep both women and men in a kind of slavery of a false narrative. The knots and "nots" are undone by her willingness to live and name the suffering they bind us to.

The second profound theme of Annette's story is her epic version of the hero's journey to reclaim her personal sense of sacred worth. Unlike many, Annette did not forget the bliss of union with the Divine and would gladly have given up earthly existence to reunite with God at almost any point. This was not to be her path. Instead, like a passion play based on Joseph Campbell's *Masks of God*, she was called to travel to all the corners of the earth to learn and commune with the infinite faces of God via teachers, shamans, and gurus and to return to share with us the Truth: all faces are the faces of the Divine, every expression shows but an aspect of the great mystery. There is no one truth that will set you free except that we are all vessels of God; so are you and me and Annette and everyone.

I have known Annette for over twenty years. I experienced a soul retrieval through her journeying on my behalf. She often visited my art studio and created countless collages from the most ordinary magazines that in her hands became exquisite tributes to the Divine Feminine. Every aspect of her life has been a teaching of the capaciousness, the breathtaking variety, the infinitude of the Divine. In her work as a therapist, shaman, and lay minister in the Catholic tradition that denies women the priesthood, she has integrated the teachings of countless masters, both men and women from ancient and indigenous traditions. Through her haunting singing voice, her poetry, her art, her humor, and, yes, her irreverent expressions, she bears witness to the Great Mother, to the God expression that is Jesus and to the holiness of material reality of the natural world.

Annette teaches each of us a truth that is often lost in our current world, although it was told to us in simple enough words years ago by Einstein: "Energy cannot be created or destroyed, but simply transformed." Our experiences of loss, violation, or pain are never erased, but they remain as potentials within our energy field to be called up for further transformation as we grow and change. To imagine that there is some sort of spiritual photoshop program that cancels out the abuse at the hand of a misguided parent or the bitter words of a teacher is to underestimate God. If God contains all things, as we ourselves become more whole, and therefore more holy, must we not also contain more? Whether expressed in celebration or agony, as a physical illness or a mystical insight, if we are all connected, must we not gladly own and kindly bear that which was given us? Annette teaches us that we can also change our understanding of the whys and wherefores of these strands of our story. Ultimately, no stitch is dropped, no stone denied to the builder but rather, all that, accepted and forgiven, added to the collage that we are, only having found the place of harmony, the right spot to rest the hand over and over again.

Born to be one of those who rebirth the consciousness of the Divine Feminine, Annette Hulefeld has shared her map to follow the "grief of holy longing" that will make and remake the world, enlarging it over and over as we come face-to-face with whatever aspect of the Divine we need to know at this moment. Both women and men, as they read her story, will find solace and strength to bear and to understand their own cross, the place where their story intersects with the ever-unfolding story of God. I, for one, am eternally grateful and deeply moved.

Pat B. Allen, PhD
Berkeley, California
October 2018

PART
ONE

Riptides

CHAPTER 1

No Intention of Being Born

Our birth is but a sleep and a forgetting;
The Soul that rises with us, our Life's Star,
Hath had elsewhere its setting
And cometh from afar;
Not in entire forgetfulness,
And not in utter nakedness,
But trailing clouds of glory do we come
From God, who is our Home.

—WILLIAM WORDSWORTH

Life began on May 25, 1942, at approximately 2:55 pm, although Ma claimed to have little memory of this event. She recalled that I was reluctant to come into the world and decided to appear only after I heard the family doctor declare, "She has no intention of being born. We'll have to pull her out by a caesarian section." As Pa remembered it, Ma went into labor after she ate a grilled cheese sandwich, minus the usual bacon and tomato slices, and washed it down with a glass of chocolate milk. I suspect that, once I heard the threat of being born under the knife, I decided to take things into my own hands and come forth naturally.

I often wonder if other people remember hesitating before entering this life, having second thoughts about the mother who is about to hold them. I believe that my old-soul baby bones knew that Ma and I were allergic to each other. Her umbilical cord was thick with nutrients of terror and distrust, whereas my intuitive soul was alive with God's peace. Since birth, I was nurtured by my eternal connection to Source, a memory that made it easy to be attuned to the spirit world. I'd agreed to be an angel for the Divine, delivering a basket of heavenly goods that would magically help people remember they were loved. But coming through my mother's birth canal muddied up this spiritual dream in ways I could not have imagined.

Ma and I were fierce competitors from my first breath of air. I believe we already knew the script we'd agreed to. We developed an invisible, deadly energy field between us that disguised the intention of Soul to live itself through me. Ma was obsessed with keeping me in her protective bubble, safe from the snares of the world, and I wanted nothing more than to be happy playing with God, catching sunbeams, and riding the wind. During my twenties, I had a recurring dream, which, at first, I dis-

Why have a human body when Spirit was so delightful?

missed as funny and irrelevant. In the dream, I was a jolly, chubby, cherub-looking six-month-old baby riding a motorized cloud. I'd soar ecstatically through the vast heavens, swooping down occasionally to earth. If I sensed any distress on earth, I'd jettison back home to God, leaving behind clouds of dust. Why have a human body when Spirit was so delightful? But the dream reflected my life's path and how often I tried to escape my mission for this lifetime: to confront the curse of dispossession and the stain of abuse that shaped the lives of every female member of Ma's family, going back several generations. I was no exception. My humanity dreaded this difficult task, and I often disassociated from life—and returned to the safety of God's love—through spirituality.

Life, however, always pulled me back. The impulse of my personal evolution tackled me over and over throughout the years, reminding me of one simple truth: I came into the world with a song to deliver from the Divine—a song that embraced the sacredness of my human body, a body that was one with the Divine.

By the age of sixty-three, I'd come to appreciate how my life had unfolded, and how a unique collage had been created and had emerged. And then my dad died.

Pa was an ordinary, roly-poly, soft-spoken, and good-natured guy. He had an infectious, hearty laugh and nothing triggered his silliness like sitting on a whoopee cushion or farting for real to annoy my mother. He'd rhythmically clack his false teeth together when Ma scolded him for his undignified behavior. Pa delighted in food, which was his drug of choice after he quit smoking three packs of Camels a day. He shone like a hundred-watt bulb while describing his favorite breakfast: eggs, ham, and pancakes at Denny's restaurant. Ma scowled and clucked like a wet hen when he snuck chocolates or crème-filled doughnuts from the cupboards for his midnight snacks. I never blamed him for his choice of comfort. My mother was a force of nature, one of the most consistently unpleasant, negative people I've ever encountered. Pa had the genuine heart of an angel and loved her to a fault. He'd admonish me when I complained about Ma's constant criticism. "I don't want to hear a thing from you. You have no idea where she came from or what she's lived through." End of story. I suspect that, during the early years of their marriage, he hoped his love would soften Ma's ragged edges. Maybe if he showed her enough love, she'd realize she was different than the insane family she was born into.

Pa retired from his tax business at the age of eighty-one, and the happy-go-lucky businessman I knew quickly shriveled up. His body developed congestive heart failure and kidney disease. His refuge from my mother's never-ending volley of anger, and her *nothing is good enough* mantra, was the basement of their home. It was a smelly, moldy, dark space filled with Ma's hoarding collection of craft and art supplies. He rarely complained about his dungeon, as it was the one space Ma could no longer invade. Her severely arthritic knees kept her from climbing up and down stairs. She could yell at him from the top of the stairs, but he would turn off his hearing aid. All he needed was his trusted TV to watch baseball games, his recliner chair, and hidden stashes of chocolates.

The straw that broke the camel's back happened when Pa was having a heart episode. He called up the basement stairs for help, but Ma didn't hear him because she was on the phone. When she gabbed, it was loud and long. Pa dragged himself up the stairs, slumped over a kitchen chair, and asked her to call 911. When the paramedics arrived, they tried to force open the back door that had swelled up from the stifling summer heat. Ma screamed, "You idiots! Stop! You're destroying my house. Stop it right now." At her command, the medics raced to the front door, stepping into the parlor with a stretcher and oxygen. Ma's hysteria rose to a fever pitch: "You can't bring *that* in here, you jackasses. You're going to scratch up and damage all my furniture." Dad had to be carried out in the arms of the medics.

When Pa returned home from the hospital, as he climbed the back stairs, he leaned against the porch railing, and said to me: "She's killing me. Her damn furniture is more important than I am." I put my arms around his shriveled spirit, while thick tears slid down his pale cheeks. "I know, Dad." That was not the moment to remind him that Ma's life was fueled in large part by fear that he would die and abandon her. I'd escaped her cruelty by taking the high road he'd suggested years ago—I moved twelve hundred miles away and rarely visited. "I've missed you so much." I hid my tears, feeling defeated that I'd not protected him from Ma's insanity and that I'd missed one of the warning signs of Alzheimer's—uncontrollable rage, which Ma was clearly exhibiting. My heart sank to see his shoulders sink down into his ribs, taking on the appearance of two worn-out tires that could no longer be patched up. It's one thing to detach intellectually from a situation, and another to touch your dad's wounded heart.

Several months later, after two grueling years of dialysis, Pa chose to stop his treatments and, in so doing, end his life. When Ma was placed in a nursing home, Pa lived in an assisted-living facility, which were some of the best times of his life. He ate regular, deliciously prepared meals, golfed with his buddies, and flirted with every woman in the facility. I still giggle remembering how, when I'd visit and walk with him around the building, invariably, sweet little ladies opened their windows, and twittered, "Oh Ray, Oh Ray!" As his days on the earth wound down, Pa moved into the same nursing home that Ma was in, and his room was right around the corner from hers. Two days before his death, he asked me to wheel him into her room to say goodbye. A bone-deep weariness had settled into his deteriorating body, along with a peaceful acceptance of his finality. At first, when he saw Ma, he bowed his head, but then he slipped his hands through the bars of the bed, gently touching the sapphire-and-diamond bracelet on her wrist. It was the last anniversary gift he'd given her. His bruised, blotchy hand returned to his lap. "Marie, it's time for me to say goodbye. Where I go, I will prepare a room for you to come. I have always loved you. I will see you sometime. Now, don't cry."

Her dementia lifted in that moment, sucking her life force into her ultimate nightmare. "You can't leave me!" Her body collapsed into a corpse-like position and she muttered, "I love you too, Ray." Overcome with swirling, stunned emotions, I pushed Pa's wheelchair out into the corridor. Call him crazy, label him dysfunctional, Pa was still a Jesus nugget in that moment. He promised she'd never be abandoned and he'd wait for her. Given that my dad claimed to be an atheist, it was ironic that he chose his last words from Holy Scripture.

I sat with my dad until his swollen body suffocated itself and invisible wings delivered his spirit back into the heart of the universe. I firmly believe he left this earth several hours before his pacemaker gave out. And that was a blessing because he was denied morphine until the last half hour—his caretaker felt it could be addicting. As Pa's loud gurgling finally stopped, creating an eerie silence, I looked out the window and noticed that two pinwheels, spinning in opposite directions, came to a standstill. All I could manage was to tenderly close the lids over his vacant eyes and whisper, *Hey Pa, I love you—watch over me, please.*

I made sure Ma attended Pa's wake and funeral service, although my brothers were slightly annoyed by this decision. But the gods were on my side for this one. As I wheeled her in into the funeral home, I felt a twinge of sorrow for her. In her right mind, she would have been mortified at her appearance. Her hair was unkempt, and cowlicks were sticking up like rooster tails. In her younger days, she took great pride in her fashionable wardrobe, but now her dress was a faded, baggy flowered print shift, and her fingers were naked. The nursing home staff removed her flashy jeweled rings (some fake and some real) from each of her fingers. She stared at Pa in the coffin and suddenly leaned forward and touched his hand. "Well, you know I was a witch, but I loved you." Had I not been so engrossed in feeling sorry for her, I might have fallen into the coffin, head first.

Pa was a proud veteran of World War II, so my brothers and I made sure he had a military funeral. He would have gotten a chuckle from the military three-volley salute at his gravesite, carried out by four very elderly, frail veterans. I'm not sure what he thought when hot spent cartridges ejected willy-nilly into the crowd of mourners. Then, when one of the veterans smartly returned the rifle to his side, he struck the ground a bit too hard and his rifle fell into pieces. My brothers and I managed to suppress the urge to burst out snorting with laughter, containing ourselves until we rode back to the funeral home in the hearse. I am sure the driver was ready to have us committed to an asylum. We regained our composure for the reception after the service, which was an ordinary feast of delicacies for a simple, small-town man: beans and franks, ham salad, and stale cookies. We were certain Pa was overjoyed with our choices. Ma would have been mortified by our bourgeois taste.

Afterwards, back home, I poked my head into the living room, where my older brother was packing up Ma's china for auction. I then decided to make one last visit to my childhood bedroom. It was piled up with old cigar boxes stuffed with cards and letters Pa had sent to Ma over the years, along with funeral memorial prayer cards and old recipes. Reluctantly I picked up bundles of stuff, all neatly held with brittle rubber bands. I am neither sentimental nor a collector, so my immediate inclination was to pitch all the "junk." But then, out of nowhere, two discolored triple-folded sheets of paper floated down, landing on my foot. A cold shiver gripped my guts for a moment and traveled quickly through my veins. *Had Pa's spirit drifted in through the window?* Trembling, I picked up and unfolded the papers. I intuitively knew that, in spite of the beautifully crafted Catholic penmanship, this was an omen of bad news. In the upper right-hand corner of page 1 was my birth date and time of birth. Although I had some knowledge of what an astrology reading looked like, I was dumfounded to think Ma would have subscribed to something she'd believed was "straight from the devil" rubbish. The time was also different than what is recorded on my birth certificate.

I shouted out to my brother, asking if he knew of any astrologers in our family. "Yup . . . one of our cousins. Ma said she was nuts. Nice, but nuts." As if a photo album unfastened in my mind, I remembered this cousin of mine who was a strikingly beautiful woman with wavy, copper-red hair. She was a brilliant violinist, and when she sang arias from *Madame Butterfly*, I was transported into other worlds. I wasn't told about it, but my cousin ended her life when she was in her late thirties. I vaguely recall overhearing someone whisper at her wake, "Poor thing, just one of those bad-luck accidents." I was seven years old and remember gently setting down the chocolate chip cookie I was munching on, having a funny feeling in my tummy but not grasping the drift of events.

Ma had asked this cousin to create an astrological reading about me when I was born? Or it was a gift? Slightly dizzy, with my heart pounding, I rapidly scanned the personality traits predicted for me. *You are excitable, mentally agile, insist on doing things your own way, easily influenced by kindness, and have a flair for the written word.* Further, I had an *affectionate nature, untapped artistic and musical abilities, pioneering abilities, ambitions to be in high office, and a climber of every kind of obstacle fate would put in my way.* All of this was relatively accurate, including my seeking higher office in the political world. The reading foretold that *I would lose a brother or sister, and that I would lose my father at an early age, not necessarily by death but because he would leave no provisions for our care and welfare.* Pa declared bankruptcy three times while I was growing up, and Ma had two miscarriages.

As I flipped to the last page, I was distracted by a scratchy, elevated bump under my fingertips. It was a distinct streak of yellowed white-out, concealing the last sentence on the page. My voice cracked as I nervously asked my brother to get me a pocketknife. He was muttering obscenities about all the work he was stuck with and told me that the knives had already been packed away. I'd been raised on the "necessity is the mother of invention" slogan, so I went to work on the dried ink with a buffalo-head nickel. *Sweet Mother of God*, I gasped, as the following words appeared: "*People afflicted with this sign can cause injury to others or even death to themselves at an early age.*" *Sweet Jesus*, there had been six suicides in my mother's family, and I'd wrestled almost daily with the dread that I'd kill myself before I was forty.

My knees buckled, and I flopped onto the floor in slow motion, the paper clenched in my clammy palms. Two pieces of paper, one sentence, a bomb detonating in my brain. As if I were riding one of those nauseating carnival rides, all I wanted was for someone to slam on the brakes. To steady myself, I knelt on the wood floor and prayed.

My inner turmoil sucked me back into a vortex of childhood memories. I could see the original pink cotton-candy walls of my bedroom, which glowed as if drops of blood-red dye had fallen into the paint. And there was the robin's-egg-blue furniture Ma had painted, then added ornamental brush strokes that looked like evil fish eyes to me. They were a constant reminder that Ma never let me out of her sight. I could hear myself silently screaming, *Stop it, stop it. You don't have to remember how Ma fondled you like a baby doll, how she played with you when the lights went out. Stop it. Don't lift the lid of that old desk you used in grade school. Forget the cryptic doodlings you hid there to mask your horror at what your mother was doing to you. Jesus, help me.*

Like film unspooling from a reel, my childhood terrors spun out of control. I recalled how I learned to flip over the footboard of the bed to get out, trying to escape Ma's advances and her roving clutches. When that didn't work, I'd psychically leave my body at night and commune with God, visiting my buddy Jesus in the cottonwood tree in our backyard. I pretended that the statue of the Blessed Mother in the corner of my bedroom was protecting the room so I could return when it was safe. Mary was my invisible Wonder Woman.

Looking about my old bedroom, I recollected the clothes bureau, whose drawers were so warped, it was nearly impossible to open or close them. Every Friday before I returned from school, Ma dumped the contents of the drawers onto the floor and demanded that I refold everything and put it back in perfect order. I hated her for making me do this. I would silently say the rosary during those times, begging the Virgin Mother to wash away the stains of my mean-spirited thoughts.

It wasn't until my older brother slammed the kitchen door that I realized I'd disappeared into my past. I composed myself by pretending to cough, as if a fly had gotten caught in my throat. I swore at my brother. "For Christ's sake, you know how I pee in my pants when someone startles me. And I don't have any clean underwear to put on—my suitcase is locked. You are just like Ma—having to slam every door in sight."

"Well, you always were the scaredy-cat. Get a grip," he said in a voice just as ornery as Ma's, but with a twinkle in his eye. "Sort out the rest of this crap or pitch it all—time is a-wasting."

"Okay, but first tell me what happened to the Blessed Mother statue I used to have?" My brother told me that Ma had put it in the attic, but it was in her way one day, and she accidentally kicked it down the stairs. Somehow telling him that the Mary statue had been my only real mother didn't seem fitting at that moment. He'd never understand that Ma was a motherless mother and I was a motherless child. I have no doubt he would have laughed out loud, sputtering something like "Deal with it, Sis—like it or not, she's your mother. Tough luck of the draw. Move on."

I went back to clearing out Ma's closet, swearing under my breath to relieve the tension. The closet was bulging with clothes, some never worn, the price tags still intact. There were old clothes in different sizes, ball gowns, and the pink-crepe, jeweled dress Ma had chosen for herself to wear in her casket. Realizing I wouldn't have time to empty a closet packed like a sardine can, I decided instead to sort out Ma's shoes and purses. I counted: there were fifty boxes of shoes, mostly never walked in, and fifty matching purses, all neatly stacked according to color and price tag. Each purse had a matching rosary, a dime, and a white peppermint. The prettiest rosary was sterling silver, resting in a white beaded evening bag.

As I giggled over possible explanations for these three items being in every purse, my brother yelled out that it was time to take me to the "stupid" airport. As I got up to go, I paused, knowing I'd never see this room again. The house was for sale. I remembered how, when I left for college, Ma took over my room as her own. She replaced the lumpy old mattress with an expensive Serta sleeper, replaced the chipped hand-painted headboard with a massive, antique fortress made of dark oak. She had no problem making a statement that she was the Queen Mother. Where there once had been the imprint of my chubby body, she had 157 stuffed animals (I tallied them): mostly cuddly dogs, soft kitties, brightly colored birds, and a few fragile porcelain baby dolls, all neatly placed on the heirloom bedspread crocheted by Ma's aunt. At the foot of the bed were mounds of afghans and chenille bedspreads. It boggled my mind to think how long it must have taken for her to clear the bed at night and to restore her belongings in perfect order the next morning.

There was also the rocker that couldn't be rocked because it was wedged between the wall and the cabinet. It served as a throne for several long-bodied porcelain dolls sitting on magazines. Pa wryly commented that the room was an obstacle course he couldn't navigate, and that gave him permission to sleep in another room.

Feeling zapped and confused once again, I stared at the scrunched-up piece of paper in my hand. I was overwhelmed by an unnamable queasiness propelling a dash to the bathroom to vomit. On the one hand, although she clung to me like heavy-duty Saran wrap, and I often felt suffocated by her possessiveness, I'd come to peace about who Ma was. On the other hand, how was I going to make sense of this astrological revelation? The predictions weren't *that* earth-shattering. There was truth in many of the statements. Equally important, I hadn't harmed anyone deliberately, and I hadn't killed myself—although I came close. Still, my mind was fuzzy and unsettled, and I didn't know why.

While driving to the airport, I chose not to share the reading with my brother. Instead, I told him about finding all the rosaries in Ma's purses. That made sense, as Ma was very devoted to the Blessed Mother and relied on her for help. The dimes? You'd better have a dime ready to call the police. And the mints? Ma prided herself about never having bad breath. We cracked up laughing, thinking how Ma's breath was far more pleasant than her tirades.

CHAPTER 2

My Motherless Mother

We weep when light does not reach our hearts.
We wither like fields if someone close does not rain
their kindness upon us.

—MEISTER ECKHART

My mother's family history reads like a textbook on psychopathology. Grandma Helen "lived with the birds," and Grandpa Joseph "played in the fields." Grandma was mentally ill, and Grandpa had a mistress. I didn't know Grandpa very well except that he was crabby, woke up daily at four a.m., shooed guests out of the house by 7:52 p.m., and went to bed at eight p.m. He wore a nightgown that was too short, pulling it down in front when he walked toward us and pulling it down again to cover his tush when going the opposite direction. This inelegant appearance didn't fit with the fact that he was the chief pharmacist at the local hospital and had made the cover of *Time* magazine for his extraordinary collection of mortar and pestles. He was a self-made man—a perfectionist, described as a tyrant at work and an iron-fisted father on the home front.

Being a "gullible Gertie," a name I often heard to describe me, I had no idea that Sadie was his mistress and not just a friend who lived closed by. Once, they invited me to a restaurant that had a buffet. There was more food on that table than I'd seen in a year, so with bulging eyes and a greedy belly, I ate too much fried chicken, green Jell-O with cream cheese and pineapple, and warm, crusty cinnamon rolls. On the way home, I threw it all up in the back seat of Grandpa's old Studebaker. I was never invited to dinner again, although that may have been because I asked why Grandma had been left home alone.

My mother was the oldest of six children: five girls and one boy. It was only after Pa's death that anyone talked about Mom's early upbringing, so I was sixty-three years old when I learned that Ma had been placed in a Catholic orphanage when she was five years old. I was bowled over by this revelation. With three younger children at home, and one more on the way, Grandma Helen delivered her eldest daughter, my mother, into the arms of the nuns. I suspect Grandma believed the nuns had better mothering genes than her, and she hoped that God might plant the seed of a vocation within Ma's soul, keeping her from sin and close to God. According to Pa's story, as retold to us by my younger brother, Ma sobbed for hours on end and refused to eat anything except American cheese and hot milk. After two years of this behavior, the local priest demanded that Ma be returned home as she was dying of homesickness. From the age of seven and for most of her life, Ma became the chief cook, cleaner, and mother of her family. She was captain of this dynasty, carrying the torch of make-believe sanity. I'd often heard Ma's sisters remark that she was a "witch on wheels" and ruled over them like a taskmaster, but I never knew why.

Two of Ma's younger sisters followed in Grandma's footsteps and spent several years in the simple-celled rooms of Worcester State Mental Hospital. Although my mother faithfully tended to their needs, her efforts didn't stop them from taking their own lives in their early forties. Both overdosed on prescription drugs. One of the sisters had an illegitimate son, who also died tragically. He had uncontrollable epilepsy and drowned during a seizure as he played with his young children at a local pond. He was thirty-three.

And there was Ma's sweet, delicate sister who turned to alcohol to escape the blows of her heavy-fisted, battle-fatigued ex-Marine husband. Just a click of the television set when he was napping could trigger a battle in the living room. I recall so vividly, when I was perhaps twelve or thirteen, waiting in the car as Ma went to take her sister to the ER. She'd "fallen" through the window, but she refused help as her husband raged behind the doors. Ma never said a word and I was told never to ask questions.

As far as we know, there were no scandalous stories about Ma's brother, who left home for an education, served his country as a Marine, and then dedicated his life to undercover work for the government.

Grandma's youngest daughter, Helen, was a Down's syndrome child whose IQ was 30. People called her an "idiot," a label I despised. The story I heard was that, during her delivery, the doctor was "tipsy" and mishandled the forceps, crushing part of the baby's skull. I suspect this story was a desperate attempt to cover up the shame of having produced a less-than-perfect child. Perhaps Grandma felt God had punished her for getting married when all she wanted to do was be a nun. Her womb belonged to God, and she had failed. The nuns refused her application, not once but three times. No one knew why.

Whatever the truth, only half of this child's body developed, leaving her with one boob of drooping flesh that bobbed around like a tennis ball in an old nylon stocking. But charming, she was! Helen loved to sit by the window and try to catch the dust particles dancing in the sun. She delighted in the neighborhood children as they tumbled down the grassy slopes. She'd laugh until she peed whenever she passed obnoxious gas from eating too many blueberries. Her constant companion was her "bala," a small piece of plastic found in the collars of shirts that came from the cleaners. She held her "bala" between her thumb and index finger, rhythmically swaying it back and forth, back and forth. She grunted loudly if you dared touch it.

Helen had a vocabulary of three phrases: "foosh you" (fool you), "you bazo" (not sure what she meant), and "wuv u" (love you). If anyone spoke disparagingly of her, I'd get on my soapbox of religious righteousness and let them know how special Helen was to Jesus and they'd better be "aware of her goodness!" One time, Ma pushed a woman into a clothing rack when she made fun of Helen's out-of-shape "hippo" body. I feared that Ma would be arrested, although I was secretly proud of her.

When Aunt Helen lived with Grandma, who often slipped into a semi-catatonic trance seated in her bedroom, Helen would twirl, dance, and sing a gibberish *la lala, la la* tune in the front room. No one was purer of spirit or happier than this innocent soul. The only time Helen cried was when Ma or I sang the "Ave Maria." As soon as she heard the first notes of this song, Helen would lay down her cherished "bala," plop her rather wide, squishy rear-end into the nearest chair, close her eyes, and weep. When the song ended, she'd smile ever so lovingly and blow a kiss to me. I never doubted that the tender fire of her love came straight from the heart of the Blessed Mother. I've often wondered if she was sent to this family as a healing light to soften the gloom of insanity and suicide that rested on us like a shroud.

After Grandma died, Ma cared for Helen in our home, and how we loved to see Helen get away with things we'd be throttled for. If Ma left Helen on the toilet too long because she was yacking on the telephone, Helen would ceremoniously unroll all the toilet paper and stuff it in the bowl—plugging up the pipes for days. At other times, Helen would wake up in the middle of the night and pull down all the towels and sheets onto the floor. Her best disruption, however, was when Helen devised a scheme to stop Ma from taking her plate from the dinner table too quickly. Ma demanded we eat all our food with little talking and minimal chewing. Within five to six minutes, she'd snatched our plate, and any leftover food either landed in the dog's stomach or in a Tupperware bowl. Helen didn't like this routine, so she'd wrap her arms around her plate, dunk her face into the middle of the food, and snort like a happy piggie. Ma tried not to laugh while she wrestled the plate away from Helen.

Helen lived to the age of fifty-four, an unusual achievement for someone with her disabilities. Ma fought tooth and nail to be her caretaker until she could no longer handle the physical task of lifting her. It warmed my heart that Helen left this world on the feast of the Immaculate Conception, December 8th. I have no doubt that Helen dissolved into pure light when her Mother welcomed her Home.

Grandmother Helen's daughters had troubled lives, but Grandmother Helen's life had a deranged mysticism to it. I was captivated by her stillness, a genuine madwoman with dignity beyond words. To me, she was a vision of the Heavenly Mother with a haunting Mona Lisa smile, a woman clothed in a blue crocheted gown, a child's tiara secured in her pure wispy silver hair. She'd pull her long tresses into a soft bun that nestled so perfectly in the nape of her neck. Sometimes, I'd peek inside it, imagining I'd find a lost sparrow. Grandma had tiny child ear lobes, which she adorned with shimmery blue earrings of clustered crystal. Their beautiful radiance danced on her porcelain skin when she sat in the light of the sun. Her smooth hands rested like mourning doves in her lap, a linen handkerchief, delicately edged with tatted lace, barely touching her little finger. I loved her so.

Like the white-out on my astrology chart that hid Ma's terror about my life, so did Grandma's pure elegance mask the chaos in her mind. Given the turmoil in my own mind, it had to be God's presence within us that allowed Grandma's sanity and goodness to come out when I sat with her. Within each other's presence, we sparkled like glowing fairy dust. Sadly, these awakenings were fleeting. We both felt exiled from God, each having an abnormally high reactivity to being human, each of us repulsed by unkind people and by situations that didn't reflect God's love and peace. Grandma and I were gifted with genes of silence, hers containing her chaotic mind, and mine shielding me from saying words that would trigger Ma's rage. No wonder she thought I was autistic.

Some of my fondest memories with Grandma Helen took place when I was around seven years old. Ma was reluctant to visit her mother not only because her house was a messy pigsty but also because Ma was certain I loved Grandma more than her—and that was unacceptable. "You are MY daughter—remember that," she would say to me as we pulled up to Grandma's house. However, once a month, I could visit while Ma took voice lessons from Mrs. Como, an incredibly rotund, kindly widow who lived on the first floor of a two-story home next door to Grandma's. When Mrs. Como opened her mouth and said hello, it was as if the world stood still in reverence. How I loved to be rocked in the arms of her deep voice. Mrs. Como wanted me to take lessons also, but it was clear there was only room for one singer in the family, and I wasn't the chosen one. I had perfect pitch, but Ma said my voice was too high and too clear—qualities that would get me no further than a solo in a church choir.

When the day came for a visit, we'd pull up to 45 Paine Street, and there was the yellow Victorian house. Shabby and run-down as it was, I loved it. The steps leaned one way, the toothless banisters another way, the walls and paint not wanting to be seen together so bits of old paint would gather in the worn dents of my Buster Brown shoes. There was a grand wrap-around porch that slanted at such an angle that, on a rainy day, rivulets of water washed away all the stray papers and pigeon poop left on the porch. Ah, the grandeur of this creaky porch! It had a danger sign taped on one of the cracked floorboards, warning you that the porch might fall if you were too fat—and I was plump.

Once through the doors, while Ma practiced her musical scales next door, I was granted an audience with Queen Helen. Sometimes I was so happy to see her, I forgot my manners and leapt over the bed, or tap-danced on the unpacked boxes in her bedroom that were covered with old chenille bedspreads. I'd pretend they were red velvet carpets. One of my favorite rituals with Grandma was presenting her with paper doilies I'd made using red watercolor and gold-leaf paint. We were quite poor, so buying the gold-leaf paint was an extravagant purchase. When my mother wasn't home, I'd sneak into the parlor and reach deep down into the chair my father sat in to retrieve lost coins that were buried near the springs. I was convinced this was money from the angels to help make Grandma happy. I also babysat during the day for five cents an hour to buy even one little ounce of this precious paint. Occasionally, Ma allowed me to babysit after her four p.m. lock-down, but that was for rare occasions, and only for the most elite people in town. I loved this, as I made ten cents an hour. I'd put the paint bottle in a cigar box, wrap it in my doll's blanket, and shove it behind my bed until I could paint without Ma's interference.

In return for my painted doily, Grandma Helen, who was sitting in front of a white vanity table with a three-way mirror, would ask me to close my eyes like a sleepy kitten and then wait until she made a funny whistling sound. That was the cue to open my eyes and form a cup with my hands, and Grandma would gently drop one of her blue-crystal beaded earrings into the palm of my long piano fingers. Each time we repeated our ritual, she gave me the same earring. I was somewhat puzzled that she never saw me return the earring to her jewelry box. I figured it was a secret game between us. However, when I was in my mid-sixties, I learned that Grandma had been legally blind for most of her senior years. That was the reason she stared straight ahead and didn't move. I was clueless that she never saw me, just followed my voice. I didn't know that those deep, recessed eyes, which opened and closed like the mechanically timed shutters on a cuckoo clock, were blank pages of gray fuzziness.

In spite of her blindness, Grandma crocheted exquisite lace ball gowns and sweaters. I was intrigued that she never looked at the crochet hook, relying on the memory of her fingers to be her eyes. Come to think of it, I am grateful she couldn't see her face in the mirror. Most of the time, she looked like a sad basset hound, waiting, dying for affection. I remember how she told me never to frown, as that wouldn't look good when it came time to lay in a casket. I also don't honestly remember hearing Grandma speak to me. She mumbled sounds at times, or occasionally blew spit bubbles, but that was about it.

During the periods when Grandma Helen was not institutionalized, she was beautifully groomed and, actually, her physical appearance was pristine. Her closets, however, needed a dumpster for the mountainous piles of unworn clothing tossed on the closet floor. This was quite the opposite of Ma's closets, which looked like bulging discs ready to explode but where everything was on hangers and sorted by colors. In Grandma's room, boxes served as end tables, unopened bills and books with dog-eared corners lay around like lazy toads in a murky pond. But the most impressive sight was in Grandma's kitchen where there were chipped ceramic dishes stacked haphazardly like the Mad Hatter's tea party in *Alice's Adventures in Wonderland*. The cups and saucers were balanced six to ten cups high, frying pans were decorated with burned Land O'Lakes American cheese drippings and the remains of scrambled eggs. I always wondered if the grease and the half-eaten peanut butter and marshmallow sandwiches were the glue that kept the dishes from crashing to the floor or into the kitty litter boxes. Heaven knows, I knew better than to ask for a drink of water or open the cupboard.

Even more distressful than Grandma's kitchen, however, were the times Ma took me with her when she visited Grandma at Worcester State Hospital, a public institution for the mentally ill. When Ma went through the locked security doors to see her mother, I remained in the foyer—I was too young to go into the mental wards. Instead, I played the card game of old maid with some of the sedated, senile male patients, semi-restrained in wheelchairs. They were too out of it to cause me any harm, of that I was sure—and they were safer than Ma. One time, when I heard Grandma screaming, I peeked through the screen-covered window to see her streaking naked down the hallway. Ma never uttered a word about these visits, never asked if I was okay. I knew she was upset and scared because, sometimes on the way home, she would stop at Friendly's ice cream shop for a small cup of maple walnut ice cream, which we shared. Her silence was more refreshing than the ice cream, but it helped the nausea thinking about the nurses trying to tackle Grandma and strapping her to the bed.

I never realized the power of my relationship with Grandma until we both entered institutions in 1960: I went to Loyola University in Chicago for pre-medical studies, and Grandma once again attended Worcester State Hospital for another course in the basics of sanity and world living. During my Christmas break, Grandma was given a pass to come home for a holiday dinner. When she crossed the threshold of the living room that day, I was stunned at the change in her appearance. There was no tiara, no crystal earrings, no sweet smile. Her hair was long, stringy white with yellow-tinged split ends, flying and crackling from the lack of moisture in the air. She looked like a Native American elder, shriveled under the heat of a desert sun. Grandma shuffled across the bare wooden floor, limp as a rag doll, the effect of the cocktail of drugs she was administered. She was stumbling on her brittle limbs, until she saw me sitting on the old piano bench. When she heard my voice, and touched my fingers, her face illuminated with a rapture I will never forget. She came alive, hydrated with love. I did not eat or go to the bathroom or shift my position the entire day. I made a royal mess attempting to spoon-feed her mashed potatoes and gravy that day!

When it came time for Grandma to return to the hospital that evening, she screeched louder than a barn owl as I unfurled her fingers that were embedded in the palm of my hand. I tried to wrap her in my arms, sing a soothing lullaby, and assure her I'd come back to visit her again—I'd never leave her. I wanted to create a magical kingdom with unicorns where dreams came true and life had a happy ending. But all I could do was listen to the sounds of her anguish ricocheting in all the chambers of my heart.

When I was home from college in the summer, I'd visit Grandma in the hospital whenever I could. Each time, I found that she had further regressed into a tottering robot, her insanity growing like a deadly fungus. Sometimes she knew me, but at other times she bawled hysterically that I never came to see her. Sometimes I wonder if she thought I was an apparition bringing her angel wings to fly back Home. Grandma's days were spent in solitary confinement, where she mimicked the sounds of her old Singer sewing machine, desperately moving her fingers as if to sew the hem of her hospital gown. She'd pull the cloth through the invisible machine, careful to keep the seam straight, oblivious that another inmate was hollering obscenities as she climbed up the chicken wire that covered one wall of her cell.

On one occasion, I baked a blueberry pie, Grandma's favorite. She lunged at me, grabbing the entire pie and plunging her hands and face right into the middle of it. When Grandma's daughter Helen did this to protect her food from Ma, it was funny. Watching Grandma devour the crust, slurping and playing in the juice like a ravenous wild animal, it sent my bowels into an uproar. She gulped down all the sugary berries with utter abandon, staining her mouth, her teeth, her skin and hospital gown. Even the tips of her long hair were tinged. For one moment in time, her unspeakable terror and pain were forgotten in glorious slurping.

When I was twenty-four years old, my dad called to tell me that Grandma died by falling down the stairs and breaking her neck, probably from sleep-walking. My mother, who always put a façade of respectability on family embarrassments, claimed her mother went to sleep one night and never awakened. I wondered if she'd heard the voice of God and went through an invisible door, embraced by the freedom of death. Perhaps each version of the story has elements of truth—I will never know. The truth for me—and I still get misty-eyed thinking of it—is how this fragile woman retained her dignity by pretending she was the queen while the rubble of her lost kingdom lay at her feet.

Over the years, I've been intrigued at how similar I was to Grandma Helen—in terms of our challenges to be in our bodies and wrestling with our minds. We were both gentle flowers of God who remembered eternal life and preferred it to daily life. Both of us had a passion for God, desiring nothing more than to enter religious life. For Grandma, being denied entrance into the convent three times shattered her already bruised existence. She succumbed to being a lady-in-waiting for her Savior to rescue her. Given the trajectory of her life, it is easy to label her as a mentally ill woman. But that is not the whole story. She carried strong mystical seeds in her love for God, seeds that shriveled in the aridness of her broken mind. Grandma also had the potential to be a shaman initiate. As I found out later through my own journey, the shaman faces illness or death-defying situations, is transformed by the trauma, and is restored to health for the greater good. The shaman also has an innate gift to navigate the unseen realms of Spirit and brings back information for the healing of the community.

Grandma certainly communed with God, with Nature, and, in particular, with the wind as it whistled through the branches of the oak tree outside her window. However, the intensity of despair that swirled in the belfry of her mind sent Grandma tumbling into the unspeakable abyss of psychological illness and mystical madness. A teacher of mine commented that the mystic and the psychotic dive into the same waters. However, the mystic swims and the psychotic drowns. Reflecting on Grandma, I get the shivers knowing I faced similar resonance fields.

Like Grandma, I slipped into the pit of darkness, wanting to escape the world, my mother, and my body. And yet, the impulse of my life force never forgot that I'd agreed with Source to come into life for a singular purpose: to untangle and evolve these family roots of insanity, reclaiming and possessing once again the divine core—the mystical nature of being a woman. Very honestly, I was a reluctant shaman in this. How astounding that, although the shame of incest with my mother burned like a branded ember in my body, the spark of God would not accept this judgment and kept demanding that I be transformed. Just as Ma refinished wood furniture as a hobby, I chose to strip myself of the damaging distortions I had about myself, and it was a full-time job.

CHAPTER 3

Meme Called Me by My Name

Some people come into our lives and quickly go . . .
Some . . . stay for a while, leave footprints on our hearts
And we are never, ever the same.

—FLAVIA WEEDN

What I know of my father's heritage is that his mother and father came to the United States from St. Denis, Canada, a few years prior to Dad's birth. Grandpa Elzear, whom we called Pepe, lived on a farm, and was one of eighteen or nineteen children. His wife, Grandma Mabel, had nearly as many siblings, and she was named Meme.

Not long before my dad died, I learned that Pepe had a gift for curing burns and that Ma had taken me to him to heal the severe eczema rash I had as a child. For the first seven years of my life, I wore gauze bandages to cover the oozing sores in the creases of my elbows and behind my knees. I kind of admired my half-mummi-fied look. I was grateful for my mother's care, except for her threat that, if I didn't stop scratching, she'd tie my hands and strap me to the bedpost. But I had eczema, and not burns, and Pepe's prayerful incantations didn't work. According to Pa, Ma was furious that I wasn't cured, calling Grandpa a "quack" right to his face. It must have been an ugly scene. My dad also revealed that Pepe stopped doing his healing work shortly after his apparent "failure" with me. I was the event he could point to, but my dad indicated that Pepe was ridiculed by the church people in his town for being a faith healer. There was suspicion that, because he wasn't an ordained priest, perhaps he was bringing healing through the power of the "evil one."

The part of Pepe's story that interested me most was that he used a specific prayer in his healing work, a prayer that had been handed down through a long lineage of male healers in the family. Apparently, the tradition could only be passed from father to son. Neither my father nor his brothers wanted anything to do with what they thought of as spiritual "voodoo," even though Pepe was a conservative, faith-filled Catholic. My dad's sister was afraid to even recite the prayer, fearing "something bad" would happen to her for going against the tradition. I knew Pepe would never consider me as a "transmitter" of this gift for future generations. Not only was I a woman, but, more abhorrent to him, I was divorced. After he was told about my situation, whenever I visited, he would turn his chair, face the wall, and refuse to speak to me. I could feel the steam of his anger against me, and it really burned a hole in our relationship. In spite of this, I visited him in the hospital a few days before he died. I reached over and whispered, "I love you, Pepe." Tears trickled down his face and mine. His words were barely audible. "Oui, je t'aime. Yes, I love you."

Pepe was an accomplished carpenter, and, along with three of his four sons, he built homes, carved grandfather clocks, and built birdhouses for purple martins. He was a quiet man for whom smiling was a luxury. Dad described him as a strict disciplinarian—someone you'd never cross. I wouldn't be surprised if he carried a hidden sorrow, as I did for many years of my life, from not being accepted for his spiritual gifts. Not being able to share a God-given talent is a grief no hammer and nail can repair.

After Pepe died, my father's sister locked the hand-written healing prayer in her bank vault, sealing it in plain white paper. At my insistence, my dad convinced my aunt to give it to me as I was involved in healing prayer services. Once I read the prayer, however, I knew I could never repeat it in good conscience. It contained damning assertions about people "not being good enough" and that exorcism was our salvation against the evils of our bodily nature. I placed the prayer in the back of my Bible, grateful that I was not chosen to carry on this tradition.

• • • • •

Meme had a radically different disposition than Pepe. She was a roly-poly earth angel dressed in black laced-up shoes and faded second-hand clothing. No wings for her—just unconditional love. Unfortunately, Ma didn't like her very much and maintained that Meme was a simpleton because she served cake that crumbled on your plate. The truth was that Meme didn't believe in adding more than one egg to the batter.

One of the main reasons I loved to visit Meme is that she called me by my name. Strange as it may seem, Ma referred to me as "my daughter" or "she" but rarely called me Annette. In Ma's eyes, I was only an extension of her and I didn't exist in my own right. This was deeply disturbing to me long before I had the words to explain it. Other relatives contributed to this, including my older brother who called me *fatty* or *elephant sister*. Uncles and aunts referred to me as *sweetie pie* or *chouette*, a French word for cabbage head. And Dad always said, I was his favorite daughter or his precious *sweet, sweet*. But then, when we arrived at Meme's home, she'd be standing at the front door with open arms and out would come the words: "Ah, my Annette!" I could feel pink glitter magically cover me in that moment. As she smiled, I felt as if God were gently tickling my ribs. To be named was to become special—to be loved for being me.

Meme was an accomplished pianist. Her rotund body sat on the small piano stool, her bottom cheeks jiggled in tune with the music. Her ear-to-ear grin was wide enough to cover her hips. Like Grandma Helen and her daughter Aunt Helen, Meme and I loved to hear Perry Como sing the "Ave Maria." She'd laugh and cry all at the same time, bringing out the Kleenex box and straightening the pearl buttons on her simple flower-print cotton dress. God, Ma disliked it when Meme and I cried so much. Maybe it was because I sat in Meme's lap and not hers. We always knew our visits were coming to an end when Meme started playing "Roll Out the Barrel" on the piano. On our ride home, I curled up on the back seat like an opossum, wrapped in Meme's sweetness and waving out the back window as Pa drove off. It helped soothe my bellyache as Ma fumed to me and Pa like an old chimney stack over Meme's choice of music. She felt it was for the "common folk"—and beneath our dignity.

I recall a Christmas present Meme gave me when I was ten years old. It was a light-blue flocked and lined organza housecoat, trimmed in delicate white lace. Today, more than sixty years later, this housecoat is stored in my attic, still wrapped in its original tissue paper and in its Filene's box. Prior to that, I hid it under my mattress. I never wore it. I remember being very determined to protect Meme's treasure from Ma's touch.

Meme died of undiagnosed pancreatic cancer at the age of eighty-seven. My dad had the decency to call me three days before she died, stating that she "wasn't feeling well." I sent her a simple love letter, priority mail, thanking her for the blue housecoat, for the fun we had singing and playing the piano, crying over the Blessed Mother, and making jigsaw puzzles together. My letter was used as the homily for her funeral. Neither Ma nor Pa informed me of her death until two weeks afterwards.

CHAPTER 4

Memories Better Forgotten

I call to you for help, O God.
Do you not hear me? I want to come Home.

—ANNETTE HULEFELD

Our family moved to Catonsville, Maryland, in late 1943 to accommodate Pa's job as a tax auditor with Shell Oil Company. I have vivid memories of myself skipping at dusk to Mr. Jung's backyard to catch fireflies, proud of the tiny holes I'd punched in the lid of mason jars so the flickering lights stayed bright. I hear Ma scolding me for talking too loudly on the bus, asking if Negroes turned that color from drinking too much chocolate milk.

There are other memories—sickening ones—made within the greasy flower-patterned wallpapered rooms of that yellow Maryland house. The neighbors probably saw me as a quiet, well-behaved child with beautiful, soft brown ringlets of hair that bounced like springs as I played hopscotch on the sidewalk. They didn't know how I dreaded going into the dimly lit, smelly apartment of the dirty old man who lived downstairs from us. But I'd been taught to comply with the commands of adults if they needed help, and my friend Jesus said to love your enemies. I loved Jesus. And the old man asked me in to put his groceries away and have a cookie. I've never forgotten the nervous wiggles that jiggled around my belly button that day with the nasty man. Never. The details cannot be retrieved. But I do know I walked carefully on my skinny legs as I came to the dinner table that evening so I could hide the marks from his scratchy, old bent fingers. He told me not to share our special time together or I'd be in trouble. While I had the outward appearance of a fragile, angelic sweetheart, I was older than dinosaur bones when I made my pact with God that night, as I said my prayers. *Dear God, please come get me. Please. Don't leave me here. I want to come Home, and if you don't take me Home, I will come anyway.* Surely God loved me enough and I was a good-enough little girl to die before I really grew up.

Looking back at this time of my life, I have a better understanding of a dream I've never forgotten. In the dream, I am a radiant four-year-old child who delighted in swinging on the stars and dancing on the moon. I had a big paint box that came alive as I splashed glittering rainbows across the cloudless blue sky. I wanted everyone to see the wonders of the God with whom I was so ecstatically connected. One day, however, I realized no one was looking at the rainbows and no one really cared about all the sparkly colors. Tears welled up in the pockets of my eyelids as I shut the paint box and tenderly hid the colors in the nooks and crannies of my quivering heart.

I figured God answered my prayers when our family returned to Worcester, Massachusetts, because Ma's allergies were so severe in Maryland. I was wrong about God being on my side. Life in Worcester was more unpleasant than eating mashed turnips and potatoes every night for supper. We lived in the same run-down apartment building as Ma's uncle and aunt. They were two lackluster sad sacks who drooled with joy when we children came in for a visit. This great aunt looked just like the picture on the labels for Campbell's tomato soup: pudgy, with sappy upturned smile, and empty as the soup bowls we finished, along with the grilled cheese sandwiches she fed us. At least she had Band-Aids, as I invariably got splinters in my hands from the rotting banister of their rickety wood porch. She was too naive to realize that I got these, trying to get away from her overly attentive, perverted husband. He was worse than the old codger in Maryland, picking me up onto his shoulders so his smooth, never-washed-a-dish soft hands, could roam around inside my undies. I tried hard to keep my lips tighter than a zipper when he'd try to burrow in for a secret kiss. He'd nuzzle my ear and whisper things in French I couldn't understand but sounded bad. I wanted to pee on him so I could run away. But, as a well-behaved child, I just prayed and became stiff as a board, pretending he wasn't there and I wasn't there. I don't like to admit that I prayed he'd get sick and die. Why God didn't strike him dead was beyond me, but maybe he didn't want him in heaven. If He didn't like him either, maybe I wouldn't be punished for wanting him dead.

My brother and I attended Holy Name of Jesus School, where the lessons were half in English and half in French. We wore dark-blue uniforms, with plastic white collars, and little red neckties. One day at school, I felt an alarm bell go off inside my belly. I knew something was very wrong at home and I had to be there immediately. Panicked, I pretended I needed to use the bathroom but went to my brother's classroom instead. Ever so gently, I knocked on the thick wood door. When the nun didn't answer, I carefully turned the doorknob and slipped in quiet as a mouse. I timidly asked if my brother could walk me home because I was sick. The nun became enraged that I dared disrupt her class. She took me out of the classroom to the top of the stairs and started to shake me—a shake that turned into a shove, that sent me head over heels down two flights of stairs. I couldn't stand up immediately as lights and stars were flashing before my eyes. After a few minutes of stunned silence, I was worried that my long banana curls wouldn't cover up the swollen bump on the right side of my head. No one came to help me, so I walked home alone, determined not to tell Ma about my pounding headache.

Ma was furious that I came home alone. "Don't you know someone could throw you in a car and take you away?" This bothered her more than my excuse: that I felt sick and was worried I'd throw up on my uniform. We were poor, and I only had one uniform to wear. Ma was actually angry, however, because she was taking Grandma to the institution again and she didn't want me to know. But I did—that was the "something wrong" that I felt. I was more concerned about Grandma than I was about Ma going to the school and finding out about my "accident." I don't think she would have believed my version of it because the nuns were holy and I had disobeyed the rules. My head pounded that night, and I cried myself to sleep. I shed my tears for Grandma because I knew she missed me.

In 1947 we moved to Putnam, Connecticut, a run-down textile mill town, where Dad opened up a service station. Putnam was filled with down-to-earth folks who had high school educations and whose entertainment was playing bingo or hanging out in front of the hardware or appliance stores. These were meeting places to gossip about the weirdoes in town, including the story of the five-hundred-pound man whose suspenders barely held up his overalls. Many of the homes were shabby, as if their owners were pioneers who barely made it through a summer drought, while others, perched on the hill near the town hall and the funeral home, were rather elegant. Putnam was as unimaginative as its small grocery stores, small apartment rooms, and small school classrooms with fifteen pupils.

The town was provincial enough to indulge Ma's need to be larger than life, and penny-ante enough to confirm her sense that "I am in charge of whether my kid lives or dies." God knows, all the neighbors, churchgoers, and storeowners knew Marie and her kids. The phone in Ma's kitchen jumped off the wall if we dared to be rude, fart in church, pee on the cement sidewalk from laughing, or spend seven cents on penny candy instead of five. Ma immediately rescued her name from her misbehaving kids by scolding us: "I never brought you up to be hoodlums—you are a disgrace to our family."

When we first moved to Putnam, we lived in a small second-floor apartment, right above the gas station my father purchased. The gasoline fumes penetrated my nostrils, leaving me with bad headaches. Ma huffed and puffed about the stench but said it was the sacrifice we had to pay to get food on the table. Like the other places we lived in, the entrance had bowed, steep stairs that led to an enclosed, slanted porch with warped floorboards. I didn't care that the porch was dilapidated. This was my sacred space to play priest. My vestments were borrowed from Grandma's collection of threadbare chenille bedspreads—the pink-and-white one was my favorite. My metal dollhouse was converted into a church. Necco wafers became hosts and Concord grape juice was the wine. I paid my older brother to be an altar boy. All I asked him to do was genuflect when I lifted the candy host after consecration and ring the tiny bell. I knew he didn't like church, but I was still shocked when, one day, with one swift kick of his foot, the dollhouse crashed to the bottom of the stairs, each room collapsing into twisted pieces of metal.

Not all was terrible after moving to Connecticut. The best perk was that I was delivered from some of the "weird" relatives we previously had to stay with. Unfortunately, Ma was still Ma. Even as a teenager, I didn't care much where we lived as long as I had a room with a lock (which never occurred), a bed that was my own (never until I moved to a college dorm), and shades on the window so I could pretend to disappear into the magic of the universe at night. I loved that my imagination could take me to faraway places—it kept me sane. I also loved playing the piano, but I dreaded practicing. Ma could not restrain herself from nagging: "That's wrong, play it again. You have talent, so stop playing like you have three hands." Sigh.

I loved it when Ma sang for a funeral because I could be alone, sit in the corner of my room, and read Nancy Drew mysteries. Sometimes during those days, my real Mother would visit me and tenderly hold my tears and loneliness. I'd watch in fascination as a blue, misty light slowly appeared like a ghost, floating toward me from the corner until I was wrapped in the softness of the Blessed

Mother. Sometimes she sang with the most incredible lilting sounds, purer than a harp in a high wind. Other times, Mary's touch awakened a yearning in my soul to become a Carmelite nun or a priest. As a starry-eyed optimist, I held out hope that, by the time I was old enough, the rules would have changed and I'd be Reverend Annette. However, over the years it became obvious that, unless I had a sex change, I was out of luck pursuing my true vocation. I admitted to the Blessed Mother that my top choice was to die at an early age, but, short of that, I'd settle for singing, praying, and baking bread for God all day long as a cloistered nun.

During the years we lived in these cramped quarters, my older brother contracted polio at the age of ten and was placed in an iron lung. I was clueless what polio was and equally oblivious to the seriousness of his illness. I just figured that, if Ma was blowing her nose and crying in the bathroom instead of forcing me to eat my vegetables, it was serious. I decided to ask the classroom nun if I could pray the rosary in front of the Blessed Mother statue in the schoolyard. I was convinced that, if all the children prayed with me, my brother would be cured. Surely, my Mother would answer the prayers of her devoted handmaiden who attended daily Mass and Communion, prayed First Friday devotions, and slept with the rosary. And even though my brother had destroyed my dollhouse church because he didn't like God, I was sure God would be pretty upset if I didn't pray for him to live. The nun granted my request, and we hit the jackpot: my brother was cured. He came out of the iron lung that same day. Ma didn't think it was a miracle, however, because he developed a limp, so the cure didn't count.

Up until fifth grade, I was the teacher's pet and never misbehaved except for putting my chewed-up bubble gum under the desk or chair. I sometimes got in trouble, such as the time I placed my school bag next to the radiator, forgetting I'd left old, cracked hard-boiled eggs on the bottom of the bag. The pungent sulfur odor tested the nun's patience with me, and she refused to accept my explanation that someone must have passed gas. I'd have been better off owning up to the eggs!

A year or so after my brother recovered from polio, we moved out of the apartment and into the house that became our family's home for the rest of my parents' lives. That year, I contracted mumps, then meningitis, followed by rheumatic fever. Ma was advised that I be kept in a hospital, but Ma was adamant that she was a more superior caretaker than any trained imbeciles. Her words. I was bedridden for a year and a half, only getting to my feet once every few months for a blood test at the hospital. Other than that, I used a bedpan, ate lots of doughnuts and custard, and gained a tremendous amount of weight. When I saw my face in the mirror, I was shocked at the ugly, homely face that stared back at me. Surely I couldn't have morphed into a Halloween monster, but I had!

I was petrified to be at home with Ma twenty-four seven, but the amazing thing was that she stopped yelling at me and spent most of her time talking on the phone apprising others of my awful situation. Ma was resuming the role she'd had with her family, giving up her life to care for her sick daughter. This is not to diminish her doting care nor the fact that she minimized her judgmental attitude, except when a solicitor came to the door or a bill collector called. Ma drank in the praise that her friends heaped on her. "Marie, there is no better mother than you. Annette is the luckiest girl in the world to receive such care." These compliments were a 180-degree turnaround from what her friends usually said to her: "Oh Marie, you've got to stop complaining—your daughter is the best, your husband a saint . . . you have no idea how lucky you are."

During my illness and for several years into my teen years, the person who kept me this side of sad was Cecile, my very best friend. She lived across the street and, factually, she was as dumb as I was smart, and it didn't matter a sliver to us. We were inseparable. Cecile developed epileptic seizures a year after my bout with rheumatic fever. She'd call and say, "I'm feeling goofy. Can I come over?" She'd bop over, slide under the kitchen table alongside our dog, and convulse. This freaked me out at first, but we both coped by teasing each other about our kooky legs. When she was having her seizure, her legs wiggled like worms hit by lightning, and mine were fat clunkers that could barely move. That made me her guardian. Cecile's mom abandoned her for extra-marital affairs, and Ma, to her credit, took responsibility for Cecile's welfare. And while Cecile and I cracked many jokes about Ma's crazy behavior, I never spilled the beans about Ma's abuse—Cecile needed Ma to take care of her, and I didn't want her to worry more than she had to.

Cecile was my one friend who understood my religious nature and supported me in carrying out my priestly duties when I decided to officiate at funerals for my dead animals. She approved when I hired the girl next door to wail at the top of her lungs, and I gave her five cents if she gave a stellar performance. She usually did. I was defrocked from my holy orders, however, the day Ma found out I'd buried Grandma's Siamese cat in my doll cradle. I tried to keep this from her, but my brother snitched on me and sent Ma over the edge. She was incensed that I'd ruined her handiwork. She had painted delicate flowers on the sides of that cradle, and I'd dishonored her talent. This was far more devastating to Ma than the neighbor who complained that I was making fun of God by praying and singing for a cat. I'd sung for my bunny rabbits, hamsters, and even a toad, so I didn't understand why she suddenly was offended.

Between the ages of ten and twelve, I had a dreadful fear that I was really crazy, like a spiritual version of Grandma Helen. On the one hand, I was this cheerful girl who never complained, and I was grateful to God that I was suffering with my friend Jesus. Priests and nuns would say to me, "You must be very special to suffer so much illness. God's chosen people have a life of trial and tribulation." I loved being special and seen as a saint. On the other hand, I also wanted to spew out all my venom against my mother. *Don't you understand? I am suffering to wash away her sins against me.* I was horrified to think I had an "evil" mother, but it was even scarier to think I would rather die than live with her. It was a torturous dilemma for a ten-year-old.

I also experienced that "nuttier than a fruitcake" feeling whenever I found myself recalling conflicting memories as to my true identity. On the one hand, I was a miserable girl propped up in bed with several pillows, staring out the window, imagining I was nothing more than a mound of lumpy spaghetti with too much melted butter and Parmesan cheese on it. I stormed the heavens with prayers to Jesus and Mary to clean up the slippery mess, but I figured I was on my own. No one, not even God, was coming to the rescue. On the other hand, I was the little girl who loved to be in nature, who drank in the sun and rocked herself to sleep on the moon. I pretended I shimmered like thousands of dewdrops and dressed in glittering leaves and fancy twigs. I believed that plants sang with soprano voices, stones snored, and birds danced to a calypso beat. I was the child who, when my mother wasn't looking, would take off her shoes and socks and let her feet open their eyes to Mother Earth. I'd hear the ants give pep talks to each other and wondered if the crickets made their noisy sound by giving each other back rubs. And I felt sad for the worms when we prayed for rain to keep the garden growing because I knew that, when they came up for air, some shoe sole might smoosh them to death. I never told anyone of the many friends I had when I walked barefoot in the dirt or in rain puddles. I think Mother Nature helped keep me alive and kept me giggling when most of my life made me want to cry.

My rescue finally came but not in the way I expected: Ma gave birth to my younger brother. At the time, I had no clue how people became pregnant and no idea that Ma was. My best friend told me that, when God wanted a baby to come into the world, He placed a seed right behind your belly button, which then grew like a watermelon. One day, when your belly was about to burst, you went to the bathroom and dropped the baby into the bowl. That was a day you got a baby instead of a poop. If you were going to have twins, they'd have to come out of your boobs.

When Ma was pregnant, I only remember thinking she had gained a bit of weight and her waistline seemed to keep getting higher. Aside from her over-sized breasts, Ma was a beautiful woman with a striking figure. I secretly chuckled about her pudginess because, for a few months, I stepped out of the spotlight of being the fat one. That word is repugnant to many people, but the truth is that I was not pleasingly plump, nor overweight—I was fat. I coped by thinking God saw me as a skinny person and that is what mattered. My hair was cut short and dorky, with two unruly waves on the top of my head. Because I was so near-sighted, I wore gold-framed wing-tipped gawkers with thick lenses, which I loved. Sadly, the geeky glasses didn't diminish my chubby chipmunk cheeks.

When my younger brother was born, both my older brother and I were upset because Pa delivered an ultimatum from Ma. Either we got rid of our severely neurotic dog "Blackie" (who without fail peed on everyone's leg as they came through the door), or our baby brother would not come home. It was selfish of us, but we voted to keep the dog. I was reminded of that years later when my own sons asked me to buy them a kitten. I said I was so allergic that they would have to choose: a cat or me. My youngest son went into caucus with his brother and emerged five minutes later with a simple statement: "Sorry Mom, you lost." Ma was not happy about our choice either, but from the day my brother was placed in the cradle, her behavior toward me switched completely. I was released from the burden of having to fill up the black hole of her neediness. At twelve years of age, my body finally was my own.

I had no way to speak up about Ma's violations. Even years later, I chose not to protest. Instead I turned on myself, waging an inner rampage of negative thinking, shredding my self-image. I was petrified that, if I exposed Ma and her family, I'd be the one in the spotlight, not her. I'd be the damaged goods, too dirty for anyone to love, the unclean leper God could never heal or embrace as Beloved.

At the age of eighteen, when I considered entering the convent, I chickened out. I wasn't sure what would have been more distressing to the Mother Superior: hearing voices from God, or being sexually abused by your mother. I was sure I'd be affirmed for being in love with God, but internally I couldn't reconcile that with the imprint of sinfulness on my body. No matter how I tried, I was plagued with the thought: *Where are you God? Jesus, what have I done to offend you?* Why didn't God stop members of Ma's family from turning me into a sugar bowl of sweetness they could dip into for their satisfaction? Didn't he see how often I threw up after yucky people played with me like the favorite baby doll in the family toy box? *Where were you God?*

My younger brother was Ma's crown prince, a child who was more effervescent than a giant bubble machine. It was clear he was a genius. When he was six months old, he began forming simple words with the letters of his Lucky Charms cereal! I taught him his alphabet, and when he was one year old, he was reading simple books. By three, he could read the word "Massachusetts" or "Connecticut" and other highway signs. At the age of four, he'd get bored with age-appropriate books and start reading my high school textbooks. He was also a musical prodigy, brilliantly performing Rachmaninoff at the age of nine. My younger brother was like a symphony for all Ma's unsung dreams. Finally, Ma produced a child who rose above the gene pool of tragedy and insanity, a living sign that the family curse was redeemed. Unfortunately, he called me "Ma" all the time, and Ma never forgave me for that.

When my brother was six years old, I left home to go to college, and at nineteen I was married. After that, we had very little contact. Years later, when I found out about the horrific experiences he faced from the age of eight until his late twenties, including

I was petrified that, if I exposed Ma and her family, I'd be the one in the spotlight, not her.

sexual abuse from clergy, I vomited in agony, sobbing for days. My guilt at having abandoned him, leaving him helpless at school because I had to save myself, still brings a wretched pain in my heart.

When we reunited in my forties, he was the crackerjack comedian. He'd say "hello" or something inane, and laughter would unhinge every bone in our bodies. His laughter was never a trickle or a slow-moving stream. It was a body-shaking experience, like a cosmic eruption of light particles and waves of sheer joy. After five minutes of howling and giggling, our sides ached as if we'd been pumped with laughing gas. Our mouths would be so wide open, a bird could fly in. Sometimes we'd be asked to leave restaurants because our snorting and screeches disturbed other patrons. I am grateful beyond words for my younger brother, whose belly-laughter in my later years helped dislodge the deep torment that choked the very core of our lives.

CHAPTER 5

The Flood

*For fire will stir all the air, and water will cover all the land.
In this way, all things will be cleansed.*

—HILDEGARD OF BINGEN

When I was thirteen years old, our town had a mini-version of Noah's flood. It was one of the worst deluges in Connecticut's history, caused by torrential rains from two hurricanes that struck within a period of six days, between August 13 and August 18, 1955. Earth and sky unleashed a cosmic clash of unprecedented raw power. A micro-tempest was stirring inside our home too. Ma and Pa were bickering in whispers, as I was sitting by my bedroom window, engrossed in the rhythm of fierce raindrops on the windowpanes. On this particular morning, Ma was determined to go to the grocery store, defying all warnings from Pa, the weatherman, the police, and common sense. The statistics say the river had risen 13.68 feet on that day alone, and the waters were ferociously battering the underbelly of the bridge. The warnings of the cops were drowned out, and both Pa and the police knew that trying to make Ma think rationally was as futile as trying to control the fury of the waters. How she crossed the bridge without being blown away was an act of God, or her own life force that defied death. Maybe both.

As the storm raged, I had this eerie feeling that the end times had arrived and there was an excitement about this. Lightning sizzled through the gray, murky skies, striking the magnesium plant on the riverbank. Hundreds of barrels of magnesium powder spilled into the river that was already contaminated with forty thousand gallons of fuel. This resulted in rapturous explosions booming their applause as ominous clouds hovered over the river that literally was on fire. It was as if dragons from the bowels of hell had been unleashed. Debris from collapsed buildings, uprooted trees—everything the floodwater swept up—wildly bombarded each other, as if trying to escape the fiery inferno. The rampage of the Quinebaug River went through the center of our town, crushing the main steel and wooden bridge as if it were a cheap erector set. In the evening, it was twisted steel dangling in the humid air, a ghostly spectacle under the barely visible moon. The *Hartford Courant* reported that black smoke extended for a twenty-mile radius. The toxins contaminated the drinking water, and warnings were posted about the possibility of a typhoid outbreak. Several people reported seeing droves of cockroaches crossing the streets, armies of them, sending shivers up people's spines as they heard the *click, clack, click* of the roaches' bodies.

At the height of the flooding, streetlights and street signs barely peeked above the waters. Business buildings were swollen with water, bulging like huge toads, while the post office disappeared, sucked in by mounds of oozing mud.

My imagination ran wild, reflecting the twisted emotions I was struggling with. Maybe the cockroaches were Ma's sins and her family's craziness being exposed, and God was going to save me. Finally, the secret would be out in the open and the guilty would be judged. Maybe the waters of the Great Mother would cleanse what I loathed most of all—the defilement of my body. Maybe Ma would never return home. Granted, I was being melodramatic, seeing this cataclysmic event of nature as the intervention of a righteous God, swooping in to punish the wicked and save a forlorn young teenager. And I felt numb from the shame of wanting my mother dead.

Pa was a man of few words, particularly when it involved Ma. When she failed to return home, he forgot the dangers of the weather and went looking for her the next day. "Take good care of your baby brother—I won't be gone long." God only knows what roads he found outside of town to travel on, or where he really went, because no one ever talked about his absence. But two weeks later, he returned, bringing Ma.

Pa had found Ma at the home of her friends who lived on the highest hill in town. As I look back, Ma's actions were outrageous and downright insane, but I think that her beliefs about caring for her family far outweighed any potential for personal danger to herself. Grocery shopping was no less important than going to church on Sunday. It was the outward sign of being a good-enough mother, something her own mother failed at miserably. Just as she fed and cared for her siblings when she was a seven-year-old child, Ma again heard the call of duty, and, by golly, she'd do it in Marine fashion. Her Catholic mentality of sacrifice and shame, along with sheer will, propelled her to defy the forces of nature. No one could accuse her of being a wimp.

When Pa left to find Ma, as fascinated as I was by nature's spectacle, my main task was to care for my eight-month-old brother and for Ma's sister Anna, who was on leave from the mental institution. I loved Anna just as I loved my Grandma. They were both motherless children, trashed by broken promises, and I was one speck of God's compassion, holding the broken wings of their lives.

Anna was petite, maybe 4'8" tall, very thin, and, like Grandma, she had a smile that seemed pasted in position, although hers was slightly more uplifted at the corners. Very few words slipped past her pale lips, but sometimes she thanked me when I fetched her pills. Anna was married to "Earl the Pearl," a non-talkative man with a personality flat as a pancake. But he did the dishes for Anna, carried the groceries up the three flights of stairs to their apartment, and disappeared into the television set until suppertime. He never bothered anyone.

When I was eleven and twelve, I frequently visited Anna, following her hospitalizations for "nervousness." Often these visits were interludes of blessing for us, times when we sat shoulder to shoulder watching cartoons, or when Anna let me wear her too-small fuzzy slippers. In such ordinary moments, she'd smile sweetly and stop fidgeting with her bird-like hands. Sometimes I persuaded her to sit on the back-porch balcony and just watch the bunnies and wolves forming in the clouds. Under most circumstances, Anna appeared normal in the way she chatted and walked, but her body and skin always seemed to be two feet behind her. The day Pa left was no exception, so I prayed that the medications she took daily and the shock treatments from the previous week would sufficiently numb her neural circuits against the erratic explosions. I told her silly jokes and made hot chocolate with marshmallows to distract her from the menacing clouds outside the kitchen window.

On what would be the second to last night of the storm—August 19—Anna and I were playing a card game by candlelight, choosing crazy eights instead of the traditional old maid. We both twittered nervously when a thunderous boom shook the house like a blast of dynamite. A laser bolt of lightning shot through the open kitchen window, grazed the birdcage, and struck the black Formica table where Anna and I were seated across from each other. We stared transfixed at the three-inch crack down the middle of the table. I tried not to gag from the acrid odor of burned laminate wood, and I tried to wipe away the ghosts that floated before my eyes.

Anna's over-permed short hair rose straight toward the ceiling, hair spray and bobby pins losing all ability to stay in control. Anna's face had Grandma's eerie translucent glow, and her vacant eyes wore the trance of death.

My heart sank into my sneakers, the blood in my veins was ice cold, but I had to take charge. It didn't seem right to comb Anna's hair down into place, so I offered her some chocolate chip bits, graham crackers, and marshmallow fluff, the main food left in our cupboards. Had the bird not been chirping so loudly, I might have forgotten to pick up its cage and fill the cup with bird seed. I placed a rusty safety pin on the door to keep him safe. Unfortunately, Anna's brain had no such

> *. . . I sure in hell wouldn't return to God as a crazy woman.*

safety latch. Her thank-you for the junk food was barely audible, a mere whisper of wind. I helped her get into pajamas, made sure she swallowed her special pills, and tucked her in for a good night's sleep.

Back in the kitchen, when I was alone, God only knows why I had a premonition of my life's path that night, but it scared the bejesus out of me. I gasped, clutching my chest and gagging on my own spit. Was I the next woman in the family to follow in the footsteps of Ma's clan of insane women? I slammed my fist against the refrigerator door and made a second pact with God: never would I end up in the loony bin—never. I may have been a thirteen-year-old girl, but I knew that, with God as my savior, I'd succeed in breaking the shackles that chained all of us women in Ma's family. I didn't give up my early death idea, but I sure in hell wouldn't return to God as a crazy woman. I'd almost forgotten about my baby brother during this drama, until I heard him whimpering from the back bedroom. I couldn't breastfeed him, and all I had to give him was Carnation skim milk. I prayed to God he wouldn't die from it.

Anna was a star that slowly disintegrated from the many collisions in her life. She rarely stayed with us after that visit, and I suspect the nearly fatal encounter with a lightning bolt was too much for her gentle spirit. Nine years after the storm, she overdosed on her medications. On the night she died, I'd just returned home to recover from the trauma I experienced at the birth of my oldest son. Ma and I planned to visit Anna that evening, but Ma kept making excuses. As usual, my sense of urgency to go *now* fell on deaf ears. Ma drove in the opposite direction from Anna's apartment, and Anna ended her life at exactly the time I begged to go: 7:12 p.m. Her pills were strewn on the table and floor, her hand cradling the phone that was off the hook. As with other members of the family whose lives ended "sadly" or "without cause," Ma never uttered the word "suicide." I recall her screaming over the phone that Anna's death was an accident, but the parish priest wouldn't budge on his refusal to give her a Catholic burial. I have no idea what kind of service Anna was given, as Ma refused to let me attend the family gathering: "You'll be too upset, and your baby needs you to be calm." So instead I baked a blueberry pie that Ma could take to the service. I was probably rocking my newborn son at home while they laid Anna in the ground reserved for "sinful" women.

I found it difficult to weep for Anna. I was relieved she was finally free of her tormented mind and grief-stricken heart. I had some guilt that my love for her wasn't enough to heal her suffering. At that time, I was convinced that love was always enough—for anything and anyone. I was also ashamed of the jealousy I harbored in my heart that she died and not me. Looking back on it now, I believe the root cause of her death was a crippling perception that she was "damaged goods," an unworthy woman not only because she bore a child out of wedlock, but also because she lost her mind over it. This boy lived with Grandma, and because he called Grandma "ma," and no one ever said who his mother was, I naively never connected the dots that he was Anna's illegitimate son. After Ma died, while going through some family memorabilia, I came across Grandma's laminated obituary, and he was listed as one of her sons, not Anna's. I questioned my older brother about this, and he laughed out loud at me. How could I have been so dumb as to not recognize the family tradition of hiding secrets? My cousin was in truth Aunt Anna's son, but, by God, even death couldn't break the shroud of that shame.

The day of Anna's death was August 6, a day of dark clouds in our family. It was the day of my parents' marriage, the death of my mother's father, the death of three members of my parents' wedding party, and the burial date for two of my mother's sisters. Historically, it's also the day of the first atomic bomb exploded, over Hiroshima, 1945. For years, I was so superstitious about this day that I either tore the page off our calendar or covered it over with a picture of Jesus or Mary—and I made sure never to travel on that day.

CHAPTER 6

Elephant Sister

*Sometimes our light goes out but is blown again into
flame by an encounter with another human being.
Each of us owes the deepest thanks to those who have
rekindled this inner light.*

—ALBERT SCHWEITZER

Putnam Catholic Academy was the name of the convent high school I attended.
It was quite the challenge, not only because I was one of the day students on scholarship, but also because I didn't come from a cultured family and I had a knack for
laughing out loud at the most inappropriate moments. It was as if a very funny
gremlin lived in my belly and, with no warning, would erupt in giggles or snorts
of laughter. I wouldn't have been so embarrassed by my laughter if only I wasn't
farting and peeing in my pants too. Usually, when this happened, it would be
during the reading of the saints' lives at lunchtime, during confession, or on
silent retreats. It wasn't my intention to make fun of people or holy traditions.
On the contrary, I embraced all holy things, even painful ones such as kneeling
on wood floors for hours or praying for hours to scour my mind from "impure"
thoughts, whatever that meant. I wanted nothing more than to be ivory snow for
God. However, under the influence of the Spirit, my body had a mind of its own.
I could be ecstatic in prayer for hours, totally engulfed in God, and then my giggle
genes would bubble up, smack dab in the middle of communal prayer. The girls
around me would double over, valiantly trying to suppress their chuckles. The
nuns were not amused, however, and I'd be quarantined in the chapel, writing
an essay on why God was offended by my gas and giggles.

When I deeply considered it, I knew some of my laughter was compensation
for the vat of shame I unconsciously walked around in. But I also think I was
a resilient soul in whom God had installed a bullshit detector in the center of
my belly. It emitted a "yuk yuk" whenever I picked up something that struck me

as nonsense. I remember a religion teacher telling us that, if we were pregnant and rode in a hearse, the baby would be stillborn. If we were pregnant and rode a horse, and we were lucky, then our baby would only have horribly bowed legs. I blurted out, "You must be kidding us . . . you really believe that?" I was given detention for several days.

There was another face to me, however, that wasn't so bubbly. What I kept hidden is that as a teenager, while others were swooning over Elvis Presley and his blue suede shoes, I was pining for God. I spent hours in church, pouring my heart out to God and lighting all the candles by the Virgin's altar. I had no money to pay for the candles, so I prayed doubly hard that I wouldn't be caught or punished by the parish priest. Those candles were the flames of God that gave me hope that, sooner rather than later, I'd be that flame within God, free of my body and my mother. There was a fierce unspoken feud for my life between Ma and God. She was as dogged to keep me alive and safe as I was to seek eternal life and be God's Beloved.

During my teen years I worked various babysitting jobs to help put food on the table or pay the telephone bills when Pa was out of work or bankrupt—he went bankrupt three times. Ma was too proud to admit that Pa failed as a provider, so when she said we were going to "borrow" bread and syrup from one of Ma's sisters who lived thirty miles away, I willingly turned over my babysitting money to gas the car. This was far less humiliating than having to go to our neighbor's house and ask for pancake mix or a bottle of milk, but I did it because my little brother cried when he was hungry. During the lean years, bread, Karo syrup, and mashed turnips with instant potatoes were our daily menu. I also remember the sub-zero temperatures when we had no money to fuel the coal furnace. Those were days I'd go to school to warm up, and at night, I'd crawl under the covers with my rosary beads and our collie dog, Beauty. My older brother chose liquor instead, so I had the dog to myself. I especially relied on the huge black cotton-wood tree outside my bedroom window, the sacred space I imaginatively traveled to at night to escape Ma. It was there that I poured out my troubles to Jesus and buried my secrets in the hollow of the tree and His heart. I reminded Him every day that I was ready to go back Home with Him.

I wasn't ashamed that we were poor, as it fit my concept of what it meant to be a "real" Christian. I recall only one time when it bothered me to hand over my money to Ma. I was working as a waitress, and Ma took my paycheck and spent it to get her clothes from the dry cleaner and buy white gloves and an Easter Bonnet so she'd look good at church. I was so angry with this that I buried a white crystal rosary inside my bra. I'd read about tribal people who successfully warded off evil spirits using sage or garlic. I tried the rosary. It didn't work. It didn't protect me from the repulsion that churned inside my belly during my twenties, thirties, and early forties. Instead of speaking up against Ma, I became a terrorist against myself, grinding down my self-esteem to a mound of rot in a tree trunk.

As a high school student, I was a top performer, excelling in academics, creative writing, art, music, and drama. In spite of my academic achievements, Ma was never satisfied with my report cards, even though I only missed being first in my class by a tenth of a point. In my junior year, I finally broke the spell of being second best. I rushed to the car, report card wide open. Ma's immediate reaction was "Perhaps next time you'll do better." I reeled as if I'd been punched between the eyes and I was going down for the count. As Ma started to pull away from the curb, I threw open the door, fell into the gutter, picked myself up, and ran into the woods, disappearing for several hours. I sought a safe haven in the ravine, where a statue of the Blessed Mother waited for me. I was too shocked to be angry, too disappointed to speak. Only my Divine Mother could hold the flood of tears that poured into her lap that afternoon. Later, I found out that Ma had misread the report. She'd read my last semester's grade, which was 99.75% instead of the 100% that put me first in my class this time. Even after I found out she'd made a mistake, I was devastated—and she never said a word of apology.

This incident was cruel from one viewpoint, but it reflected the fear-based drive in Ma's mind: perfect mothers have children who excel in everything, and I could never live up to her expectations. Unfortunately, I internalized my mother's fear-based hatchet and often used it to systematically chop away at my perceived sin of imperfection, of not being good enough.

In the midst of this bleakness, however, two women came into my life during my junior year of high school, and both of them became significant role models. The first woman was my English and drama teacher, Sister Elizabeth, a daughter of the Order of the Holy Ghost. Her physical appearance was peculiar and yet riveting. She looked like a giant sea turtle that walked on its back legs with its head permanently fused to the upper rim of its shell. It appeared as if she had no neck and she walked with an unbending spine. Her arms flopped at her side like droopy stumps of flesh. Several of the students, including me, made jokes that she probably took her head off at night, and this is what made her so crabby at times.

To my absolute dismay, I found out she'd been tortured in a Nazi concentration camp. Several of her neck vertebrae had been removed. When I heard of this barbarity, I prayed several rosaries as penance, went to confession, and didn't eat lunch for a week. I was aghast at my insensitivity toward her. She had been nothing but kind to me and consoled me the time I was sexually attacked by a seriously disturbed student during a fieldtrip. Although I reported the incident immediately, I was told to be understanding of the student as this was the only way she knew how to express friendship. I was punished for shouting at the girl and was put in a separate classroom to do my homework. Sister Elizabeth came in and shed tears with me for what I had endured. And I had made fun of her short neck!

One day Sister Elizabeth announced a writing contest that focused on an embarrassing but humorous event in our life. I decided to write about the time my mother demanded I attend a dance at my brother's high school. Going to a dance was as appealing to me as eating raw oysters. Ma didn't understand that being touched while dancing brought back nasty memories of her. The only touches I enjoyed were the touch of Christ in Communion and holding my baby brother's hand. Furthermore, I was a fat girl with doughnut rolls around my waist, a Buster Brown haircut, big boobs, and oversized, round dark-pink glasses. I hadn't cared that I looked like an undercooked muffin because I was convent-bound. As a nun I'd be baked to perfection, a Pillsbury dough girl for God. But Ma was blind to my choice of career and sewed a valentine-red crepe V-necked dress for the event. The design included a drop waist, accentuating the fact that my body shape could have been a poster board for oil barrels. To top it all off, the edges of the neck were trimmed in white guaranteed-to-make-you-sneeze fake fur. Good grief, it was an ugly outfit.

My intention on the night of the dance was to shape-shift into a wallflower. But along came a gawky five-foot-four-inch sophomore who introduced himself as a friend of my brother. His arms and legs moved like a robot's, so I figured he was safe to talk with. "You are Ray's sister, right? I'd like to find out what it would be like to dance with an elephant. He says you are his elephant sister." My first reflex was to throw up on his polyester suit coat, but instead I dug my left heel into his Sunday best shoe. I don't know if I was fuming more at my obnoxious brother or at Ma for sewing a dress that made me look like Santa Claus's toy sack.

Tears welled up, spilling onto my ridiculous dress. It flashed through my mind that, if I cried enough, I'd dissolve and disappear from the dance floor. It didn't cross my mind that elephants don't melt, and they are also difficult to hide.

The day that Sister Elizabeth read my essay aloud to the class, she sat at her desk, tears streaming down her scarlet-red face as she choked with laughter. I feared she'd need CPR. I didn't want to win an award and see the headlines in the school bulletin: elephant fails to resuscitate turtle with no neck. For one day, I was a brilliant humorist, a funny would-be nun. My mother was called with the good news. I was grounded for exposing the family and for painting my brother in a bad light. He was also grounded and refused to speak to me for weeks.

Receiving the Golden Globe award for humor from Sr. Elizabeth was better than getting an Oscar for straight As. She saw me as a creative being, an artist of God, someone who could change lives through laughter. Like her, it didn't matter what I looked like or who my mother was. What was important was that pain could be alleviated by the laughter that rumbled in my tummy. Sister Elizabeth also recognized the gloomy clouds that rested on my shoulders. Several times after this essay, she found me slumped over my desk, pretending to be asleep. But she knew I'd shut the clamshell of my existence for a moment to hold my quivering heart. Gently, she'd call my name and soon we'd be smiling or reciting silly poetry. When she laughed at my jokes, possibility came alive within me. Maybe I was important. Maybe I wasn't a crazy woman. Maybe I mattered. Maybe I was good enough to be a nun. If I were to meet Sister Elizabeth today, I'd want to hug her with all the love of the universe. I'd want to sit at her feet and ask her to tell me her story, and I'd share with her how ashamed I felt that Ma had claimed my body before I could become a Bride of Christ. And I'd share with her how I envied her protective habit and those big rosary beads around the waist, along with the long black strap. And maybe, sitting face-to-face with this holy woman of God, I'd be silent, overwhelmed that I'd been so loved.

The second woman who called forth the mystical *me* was someone I called "Auntie." She was the aunt of one of my classmates, Pheonia, whose home was in Harlem. As a dormitory student at the Academy, Pheonia had little to do on weekends except chant hymns or scrub the already polished floors of the chapel. I begged Ma to let Pheonia stay with us on Saturdays. I give credit to Ma for saying yes since we had no people of color in Putnam. None.

Pheonia's eyes sparkled like carbonated soda water, and her laughter rumbled like a bowling ball slowly making its way down the polished lane. She had a rich Jamaican accent that was almost surreal when she recounted spooky stories. Her bathroom rituals were fascinating: she'd shuffle her feet, walk backward, then forward, then sideways, all the while chuckling, pretending to brush her teeth and comb her hair, until she reached the toilet. My older brother was so irritated with her behavior that he went to the neighbor's house to use the toilet, which, of course, infuriated Ma.

While Pheonia and I didn't share similar skin tones, I was not aware how different we were until the night I saw her standing next to the bedroom window in a pink nightgown—her skin glowed like polished coffee beans in the light of the full moon. She was staring at something that gave her the willies, and with no warning, she screeched like a banshee, shutting her eyes to block out the shadows dancing on the walls. I freaked out because all I could see were her big, pearly white teeth grinning at me. Then we both hollered, collapsing onto the bed with side-splitting laughter, remembering at the last minute, in prayer, to stand at the window and blow out our fears to the moonlight.

Unbeknownst to us, Ma went ballistic after some townspeople called our home, chastising Ma and Pa for bringing "dangerous foreigners" into the neighborhood. Years later, Pa admitted that the callers threatened to damage our home unless Pheonia was sent back to where she came from. Ma's response was quite impressive: "Stupid idiots—no one

Maybe I was important. Maybe I wasn't a crazy woman. Maybe I mattered. Maybe I was good enough to be a nun.

is going to tell me what the hell to do. Idiots." What Ma knew, and the townspeople didn't, was that Pheonia's parents had been murdered in Jamaica. On this occasion, orphanage memories must have softened Ma's heart and made her protective of a motherless child.

One summer day, a taxicab stopped in front of the house, and what looked like a sun-tanned jolly green giant stepped from the back seat of the cab, elegant in white gloves and a tailored light-blue sleeveless dress. What I thought was an apparition of the Dark Madonna was, in fact, "Auntie." Pheonia's aunt had traveled from Harlem to thank the "nice white girl" who kept her niece this side of sad. Auntie's six-foot-seven-inch body dwarfed all the furniture in the front room. I dared not invite her to sit on the couch for fear that her seemingly endless legs would fold up like an accordion if she landed on the weak springs. Auntie must have read my mind because she remained standing, hunched over, yet as poised as a graceful giraffe. I suspect she was intuitive enough to wonder if the taxi driver, who kept racing the motor and blaring his horn every few minutes, feared a mob might come by for a midday lynching.

After presenting me with a beautiful blue-green paisley dress with gold buttons down the front, the dark goddess politely, but firmly, informed my mother that she was taking me to Quebec, Canada, on a pilgrimage to visit a recently completed statue of the Virgin Mary. This statue reportedly had extraordinary healing powers that flowed through her crystal eyes and rosary beads. Ma never—and I mean *never*—allowed anyone to have power over her. But this woman was not to be argued with. The power of her presence felt as if Jesus had come back as an African woman. She spoke in sultry, hypnotic tones, a voice more comforting to me than pure maple syrup on buttered waffles. She produced bus tickets, not realizing that I'd never been away from home except for school, church activities, or visiting family in the insane asylum. When Ma agreed to let me go, I believed in miracles. There was no other conceivable explanation for Ma's capitulating without protest.

Within the week, Pheonia, Auntie, and I traveled by Greyhound bus to the Canadian border, where we were blindsided. Pheonia and Auntie were not allowed to enter Canada on their Jamaican visas. Had they crossed the border, they would not be allowed back into the US and be deported to the Jamaican Islands. Although my anxiety whistled at the pitch of an over-heated tea kettle, Auntie kept her poise. She insisted I continue the trip alone, under the supervision of the tour guides and bus driver. Auntie's peaceful eyes penetrated my bones as she whispered, "Go see the Virgin . . . your mama will never know you have gone alone. I will take care of everything. Wipe those tears, my love, and go back on the bus. God is with you."

Auntie winked, and I blubbered over my prayer book as I waved goodbye from the bus. Two women from Germany sat behind me, occasionally tapping me on the shoulder, offering hard candy or sometimes a sweet smile. They became my bodyguards and we communicated telepathically from our hearts as none of us spoke the same language. They made sure I had orange juice for breakfast and a hamburger and chips for lunch. I usually didn't show up for supper, using the excuse that I had a pounding headache from all the travel. The truth was I didn't have enough money for three meals a day.

Finally, we arrived where the Virgin's statue was exhibited. Until that day, Mary had been my friend and my semi-protector. I was somewhat reticent to put all my faith in her as she didn't have power over my mother. Mary's statue was about eight feet tall, and her face was lustrous, a snow-white porcelain, phenomenally beautiful. I swear I saw her breathing and I could almost touch her as flesh and blood. Never had I seen such exquisite eyes, a shimmering light blue, similar to Grandma Helen's crystal earrings. The rosary, which had to be at least five feet in length, was made of clear crystal multifaceted beads. When the sun touched their surface, the beads flashed tiny rays of light, encapsulated stars from the heavens. Her white robes were carved and yet seemed to flow like silken streams from the mountains. Like a newborn baby with underdeveloped neck muscles, my head flopped from side to side as I tried to absorb the grandness and power of this statue. At one point, I cupped my drooping chin in my hands so as not to drool all over the place. I've seen young children be entranced by fairy princesses—this was my fairy Godmother straight from heaven. In the face of such divine elegance, I felt the seduction of death calling me home, and I fell to my knees. I don't recall how long I remained in prayer or even how I returned to my hotel room. Rapture is quite difficult and painful to move out of. That evening, I had a ferocious migraine headache, and I refused the potato chips and orange soda the German women left in front of my door.

The next day we participated in a ceremony at the Basilica of St. Anne de Beaupré. Hundreds of crippled people, rich and poor alike, women chanting, men pushing wheelchairs, all reciting the rosary with the expectation that their Mother would grant them a miracle. I watched in silence. Knowing that the Mother loved me erased my pain—I didn't need anything more.

Fifteen days later, I arrived at Auntie's apartment in Harlem. Awesome Auntie told me that she hadn't called Ma—"what she didn't know didn't hurt her." In thanksgiving for my safety, Auntie and I attended Mass at the local Catholic church. I loved the gospel singing and belted the "praise you Jesus" chorus along with my fellow Christians. Auntie sat two pews behind me, which puzzled me until I remembered her whispering to me as we walked up the stairs to the church, "Do not be afraid, I am with you, sweet child." What I didn't know is that several people had posted death threats on Auntie's door accusing her of having "dirty, white trash" in the neighborhood. On the way home from the service, Auntie walked with long strides, the fluid movement of a panther sniffing danger. She bolted the iron barred doors, read scripture in her native tongue, and wrapped me in her arms until Pa's pudgy knuckles tapped on the door. He wasn't invited in. She gave him one directive: he was to drive at high speed, without stopping, until he reached a certain street. Auntie shoved me onto the floor in the back seat and covered me with pink blankets and shopping bags. At the designated juncture, it was safe for me to sit up and straighten my hair and rumpled dress.

When we arrived home, no one said hello or welcomed me back except for my little brother. He missed me and was miffed I hadn't told him where I'd gone. Ma curtly told me to be quiet about everything, and she told people I'd been taking care of Grandma Helen. Neither Ma nor Pa ever mentioned the trip to me again, never asked about Canada or the Virgin. At bedtime, Ma demanded I hand over Auntie's gifts, which she promptly dumped into the garbage can, along with the remnants of our Sunday meal of hot bagels, cold butter, and milk with Hershey's syrup. In the middle of the night, I reached into the garbage can and cut two buttons off the paisley dress I treasured: souvenirs I kept along with the bus ticket.

Pheonia didn't return to the Academy, and my letters came back with "addressee unknown" and then "refused." Although I was very confused and wondered if I'd done something wrong, my grief was more about having Auntie, a good-enough mother, ripped away from my arms.

A month before I graduated from high school, my appreciation of Ma's resiliency under adverse situations unfolded dramatically. It began after midnight one morning in May, a few days before my eighteenth birthday. My dad was traveling for his job, my four-year-old brother was sound asleep in the back bedroom, and who knows where my older brother was. I'd created a tent in my bed, a flashlight in hand, probably re-reading *Love is Eternal*, my favorite novel about Abraham Lincoln and Mary Todd.

That night, I heard moans coming from Ma's room. At first, I wasn't concerned because oftentimes when Pa was away on business, Ma would sob in her room, and try to muffle the sound by rattling her rosary. The faster the clickety-clack of the beads, the more we knew "mama wasn't happy." Then, suddenly, an ominous, heebie-jeebies feeling came over me. As if wild fire shot up my spine, I bolted out of bed, stumbling headlong onto the floor. Trying to regain my balance, I stubbed my big toe against a wooden chair. Ignoring the throbbing pain, I called out, "Ma, are you okay?" No answer. Ma's door opened, and the light from the neighbor's floodlight cast a bone-chilling shadow as Ma stumbled past me. She was hunched over, blood gushing and running down her legs, out under her feet, and splattering onto my bare feet. The ghostlike color of her face and her drooping eyes told me death was stealing her life force. She grabbed several white bath towels from the linen closet, but they rapidly turned into sopping bundles of blood. Ma lunged into the bathroom and collapsed next to the toilet. She managed to get back up, plop onto the toilet seat, and then staggered back to her bedroom. I was frightened out of my wits gaping down at the sea of blood—Ma's life—squishing under my feet. "My God, my God Ma . . . are you dying? My God. Holy Mary, pray for us."

Ma was barely audible, "Call the doctor—tell him I'm hemorrhaging." My fingers were cold as ice as I reached for the wall phone and dialed Ma's physician. The doctor answered but told me curtly that I was too young to understand the meaning of the word "hemorrhage." He told me to call him in the morning if Ma was still bleeding, that it was probably just a heavy menstrual period. He told me to stop being so "hysterical" as I was just making things worse. "It can't be that bad, go back to bed." This was one of those rare moments when I knew the authority figure was dead wrong, that I was not a lunatic for seeing the gravity of Ma's situation. I dialed for an ambulance and was enraged to find out that, in order for the medics to respond, a doctor had to give the orders. My observation was irrelevant. As I hung the phone up, I was seething. *Jesus, Mary, and Joseph—will it be my fault if she dies? What am I going to tell Pa? And where the hell is he, anyway?* Shit, I was in trouble. She was in trouble.

Some merciful spirit from within me gave me energy to call the doctor again. This time I channeled all Ma's indignation. "Doctor, you are a stupid idiot—she is *dying*—there is more blood on the floor and on the sheets than in her body. Do you *hear* me? If she dies, it will be your fault, and I will tell everyone in town you killed her. Do you HEAR me? My mother is HEMORRHAGING to death. Call the ambulance—NOW!" I slammed down the telephone handset so hard that it spun out of control and punched me in the jaw.

Fifteen minutes later, the paramedics arrived, and they wrapped her unconscious body in clean sheets. They shook their heads in disbelief, wiping their bloodstained boots on the small carpet in front of the door. The only thing they said to me was to get some sleep. Knowing my brother would wake up in a few hours for his breakfast of Cheerios or Lucky Charms, I set about cleaning the house. I gathered up the blood-drenched nightclothes and towels and put extra bleach and soap into the washing machine.

A day later Dad came home. We didn't have cell phones in those days, and Pa never called us when he was traveling. I asked him to go to the hospital. I figured someone would have called me if she were dead. Thank goodness Pa didn't yell at me after he visited Ma. Pa never knew the secret I kept from him: that night when Ma's doctor asked if I had "found anything" on the bed or in the toilet, I said "no." But the truth was that I had found a large, solidly formed "blood clot" Ma had left in a basin on the side of her bed. I flushed "it" down the toilet. Until the doctor asked that question, I thought the dark red blob was a result of Ma's bad monthly period. I wanted to hurt myself once I realized that I'd abandoned a baby brother or sister into our sewer pipes. God help me. I felt like a murderer. Maybe I was as "stupid" as Ma claimed I was.

Miraculously, Ma recovered and attended my high school graduation a week later, weakened and yet elegantly dressed in a beautiful lavender lace dress, wearing her favorite dark-red lipstick. A good mother would never miss an important school event. She never said a word to anyone about her slightly protruding belly or the miscarriage or her brush with death. Come to think of it, she never asked me if I was okay or if I had found anything in the basin. Silence is not always golden.

CHAPTER 7

Falling into the Abyss

Women need a literature that names their pain and allows them to use the emptiness of their lives as an occasion for insight rather than as one more indication of their worthlessness.

—CAROL CHRIST

In the spring of my senior year, I received a letter that knocked me for a loop. I'd been accepted at the prestigious Juilliard School of Music, and they'd offered me a four-year scholarship! "This can't be . . . this must be a mistake." I was completely confused because I would never have sent in an application, knowing full well we couldn't afford the tuition. Apparently, my voice coach and piano teacher appealed to the college on my behalf, and I was given the golden prize. This nun had treated me like Ma did, critically dissecting every note I sang, every note I played. Once, she stomped out of my voice lesson, went to where the other nuns were eating breakfast, and shouted, "This girl is so stupid she thinks I am complimenting her when I tell her she sounds like a flute. It means she has no depth and too much high range." God, I was mortified.

In the end, I turned down the scholarship, and my teacher walked out of the room. I tried to explain to her that I wanted to either enter religious life or pursue medicine—but that was a half-truth. The students at this world-renowned school were from well-to-do backgrounds, and they were exceptionally gifted. I had no confidence I could compete with this "crème de la crème" talent. I was a country church-mouse of a young woman and would be devoured by the sophisticated cats of the big city. For some odd reason, Ma kept silent about my decision not to go to Juilliard. I told her about being accepted but not about the scholarship.

My heart's desire was to be a nun. I'd sent in an application to be a Carmelite nun—nothing made me happier than thinking of spending my life praying, singing, and baking bread. Had it not been for some small print in the application, I'd most likely be a Mother Superior today. It is humbling to admit that my passion to be God's chosen bride fizzled when I read the words "bring a year's supply of old rags." When I realized this meant I'd have to wash out my menstrual blood with my bare hands, I felt so repulsed that I pushed the pause button on my vocation. What impacted me even more was a rare conversation I had with my dad. We were walking from the parking lot to a school event, and I shared my desire to be a Carmelite nun. Pa's reaction flared out like dragon fire, an emotion I'd never seen in him before. His objection was simple and to the point: "Don't give up your life for a bunch of dried-up, stodgy old farts. You are better than that." He asked that I go away to college for one year and then reconsider. "I don't care what you study—just do what you love." For Pa, doing what I was passionate about didn't include God. I was going to reply that God was the most important person in my life, but my gut instinct said, *be still.* I have no doubt that, had I shared with him how I heard God when the flowers sang to me, or loved the opera the crickets created, he'd have given me a one-way ticket to Timbuktu so I wouldn't become one more lost soul, like Grandma and her daughters.

I don't give up very easily, so God sent me one more message that religious life was not in the stars for me. There was a particularly ingratiating nun who was intent on snagging me for the convent. Often, she would follow me out of the chapel and get right in my face and ask in a whisper whether I heard the call of God. Her bad breath was reason enough to avoid her. One time, exasperated by her stalking me, I confessed that I'd join an order if I'd be allowed to study medicine and be a missionary. "How arrogant of you to have such ambition and defy God's will," was her response. A friend told me later that she had been an accomplished pianist prior to entering the order. As an act of obedience to God, she surrendered all she loved and became a teacher, which she disliked immensely and, frankly, had flopped at. The final straw was when she laid on "the curse." "If you marry, you will have two sons, and both will die at an early age." As I turned away, her final words sizzled in my brain: "It will be God's punishment for your disobedience." God surely wouldn't let that happen, or would He? Something snapped within me like the elastic on a too-tight bra: I unplugged from the house of the nunnery.

As the images of music and a life of silence faded, I circled back to my aspiration of being a medical doctor. In my freshman year of high school, I had developed a serious crush on Dr. Tom Dooley, a world-renowned third-world medical missionary who worked in South East Asia. I attended one of his lectures at Holy Cross College and was so enthralled with his presentation that I forgot how painfully shy I was and pushed my way through a swarm of people to shake his hand. His kindness prompted me to ask if he'd consult with me about a paper I was researching on the impact of drug addiction on disadvantaged populations. He gave me his address, and internally I swooned like a love-struck teenager. During some written correspondence, he openly shared his zeal for God and his deep connection to nature. Dr. Dooley also encouraged me, at all cost, to follow the desire in my heart to serve underprivileged people. I slept with his notes under my pillow for three years, hiding them from Ma's snooping eyes every morning in a schoolbook. I figured if Ma could sleep with a can of Bon Ami (good friend) cleanser under her pillow, and a bottle of Lysol next to her bed, I could give myself permission to rest my head on healing words. It gave me the courage to apply to pre-medical school. This was Ma's first choice for me, and I had to resist the temptation to ditch everything because she was for it. Externally, Ma appeared supportive, but had I chosen a different field of study, she would have made it clear that my choices were irrelevant or impractical.

While I applied to several renowned colleges, I had an intuitive hunch that Loyola University of Chicago was the best choice for me. I deliberately rejected any apprehensions that being on a campus with mostly males would scare the liver out of me. Leaving home was my priority, so why sweat such small things as never having been on a date and not knowing how babies were made. "Suck it up!" was my motto along with "Hail Mary, pray for me."

Despite several undiagnosed illnesses and bouts of migraines, I was a straight A student my freshman year . . . except for a D in logic. My teacher commented to the class that he was only passing me so that no other teacher would have to deal with my way of reasoning! And in spite of my grades, the all-male faculty recommended I drop out of pre-med because, as they said, "you are too tender-hearted and vulnerable to pursue a medical career." These men were well-intentioned, I am sure, but I decided to stay with pre-med, giving myself the summer to make a final decision.

Returning home was as pleasant as sleeping in the North Woods without bug repellant. When Ma picked me up from the bus station, she was appalled that I'd put on so much weight. Granted, I did look like a gigantic helium balloon, but when she screamed, "Oh my God, you are FAT!" the wind was taken out of me.

Within days, she marched me to the family doctor, demanding I'd be put on diet pills. "What a disgrace she is. This is no daughter of mine. I can't be seen with her when she is so obese." I didn't know the diet pills contained speed, so I was amazed how my appetite disappeared and how energized I felt. I worked two jobs, from six a.m. to midnight, and by the end of the summer, I shed over seventy pounds. I could wrap my work uniform around me twice.

What really motivated me to lose weight was the thought of taking up music again if pre-med wasn't suitable for me. At college, I'd auditioned for the role of Anna in the musical *The King and I*. The director was blunt: "Honey, you have the voice and the acting ability. You'd be perfect for the role, but your body has to go. Anna cannot be overweight." Although the role was given to someone else, I was given the confidence that I had talent.

I decided to try one more year of pre-med studies, but there was another plan unfolding that I did not expect. The day I returned to the campus to begin my sophomore year, the dorm mother was standing at the top of the stairs, barring me from the dormitory. "These orders are from the bursar. Your bills were not paid. You have to leave NOW." I was so flabbergasted I barely could speak. "Don't you remember who I am? I was chosen as president of the dorm?" She turned her back, then locked the door. I managed to regain the use of my rubber legs, sprinting to the bursar's office. Once again I was told, "Your bills are not paid. Now leave the premises," and the door was slammed in my face. This was outrageous. Of course, Dad paid the bill. Ma's outrage arose in me, and I pounded on the door, screaming that the bursar was a liar. It felt like my brains had dropped onto the pavement and some monster was scrambling them for dinner. The short, dour priest jerked the door open again, yelling over my protests, "I said, your bills are not paid. Leave or I will call the police."

I found a pay phone and told Ma to wire money for me to come home. She bellowed to my dad. He, true to form, said, "Quit being a nervous Nellie. I paid the bill. I have the receipt. I'll call the bursar. Nothing to worry about." But Pa was telling a brazen lie. He hadn't paid the bill and the bursar was correct. The coup de grace was that, even if I paid the bill, I wouldn't be allowed to return. My dream of becoming "somebody" had been steamrolled.

My father left on a business trip the morning I returned home. As usual, there were no apologies, not even one word about why I was home. I felt like a paper doll cutout, wondering who or what in hell would send me to the next shredding station. I forgave Pa for his betrayal, knowing it was not his intention to harm me. I suspect he was beaten down from all the times Ma verbally pummeled him for being an insufficient provider. I understood it as personal failure, the dark molasses kind that tangles you up in a sticky ball of deceit, and you feel helpless to escape. I chose to minimize Pa's deception and instead latched onto the hand of my old friend, shattered illusions, and sank into the darkness of "nothing matters." Ma dealt with Pa by locking her bedroom door and blowing her nose fiercely to cope with her tears.

To Ma's credit, within a week, she drove me to the nearest college, where she had connections with the dean. I was permitted to enroll in a late registration, signing up for Shakespeare and biology. She drove me thirty miles each way to class. Like the times we drove to the insane asylum to visit Grandma, these daily trips were carried out in silence . . . and I had a lot to think about.

I thought about someone I dated during my first year at Loyola. He was a doctoral teaching assistant, and he taught an introductory history class that was one of my prerequisites. Although I could think of nothing more boring than history, I was impressed with his intelligence, his booming voice—and he was attracted to me. His personal story interested me in that he was a former seminarian who decided to leave his chosen path on the Feast of the Immaculate Conception. He felt that Mary called him to the vocation of marriage. I had never dated before, and, given my wider-than-normal dress size and dorky wardrobe, I was very surprised that anyone would want to spend time with me. Plus, I felt quite certain I'd never be the one to fulfill his mission.

I was so obsessed with being free of Ma that I didn't see how much this man and Ma were mirror images of each other. I also desperately wanted to return to college, and, sadly, for that, I needed a different last name. Though my dreams and my gut-knowing told me "no," I convinced myself, in spite of his domineering personality, to accept this man as my husband. I can really empathize with people who marry to get a green card.

Walking down the aisle on my wedding day, I said to Pa: "I shouldn't be doing this." He chuckled. "It only lasts a lifetime, don't worry." All my cells, my blood, my bones shouted, *Wrong, wrong, don't do this.* But how could I disappoint the guests, return the gifts, and go back to living at home? I decided that escaping home trumped my misgivings and bad manners. God, with a sense of humor, even opened an exit door, but in vain: When the priest asked, "Do you *Marie* (my mother's name) take *Louise* (he was Louis) to be your lawful wedded wife (not husband)?" I gave a resounding "No." Everyone laughed at the punch line but me.

In retrospect, I've come to believe that the Spirit brings two people together in a relationship so that their psychological shadow material gets transformed. Some ancient traditions see this as trickster medicine, meaning: I knew on a soul level what I had to encounter to be the woman I agreed to be. I thought I was escaping the crockpot I had lived in, but the heat just turned up several notches. In so many ways, he became my voice, and my mother's voice, parroting back to me exactly what I was saying to myself. I regurgitated the same words in secret, every minute of my existence: *You are insane, unworthy, not good enough, and you can't live without me.* Like Ma, this man criticized the way I thought, the way I looked, the way I did things—including the way I packed the frozen peas in the freezer. He left notes taped on doors (instructions on locking them) and drains (instructions on tipping them). He threatened me with shaking fists about my relationship with God.

On April 30, 1964, fourteen months from the day we were married, our first son, John, a perfectly healthy child, was born. Following the delivery, my belly was hugely distended, and I felt unusually weak. My complaints were dismissed by the staff as nothing more than the fears of a neurotic young mother. I finally trusted my intuition, and, while bawling my eyes out, I yelled at a nurse to call a doctor. When he came in, he placed his hands on my belly and pressed. As outrageous as it seems, blood clots bigger than my eight-pound baby went flying across the room, splattering onto the walls. One of the nurses had a great sense of humor and muttered loud enough for me to hear, "Jesus, you never see this on *Dr. Kildare.*" But the obstetrician wasn't laughing. In a voice deliberately empty of emotion, he said, "Sweetheart, I have to call your husband. I don't think you are going to make it through the night. You are hemorrhaging to death."

A peace beyond understanding swept through me. I hadn't been crazy for thinking something was terribly wrong, and maybe, just maybe, I'd be released from this body, from this life. My husband was called, but he told the doctor, "You are probably exaggerating . . . she will be fine. I'll come after work tomorrow." As I was being rushed into surgery, I went past my roommate's bed. "I am not going to come back, but don't cry for me. I'll be with God." What the doctors discovered in surgery was that a uterine artery had burst, filling my empty womb with blood.

I have to admit that dying from loss of blood was a euphoric experience—like drifting into a far-off mystical galaxy. At the moment of near-death, I was engulfed in the brilliant, iridescent splendor of my Jesus, my Beloved: Light unto Light, Life beyond Life, Love beyond Love. My body was a floating orb of gossamer white light. I was surrounded by celestial music and beyond-the-rainbow colors that held my ancestors. Jesus reached forward to touch my fingertips and whispered my name. This was the moment I had waited for my entire life. I was going to die. I was returning to God. Tenderly, Jesus said, "Annette it is not your time. You must go back." Blackness descended—I was shocked, stunned, devastated.

What I remember next was the doctor saying I had given them a "run for their money." I had died on the table, but they were able to bring me back to life. I was as astonished as the doctor that I was alive, but I wasn't rejoicing. It had been my dream that, when I died, Jesus would be delighted to see me again. He'd gently wipe away my tears with white clouds trimmed in sunshine. Instead, the wounded child within me heard his words as a crushing rejection—I wasn't good enough to return Home. It was a betrayal more brutal than Ma's touch. For many years, I pleaded with God: how could you be so heartless as to root me on earth? Don't you realize I'm dying here? I sizzled with mute rage, branding the lining of my heart with self-loathing. I plunged into a bottomless pit of despairing unworthiness, crucified by my victimizing mind. For close to thirty years, I contemplated suicide, desperate to escape the imprisonment I felt in my own body.

My stay in the hospital was a mixture of helplessness and hazy memories. I'd have flashbacks of when Ma almost hemorrhaged to death after a miscarriage and how stoic she had been. She willed herself to life for her children's sake. That's what a good mother does. How mortifying to admit that I felt so trashed in life that it never dawned on me that my baby would miss having me as his mother—would miss *me*. All I could think of was how deranged I was to be willing to abandon my baby because I was enamored with God. The truth was I was terrified to return to my marriage relationship—that was the death sentence. Because I couldn't admit this, or maybe because I felt so trapped, I convinced myself I was a rotten mom. Hating myself became a dangerous pattern I turned to when I couldn't contain my rage.

Sadly, I don't remember seeing or even feeding my son. After ten days or so, I returned home to the third floor walk-up we lived in, along with dozens of cockroaches. I returned to the hospital several times during the next month for surgeries to deal with further bleeding. Ma offered to come and stay with us because she figured my husband would not be able to manage teaching at a high school, continue his doctoral studies, and also handle a half-alive wife for whom even holding her baby was a challenge. In truth, I needed the help. In spite of my physical condition, my husband expected me to make dinner and clean the apartment. I had to wash the baby clothes by hand because I was too weak to climb the stairs and get to the laundromat.

My postpartum depression was severe, and losing so much blood put me into a debilitating state of fatigue, making it almost impossible to stay awake while sitting on the toilet or on a kitchen chair. Thoughts that I was turning into Grandma Helen or Anna chilled my bones. I also entertained the idea that my misery was because of the transfusions I'd received—seven to be exact. I'd been infused with craziness from my family, so it seemed plausible that maybe I'd taken in other people's demons along with their blood—and that was the cause of my distress.

As helpful as Ma was with the chores, the relationship between her and "he who ruled with an iron mind and a cold tongue" was contentious. At times, they sounded like blue jays squawking at a squirrel on the bird feeder. Neither of them recognized how they were a continuation of the black-and-white mantra I heard throughout childhood: "I am right, you are wrong. Do what I say or pay the consequences. My word is law."

One afternoon, Ma started bitching at him for not treating her or me very well. Whatever triggered Ma's tirade, it ended with one of her trademark remarks: "You are one mean, stupid jackass . . . people like you deserve to be locked up." She put on her lipstick, picked up a carton of empty Coca-Cola bottles, and left the apartment. Still sputtering in her annoyance, Ma didn't see the last two steps of the staircase. She tripped, landing on dagger-like shards of glass and slicing her wrists in several places.

I was oblivious of the accident, although I was worried when she didn't return home for several hours. When she did, her plain cotton print dress had turned into an abstract work of art by her dried blood. Her wrists were neatly bandaged like gauze bracelets, covering layers of stitches. Ma had managed to get to the church across the street from our apartment, where a staff person called an ambulance to take her to the ER. That evening, she booked a flight home for the next morning. Loud enough for the neighbors to hear, her last words to me were "Remember, you can come home if he hits you."

Months later, I almost did leave—the evening when he hit me in the head with a glass baby bottle, which landed on my left temple. He had papers to grade and he didn't like being interrupted by the baby's crying. Surprisingly, I recall telling him that, if he ever touched me that way again, I'd be gone, baby and all. He didn't hit me again, but his physical intimidations continued: times when he gripped my arms too tightly or cornered me with a raised fist. I confessed to a priest how frightened of him I was. The priest's reply was a smack to my eardrums: "What are you doing or not doing that is forcing him to treat you this way?" I translated this to mean it was my fault for denying him conjugal rights.

Since I wasn't being punched, I didn't realize how devastated I was by my husband's treatment. But his verbal assaults and his constant lectures about my deficiencies, broke my spirit. On the outside, my skin was unblemished; it was my heart and mind that carried the bluish, purplish, and greenish bruises. Even worse, I felt I deserved to be treated this way—I convinced myself that it was God's will and punishment for the stain of Ma's abuse.

To counteract the belief that I was a sub-intelligent being, I decided to return to college and focus on being an English major. I had a reduction in tuition because of my husband's studies, and I agreed to take just one class a semester. I loved to study and immerse my imagination in literature, plus it was great fun reading Chaucer to my oldest son when he was six months old. He'd look at me wide-eyed, making up his own language to offset my old English accent. I was not allowed to be a slacker in my home duties, so most times I'd wait until my husband was snoring before the magical powers of the books could awaken and I could relish in the task of writing papers.

I was never a social butterfly, and, in fact, solitude was my best friend. Because we were poor, I had no spare change to fritter away on movies, go out to lunch with friends, or shop for anything but bare essentials. Thank goodness I inherited Ma's skills as a seamstress, so I could make all our clothes, including pants and coats. I had a hawk eye for fabric bargains, although my sons still tease me about the gaudy flowered materials I used to make ties and curtains.

Apart from classes, my connection to the outside world was through our local church. I did volunteer work and joined a charismatic prayer circle, even though my husband thought that "those weird Catholics" were cultish and a threat to our marriage. He went to one prayer meeting and was infuriated with my friends and our enthusiastic love of God. He pompously argued that praying in tongues was not logical, nor was prophesying, praying for miracles, or believing in personal experiences with God. The only way to God, he insisted, was through the church's dogma and traditions. Like Ma, he was convinced his viewpoints were gospel and not to be challenged. I understood it when even good friends stopped inviting us to events due to his offensive and rude behavior.

When I was seven months pregnant with our second child, I woke up at five a.m. one morning, "seeing" dirt swirling around a child's body and stones crashing into a ravine. The face of my twelve-year-old godchild then appeared before me, radiant as a glowworm. His crooked front teeth overlapped each other, sparkling through his silly grin. He said, "I'm fine and I love you." I sucked in a deep breath, and my unborn child shivered with me. We both understood the meaning of the vision. Three hours later, we received a call from my godchild's mom to say that he had slipped off the edge of a cliff and plunged to his death during a camping trip.

The vision wasn't frightening to me as I was used to having Jesus and spirits of the dead visit me. After I became involved in charismatic prayer, I often knew when someone was going to be ill or die. I recall one evening, as I was going to a prayer meeting, I was abruptly stopped in my tracks as a cold wind swooshed around my legs, and I "saw" a child fall off a porch and break her leg. I immediately prayed to the Holy Spirit for everyone involved in the accident. During the meeting, a good friend frantically rushed in, asking that we pray for his daughter who'd fallen over the banister of their porch that evening. Although I was cautious in sharing what I believed were normal experiences, word spread and a few people began calling me a witch, my husband being one of these critics. "You think you are talking with God, but the Devil comes in many disguises."

I don't know if things would have been different for me had I known that Ma had similar psychic abilities. One of my brothers, at my parents' fortieth anniversary celebration, mentioned jokingly that Ma was a "witch." He said that when someone was about to die, she dreamt of her grandmother rolling over in her grave. *You've got be freaking kidding me.* It was the first time I'd heard this about Ma, and now I was doubly terrified to admit we had similar talents. After Ma died, my younger brother and I returned to this conversation and we revealed our clairvoyant abilities to each other. We belly laughed about our weirdness until we were sick. Pa would have rolled his eyes in disbelief. "You are both kooks, and you got that from your mother, not me." I have no idea if Ma could detect difficulties in people's lives just by walking past them, as I sometimes did. Or if she predicted illness by sensing whether a person's energy felt hot or cold, as I did. I regret that I never had the chance to ask her about these matters. Given her family background, I suspect she would have judged paranormal experiences as a sign of mental illness. I certainly did.

Prayer and praying friends were a lifeline for me, so I'd walk down alleys and find different routes to meet the friends who picked me up for the meetings. When I came home after being away for two hours, he'd grill me like a barbecue chicken fillet. I kept many secrets from my friends, never admitting how obsessed he was with my every move. I had to account for who I was with, where I went, and what we talked about. In addition, I wasn't allowed to have any money of my own, and I felt like a beggar whenever I needed cash. He'd check the grocery lists to make sure I hadn't lied about what I spent shopping. All of this paranoid behavior on his part called out behavior in me I never would have thought possible: furtively squirreling away twenty-five cents to buy orange-slice candies for the boys, or slinking down alleys to get to a prayer circle. I learned to lie, and I became secretive as a sly fox.

Our second son, Tom, was born January 7, 1967, three weeks before the massive blizzard of January 26, the largest single snowfall in Chicago's history. Like his brother, Tom was a perfectly healthy child. Ma blew into town only days prior to attend our son's baptism, bringing her own version of a storm. Ma's lunacy popped out like a full moon the day after the storm had calmed down to high winds and blowing snow drifts. As if she were once again crossing the Putnam bridge during the flood to buy food for us, she decided to go to the grocery store that was six blocks from our apartment, pulling along a little red wagon to carry her purchases. Her makeup was pristine with fire engine red lipstick, a smart move considering she chose to walk boldly in the middle of the street. The goal of her mission was to purchase a package of cheese slices, a loaf of Wonder Bread, and Hershey's syrup to sweeten our Carnation powdered milk. A normal ten-minute walk took her over two hours to complete. Apparently, she got into a heated argument with a snowplow operator who, she felt, deliberately tried to kill her. "How dare he tell me to walk on the sidewalks, when there was nothing but snow drifts . . . how stupid can they be!" I can just imagine what went through the truck driver's mind.

I might add that my husband was equally delusional. He insisted on driving to school, battling the drifting snow under whiteout conditions, avoiding the spin-outs and stranded motorists. It took him over six hours to get home, a trip which ordinarily was a forty-five-minute drive.

Following my second delivery, my blood pressure hovered in a dangerously high range: 275/180. The doctor actually slept in the room to monitor me as my track record with childbirth was not the best. The distant shore of death crept closer to my horizon, but there was no boat to take me to the land of God's peace. There was no moment of touching the Divine in a near-death experience this time—only the birthing of daily debilitating migraines. I lived with chronic headaches after having mumps and meningitis at the age of eight, and in my teen years migraines popped up about six or seven times a month. After my first son was born, they occurred almost daily. Now the pain was so intense that I could barely nurse my baby or care for John, who was three years old when Tom was born. When I wasn't doubled over, or wrapping my head in ice packs, I was throwing up and then collapsing in a room that was devoid of light and noise. Even the sound of a bureau drawer opening or the door closing sent me up the wall. For the most part, drugs were ineffective, merely dulling my senses into a robotic stupor. I ranted at God for not listening to me. At some point, guilt and shame rode on my shoulders like twin beasts, taunting me for not wanting to be alive when I had two beautiful sons, and pounding my head about what a rotten mother I was being to them. I was a disgrace to motherhood. My husband didn't help. "This is all in your head, and you can fix it if you stop your complaining. Snap out of it." He also taunted me: "Oh, why doesn't your God take this away? Answer me that."

As my sons grew up, I learned to live with the migraines, and the boys and I had some good times, mostly when their dad wasn't home. When we were alone, we giggled and talked loud without fear of being scolded. My husband demanded total quiet when he took his daily nap and when he played solitary chess games in the newspaper. Dinner time was tense, not only because I was a horrible cook, but because we had to behave at the table—no laughing, no belching, no nothing. During the week, he'd ration out the cheese slices, counting to make sure no one ate more than allotted. I stretched the hamburger by adding soybeans that had the appearance and texture of rabbit pellets.

When I managed to save up a quarter, the kids would go to the day-old bakery across the street, to buy pretzels and Twinkies. My head hurt so much that

I never looked up to see the spitballs of chewed pretzel sticking on their bedroom ceiling. To admit that I felt like the lowliest scum of a mother is understating my case. Once the children were sleeping, I'd stand at the foot of their bed, usually sobbing, praying to the Blessed Mother to care for them.

There is, however, one memory in my treasure box that always brings me joy. It was Christmas Eve, and I walked nearly a mile to the local department store to see if they had reduced the price on a gigantic stuffed Snoopy. My youngest son loved Snoopy beyond words, and I'd been saving pennies and dimes for this but never had enough. I sneaked out of the house, got to the store fifteen minutes before they closed, with nine dollars in my pocket. The stuffed dog was still on the shelf, but the price tag was $19.00. I burst into tears. I was exhausted from feeling like hell, ashamed of being so poor, and all I wanted was this one stuffed animal for my kid. I didn't think that was too much to ask of God or life.

My old friend, hopelessness, was slithering around my heart, but just then the owner of the store came over to me, offered me a Kleenex, and softly asked if he could help. Oh dear! I poured out my story to him, and, without any hesitation, he put his hand on my arm and asked, "How much do you have?" I placed nine crumpled dollar bills in his hands and he said, "Sold. Snoopy wants to go home with you. Merry Christmas." He even wrapped him in white plastic, as it had started to snow and I had several blocks to walk. Seeing my son's face the next morning is still etched on my heart. His dad thought it was wrong to splurge on stuffed animals. I didn't care an ounce about his opinion that day—for once, I felt like a good mom.

My Snoopy-loving son became very ill when he was ten years old. He complained of his leg being very sore and he was limping. He was not a child who ever complained, so I took him to the pediatrician that afternoon. Within minutes, the doctor said that there was something "very wrong" and my child was to be taken to the Children's Memorial Hospital immediately. I called his dad to pick us up and told him the urgency. His reply was predictable—the doctor was exaggerating, and we were to come home on the bus. He was quick to remind me that Tom had pricked his thigh on a straight pin I'd dropped while sewing: "If you hadn't been so sloppy and left the pin there, he wouldn't have a sore leg."

I called a cab, told the driver I didn't have money for the ride, but would he take us to the hospital—it was an emergency. Once the tests were completed, my son was diagnosed with bone cancer. They assured me they would have a plan in the morning for treatment and said it was best that I go home. Walking away from him sent waves of tumultuous dry heaves through my belly. He was sitting calmly, holding a teddy bear. Ever so gently he waved his hand goodbye, trying his best to smile. As I walked down the hospital corridor, I had to lean against a wall. I was fainting, and I slid to the floor, slumped over like a tree slug. I clearly remember my prayer. *Jesus, no child could have been a greater gift to me. If you want him back, he is yours. Thank you for loaning him to me and forgive me for not being a better mom.*

I knew if my son died, he'd be happy with God. But I'd never get over him being there while I remained here. My husband was asleep when I got home, and he left the next morning for school, not even bothering to ask any questions. After getting my older son to school, I took a bus to the hospital. Once inside the facility, I sped to my son's room like a roadrunner. Standing by his bed was his doctor, beaming. "I have never used the word miracle—I don't believe in them—I don't know what you have done, but your child is healed. You can take him home." All the test results had been reversed during the course of 24 hours. The final diagnosis was strep throat with a treatment of antibiotics. Skeptics like his dad belittled this story, but I believed.

On the ride home in the cab, my son lay across my lap and asked so sweetly why everyone made such a fuss over him. I tried to explain that the doctors thought he had a very bad disease. "But, Mommy, Jesus came to me in the night and told me I was okay . . . why didn't anyone ask me?" Later that day, his dad accused me of being neurotic and said that all my nonsense had resulted in nothing but a stack of bills. I took great solace in Jesus that day. I had given up on him for myself, but he came through for my son—and that was good enough for me.

CHAPTER 8

Unraveling and Waking Up

When you come to the edge
of all the light you have known
... and are about to step into the darkness,
faith is knowing one of two things will happen ...
there will be something to stand on
or you will be taught to fly.

—RICHARD BACH

By the age of thirty-one, I felt like a walking zombie, depleted by physical pain, by constant verbal abuse, and by my internal demons. My head hurt so much I swore someone had dug a crown of thorns into my skull, and my stomach could barely tolerate any food unless it was soft, gushy, or sweet. Diagnosis from the doctors: "Stress." My husband convinced me that my "sickness" was destroying our family: that my praying for a cure was idiotic and useless, that the medical treatments did nothing but pile the bills on his desk. He didn't realize that I managed to attend school functions for our sons through the fog of prescribed drugs and the crucifix embedded in the palm of my hand. I have no doubt he was confused by my behavior, but his frustration and fear took on the mask of caustic fault-finding—a mask worn previously by my mother.

The rudest awakening for me, however, was realizing that Jesus was not going to be my Prince Charming and take me home in a magic carriage. My grief poured into the fragile pipes of my mind, leaving a corrosive film that even cut through my soul. Looking back now, I can see there was a power within me that kept asserting, *You cannot give up—you have a mission, and the unseen forces will not betray you while you complete your task.* But I wasn't consciously awake to the mission of coming to peace about my human nature. When the twilight was upon me, I imagined how I could accidentally die, without a lot of mess for those finding my body. But then immediately I'd be riddled with guilt, slamming myself for being so damn selfish as to put my children through this. And then, as if the garbage truck tipped its load on top of my head, the screaming in myself took on the voice, *You are the worst mother the world has even seen—they will be better off without you.* I can still recall those anguished moments when I walked into the street, deliberately not looking to see if cars were coming. At other times, I had to grip the car's steering wheel so tightly that my knuckles turned white because I was thinking, as I drove across an overpass, how a simple twist of the steering wheel would bring instant relief—the stunning silence of death.

One of my worst fears in contemplating suicide was failing at the attempt and being permanently disabled—a useless, decaying vegetable. Or if I succeeded, that Jesus would say, "You inherited insanity and you've failed to overcome it. Out of my sight, wretched worm." And yet, no matter the depths I sunk into, some seed of divinity, some seed of wholeness pursued me, determined to have me begging for life instead of death.

In all of this pain, an angel appeared in my life in the form of a beautiful, talented woman whose sense of self-worth rivaled my emptiness. I'd met her at my local Catholic church where we decided to become singing partners at Sunday Mass. At first I was intimidated by her guitar skills, but our voices blended perfectly. We quickly became soul friends.

One day she caught me off guard when she said, "I care for you so much that I refuse to be in your husband's presence. I cannot tolerate how he speaks to you and how he treats you so disrespectfully. I don't mean to hurt your feelings or ruin our friendship. He is just mean to you, and I cannot stand it." Tears stung my cheeks as her words stripped away a deep misapprehension. I'd been under the impression that most people legitimized my husband's crabby and stern demeanor because he lived with me, the "fruitcake." "Annette," she said. "How can you believe that? And if some people think that, then don't hang around them, for God's sake." My friend also recognized how jealous my husband was of my friends, and she cleverly devised schemes to get me out of the house. One of them was getting me involved in her husband's campaign to be a delegate to the Illinois Constitutional Convention. Although I had no experience, her husband had total confidence in my abilities, and he entrusted me with organizing groups, writing brochures, learning silk screening to make posters for billboards, and I even helped him strategize his hearings with local politicians.

When the campaign was over, my friend's husband made it possible for my children, who were then seven and ten, to attend a prestigious private school, as long as I volunteered to teach in exchange for their tuition. Of course, my husband was furious about this arrangement as he felt the school was elitist and would warp the boys' sense of being ordinary people. I, on the other hand, loved the idea that I could finally provide something special for them. And what could be more special than a school in which the first-grade teacher brought his St. Bernard dog to every classroom in the morning. The dog stood at each door, barked his good morning greeting, with the school's hamster hanging on for dear life to the dog's thick, furry neck! I often imagined that I was like that vulnerable hamster, protected and supported by my amazing friend.

During the campaign, even my children were involved, plastering bumper stickers on trees for election day, stuffing envelopes, and handing out leaflets at the train stations. The experience and the encouragement of these friendships buffered me from my husband's nitpicking barbs, but, more importantly, it awakened my confidence and a belief in my innate goodness. I was allowed to bloom like a garden of colorful tulips. Once my soul was watered by their encouragement, hidden bulbs of talent burst forth, and success further affirmed me.

There was another campaign worker, a woman whose personality was almost as outrageous as her hairdo, which resembled unraveled Brillo pads. She drove a bright yellow Volkswagen with a noisy muffler and a broken passenger door. I had to get in the car through the back door and climb over the seat into the front. If that path was blocked, I climbed over her in the driver's seat as she was too lazy and rotund to move, and she didn't give a hoot about her size. Of the two of us, I was the loyal collie dog and she was the erratic squirrel, racing for acorns in a windstorm. We bonded through uproarious laughter, and we claimed we won votes by making people crack up with our silliness. One particular morning during the campaign, I flippantly said to her on the phone, "I'll come flying out—just honk the horn." I kissed the children goodbye and wrapped my guilt over leaving the house in my back pocket. As I flew out, in my excitement, I failed to notice a rusty spike sticking up in the front lawn of the apartment building. I tripped and the left side of my face and neck slammed into the oak tree hemmed in by the sidewalk. Like birds that dive-bomb into glass windows get stunned, and then fly away, I slowly came to and stumbled over to my friend's car, hiccoughing with alarm.

Several hours later, I returned home, numb on my left side, unable to move my neck, nursing a migraine. My husband's response was that medical treatment wasn't available for stupidity and that pain was its natural consequence. Besides, he continued, I was already such a drain on our finances that we didn't have the money for a doctor. I managed to get to the emergency room by myself via public transportation. The treatment I was given was to place a pulley over a door, with five cans of peaches in a sack as a counterweight. I was told the weight would help stretch my neck and relieve the injured disk if I did this for fifteen minutes every four hours. Thank goodness the kids didn't eat peaches, or I might have had even more damage than the 90 percent hearing loss I sustained in my left ear.

There was comic relief in this situation as my oldest son told people I was *not* available to take their phone calls, as I was "hanging" myself. Some gasped and hung up on him! In reality, I had been like a hanged lady. Through my recent experiences, I was becoming aware how much I'd been suspended in the haunted maze of my mind. I'd felt stripped of any control over my life, totally dispossessed. I'd lived without the resources I needed to break the spell of powerlessness I was in. But now, even though my friends were expressing their concerns about the seriousness of my physical condition, I thought I was beating the odds, that I was successfully coping—until a night-time dream woke me up.

In the dream, two gigantic hands are floating in the sky. Everything is still—the kind of eerie, pea-green stillness that hovers in the sky just moments before a tornado strikes. Suddenly, a very large glass ball, wrapped in glowing neon light, tumbles out of the extended hands and crashes onto the cement sidewalk, shattering into splinters. At the moment of impact, a curled-up fetus inside the ball emits a gut-wrenching shriek that pierces my sleeping body.

I woke up with my heart pounding in abject terror, drenched in cold sweat. I knew the interpretation of this dream without a doubt. I'd tried to live in a glass bubble with God, separate from my body, and it was time to leave the womb of my spirit world and wake up. As in my near-death experience, I was being returned to earth.

CHAPTER 9

At Home with the Homeless

The human mind is like a piñata.
When it breaks open, there are lots of surprises inside.
Once you get the piñata perspective, you see that losing
your mind can be a peak experience.

—JANE WAGNER

In July of 1976, I was named Citizen of the Month by the *Pioneer Press*, a newspaper chain covering several suburbs on the north side of Chicago. The award came as a result of my work as a legislative assistant to an independent Illinois state representative. The headline for the article was humbling to me: "Christian approach is her way of tackling seniors' problems." The article went on to say, "she attracts people with problems and they know they'll be treated with dignity and love."

During the time I worked for the state legislator, conditions for chronically mentally ill people were substandard to say the least. The State of Illinois approved a policy that released thousands of these patients from institutions and deposited them in local communities without adequate social services. It was a living nightmare for the patients, their service providers, and for the communities they moved into. Working for an elected official, I had the connections and tremendous leverage to advocate for the rights of these dispossessed, abandoned individuals. In addition, having lived with mentally ill family members, I was acutely aware that deranged people were on the fringe of society's fabric, people deemed not good enough to be in the mainstream. And truthfully, I was one of them.

The legislator believed in me for reasons I never understood. He gave me just a few rules to follow: "Ask questions, be kind and confident, and never lose your marvelous sense of humor. I have no doubt you'll be the top aide in the state." As if that weren't enough, he added, "At meetings, speak your opinions, and if they diverge from mine, don't worry . . . it will lead to healthy discussions. I trust you."

"Thank you," I replied. "I won't be an embarrassment, I promise." Internally I was saying, *Are you out of your gourd? Trusting* ME*? Man, if you only knew who I really am . . .*

Looking back, I am in awe that I had an inner Wonder Woman living in me who was able to rise above the shock waves of my fears, and the trauma of my story. At times, I felt I was observing myself from across the room, marveling at the natural charm and finesse I had in establishing smooth working relationships with various agencies, and in negotiating with their directors who always found a way to take care of my requests. I was able, miraculously, to keep my battle with migraines and my queasy stomach hidden from the public. I rose to meet other people's level of confidence in me, and there was little I couldn't accomplish. I found that, without formal training, I was a natural mediator and negotiator.

While I valued the political clout I had, I often woke up in the middle of the night, lamenting that my destitute, illiterate, and sometimes obnoxious clients didn't have my privilege. I also struggled with the all-too-familiar comments I received from seasoned caseworkers: "You've got to be tougher and not be a bleeding heart. Most likely, these people didn't lose their social security or disability checks. They probably drank it away or spent it on drugs." I bit my tongue more than once, fighting the urge to lash out against such rational cruelty. And I realized more than once, their cynicism was accurate.

Several months after receiving the Citizen of the Month award, I nearly fainted when the newspaper editor called to say I'd won their Woman of the Year Award. I felt certain there was some mistake, but the editor assured me that I surpassed other nominees in my competence and my service to the community. From my point of view, the people who deserved the award were the smelly, toothless, gentle souls who sat across from me in my office. They, like me, were dried up, cracked pottery jars, needing kindness and hope for new possibilities. Their needs were just more obvious than mine. I felt a notch saner than the people I served, but not by much. I knew the mind of lunatics, their shame, their dignity, their desperation, and their strength, and I intuitively knew that love and meeting their basic needs were the answer for these "throwaway" people. Eccentric as they appeared, they were like delightful charms on the bracelet of life.

As prestigious as this award was, as beloved as I was by society's throwaway individuals, my immediate concern was how I could break this news to my husband, who had not been pleased with the publicity of my earlier award. Like Ma, he commented, "I hope this doesn't go to your head and make you think you are better than others." The prestige of the award faded quickly as shame oozed in and through my spirit. How could the award be true when I felt like a sewer rat in my marriage, a desperado wrestling with destructive inner demons? The stark contrast ripped me in two. Who was I? A fraud or someone worthwhile? But I felt supported by one of the journalists who commented on my husband's attitude at the award dinner. "Honey, if I lived with someone that angry, I'd go live with the homeless—I really feel sorry for you. You deserve better."

Five months after receiving the award, I was offered a job at our parish to create and coordinate a pilot social service program. It would include working with homebound individuals, developing outreach programs for senior citizens, coordinating and training volunteers, and maintaining a food pantry.

My answer was always, "Yes—honor their dignity. Cleanup will come later."

As with my legislative position, I had no formal training for this position, but I had a natural aptitude for working with disadvantaged people and again—a surprise to me—I had the brains to design and run a successful program! To be honest, the salary was far below the poverty level and would only attract the most dedicated Christian servant or someone at their wit's end, needing employment. I was both. The positive side was the health benefits that paid for my medications, and I figured the job was a stepping-stone to leaving home.

In training my volunteers, I was deeply committed to the perspective that presence to the people we served far outweighed any desire to fix their situations. This attitude rocked the core of many volunteers. "So, you're telling me to first sit and listen to their stories, find out what makes them tick, while I'm surrounded by stinking milk cartons, mouse droppings on the kitchen counters, dirty toilet bowls, piles of crusty dishes, and stacks of unread newspapers? That is so disgusting." My answer was always, "Yes—honor their dignity. Cleanup will come later." Slowly, as patience and kindness replaced the grumbling, little miracles erupted. The volunteers came to understand that vulnerable and underprivileged persons were like wrapped jewels, waiting to be uncovered, held, and cherished. That was healing and delivering services at its best.

A heartwarming illustration comes to mind: the encounter between a high school volunteer and an awesome, eighty-seven-year-old Russian woman. The young man was taking "Spunky Lilly" to the bank to deposit her social security check. He was also bringing along a savings account book he'd found while sorting out this woman's trunk loaded with published poetry books. I heard the well-mannered student audibly gasp. Not only was "Spunky Lilly" the author of the poetry books but her account book showed an amount of $40,000. Stupefied, he silently mouthed, "Are you kidding me?" The wizened elderly woman lived in a filthy, roach-infested one-room apartment full of half-opened boxes of memorabilia and slept on a twin bed covered with greasy, stained sheets. I motioned for him to continue with his task—taking her to the bank. Although it was a ninety-degree day, "Spunky Lilly" donned a long black woolen coat that was threadbare on the edges of the sleeves and hem. It was so stiff with grease and dirt, that she could have passed for a human billboard. As she waited in line at the bank, I stood back, not daring to laugh at the scene unfolding before my eyes. A line of black roaches walked out of the hem of "Spunky Lilly's" coat. The teenager, a true knight in shining armor, darted to her side and stomped on the creatures. Ever so gently, he asked if he could remove her coat, convincing her it was too heavy on her shoulders, and shook it over the sewer near the sidewalk. He later admitted to fumigating his dad's Audi when he returned home that afternoon. This young man's beliefs about how some people choose to live took a tumble that day, and yet, when the elderly woman put her bony, dry-as-a-lizard hand into his and placed a pecking kiss onto his chubby cheek, his eyes welled up with tears. Later that day he said to me, "Shit, lady, you were right. I wanted to disinfect her place, but what she wanted was for me to respect her. Shit, this is hard."

Another young man insisted on accompanying me to the morgue when I needed to identify the body of a woman who'd died under suspicious circumstances in her apartment. Back then, using the term "domestic violence" or "sexual assault" often resulted in off-the-record comments by caseworkers such as "She was a whacko. Probably a prostitute. She's better off now." Since her body had not been discovered for two weeks, the task at hand would be repulsive and breathtaking. The chivalrous teen and I rode the cold elevator together, and I reminded him: "This won't be pretty. Are you sure you want to do this?"

"Of course, I'm here to take care of you." However, when the staff wheeled out the body, even though only the severely discolored face was peeping out of the black body bag, he fainted, sliding against the morgue window. I ended up driving his convertible sports car home, feeling totally alive as the wind rearranged my mood.

A therapist once suggested to me that the main reason I was so devoted to working with fringe people was an unconscious, unmet need to be appreciated. Part of me believed this interpretation, but another part, deep inside, rebelled against it. Loving mentally ill people was no different than loving Grandma Helen and Aunt Anna. I have no doubt that I came into the world remembering that God's brilliance is always present in marginalized people—people the world treats as pond scum.

I have fond memories of the cultured homeless southern belle who dressed in long skirts and high-buttoned blouses, and she always chastised me for my substandard polyester pants and shirts. Like my grandma, she hid the stigma of being homeless by finding Goodwill bargains that gave her the appearance of being high society. And then there was the giraffe woman. Although many professionals would doubt my sanity, I coached this woman to be the best giraffe she could imagine. She had such decorum walking across the street, head erect, with her shopping cart for support. Sometimes she bent down to eat the flowers climbing over a neighbor's fence. Or she'd bring me a small bouquet of dandelions she had sneaked from someone's front yard. More often than not, she'd eat more than she put in my vase.

The most colorful person, however, was the brain-fried alcoholic who dressed as a gypsy for Christ. He was convinced that Jesus wore boxer shorts with printed hearts while preaching the Sermon on the Mount. When this poor soul talked, it was as if he were reading a dictionary backwards. People were astounded that I made sense of his gibberish, but it was similar to interpreting tongues at a charismatic prayer meeting. The pastor of the parish warned me that, unless I reined in this fellow's behavior, I might lose my job. This occurred after he sprinted out of my office one day, ecstatic that I'd given him ten dollars, and exuberantly tried to jump over the metal newspaper stand, near the front stairs of the church. Unfortunately, his red striped pants, two sizes too small, didn't allow his legs enough leeway to jump, so he landed squarely on his manly jewels. None of this would have mattered to the pastor if a funeral procession hadn't been occurring at the same time. The client yelled like Tarzan, and the pallbearers, startled by the call of the wild, nearly did a *heave-ho* with the casket. The pastor sent me a second warning about the "crazies" I was serving.

True to my nature, I dismissed the pastor's concern and stretched the envelope even further by involving one of the "nutcases" as a volunteer. I'll call her Sweetheart—she loved to be called by that name. Sweetheart came to my office, a bit semi-crazed, but her heart filled with a desire to bake bread for homebound seniors. She jumped over chairs, while reciting, with detailed precision, all the side effects of the anti-psychotic medications she was taking. I was startled when she sat down on the piles of paper in the middle of my desk, but I cleared a space and sat next to her.

After several weeks of talking and giggling with her, never sure whether she was going to do headstands in the corner or spin on her rear end in the chair, I said to her, "You know, Sweetheart, there's going to come a day when you realize you are not the nutcase you make out to be, and then you are really going to be in trouble. You'll be normal, with no place to hang your crazies."

She came to a screeching halt, a half-blown piece of bubble gum hanging out of the side of her mouth, and she sputtered, "Shit, oh pardon me, damn, oh crap—forget it. You got my number," she said, intrigued that I had her figured out.

"Now, do I get to help?" She added quickly, "Are you gonna trust my ass to be normal with these crabby old folks?" I sucked my belly in, burst out laughing, and said, "You pull any of your craziness crap with the seniors, you and I will both be toast. Now, here's the cash to buy flour, yeast, and sugar. Get to your baking."

As it turned out, Sweetheart was loved, adored, and totally responsive to the seniors. She had them laughing at all their quirks, their complaints, and "oh, why don't I just die" mantras. When I was fired some time later, Sweetheart quickly slipped back into her skin of insanity. Without a place to foster her normalcy, she saw no other choice but to return home to an alcoholic boyfriend, take drugs, and manipulate the public aid system. She, like so many of the people I loved, were mosaics of broken glass, and yet, when light shined between their cracks, their true colors came to life. In the end, she showed me that kindness has a far greater impact on healing than expensive pharmaceuticals. In the end, I knew I had come face-to-face with all my own demons, insecurities, and craziness. In the end, they freed me more than I freed them.

CHAPTER 10

Father Frank

A few nuns at the school my children attended invited me to attend their weekly prayer group, and I accepted without hesitation, as I always hungered to be with people who loved God the way I did. On the evening following our first gathering, all four nuns were driving home in a torrential storm. When the youngest nun opened her door and exited the car, a driver, blinded by sheets of rain, never saw her petite figure, nor her opened umbrella, and took her life with the hood of his car. Hours later, I was huddled with the nuns in the entryway of her hospital room, and their chaplain, Fr. Frank, was at our friend's bedside, as she transitioned into new life.

Though I'd been in the same hospital as him that day, I didn't actually meet the reverend for another two years, when he suddenly appeared at a charismatic prayer meeting I was leading. My eyes were sealed in the bliss of God, but when he walked into the room, I suddenly felt lightheaded. My eyes peeped open. Because we sat on the floor as we prayed, it was the length of his long feet, nestled in highly polished lace-up black leather shoes, and his lanky legs that first greeted my soul. I was taken aback at my second impression: *This was one handsome dude of God.* His flipped-up page-boy hairstyle charmingly offset the wooden cross that hung limply on a leather string around his heron-like neck. He seemed attached to a worn copy of a leather-bound Bible. I understood why the nuns described Fr. Frank as a saint, a man of Jesus, and kindness personified. He came from a cultured, well-educated family, the eldest of seven children, all of whom were successful professionals. His food for life was flavored with gentility, strong religious values, hard work, and family loyalty. Furthermore, as a Jesuit priest, he was regarded as the pride of the family.

One of the nuns who introduced me to Frank admitted that she'd had a dream in which Jesus said, "I am sending Fr. Frank to the parish for Annette."

I said, "Thank you," and didn't think much of it. I was grateful to God that I'd have spiritual assistance with my new job, and maybe even a friend I could trust.

Fr. Frank started attending our weekly prayer sessions, and, shortly after, I asked if he'd be willing to be my spiritual director—that is, a trusted person I turned to for guidance about my life and spiritual journey. At first, I was dazed in his presence, embarrassed to admit that when he prayed and when he smiled, I became like a sugar cube dissolving in hot coffee. I'd never encountered anyone with such humility and grace. There was no tension between us as we spilled over in God-filled conversations. It was as if we had been separated at some moment in time and were now brought back together seamlessly. Here was an angel of God who saw through my brokenness as I had for Sweetheart. All I could fathom was that he was a living version of Jesus. I began to renew my faith that maybe God did love me and had sent his very best to protect and guide me. He became my best buddy, bringing a divine energy that watered my parched cactus-filled existence. Always, with his arms extended out to his bony knees, his eyes closed in concentration, he listened patiently as I poured out the helplessness I experienced—not so much with the poor mentally ill folks, but with the loopholes and inadequacies of the systems that were set up to serve them. He assured me that God was with me, and, he said, "These people know you love them, and that is such a gift."

One can only imagine how Fr. Frank grappled with the messiness and wretchedness of the people I asked him to assist me with in the parish. I still giggle thinking of the time he rode with me in the back of a police paddy wagon to bring a very paranoid woman to the local mental institution. She was convinced the broccoli in her toilet was warning her that she was going to be killed, and she was making plans to destroy it first. While she, Fr. Frank, and I rode together, she snuggled up to him and stared into his deer-in-the-headlights eyes, and said she knew without a doubt that the priests were "doing it" all the time. Her eyebrows twisted into corkscrews when he asked her what she meant by "doing it."

When my husband heard that Fr. Frank was my spiritual advisor, he fumed that this relationship was the cause of our marital problems. He threatened me several time with shaking fists, claiming he'd see to it that I'd lose my job and Fr. Frank would be transferred. Since my annual salary was about $4,000, losing the job wasn't a great threat. However, losing the companionship of my soul friend felt like a death sentence. Truth be told, I was in love, but not romantically. Fr. Frank's compassion for me and his understanding of my mystical nature were the only sustenance I had as I shriveled away on the barbed wire of my marriage.

A simple smile and good morning from him as he passed my parish office was enough to evaporate my weariness.

Throughout the time I worked at the parish, my health was steadily going downhill. The craving I had for the sweetness of daily Holy Communion lost its taste. God became a stiff piece of flatness that irritated the roof of my mouth. My mind churned with thoughts of being Fraud of the Year or Ms. Loony Tune. I was a "blessed mother" to all who sought refuge under my wings, and yet, my own life crumbled like bread past its expiration date. No medication, no prayer could reverse the collision course I was on.

Without the comfort of the Divine, I turned to sweets, consuming very little substantive food, filling up on cream-filled Dunkin' Donuts, red licorice, and spice gumdrops. Occasionally, a hot dog, a piece of chicken, or a hamburger slipped in, but that was rare. I was anorexic, starving myself to death for a holy reason: I would make reparation for being a not-good-enough woman. I wanted to be the apple of God's eye, but now I gave up, certain that God had become a traveling salesman, like my dad. He was never there when I needed him. But Fr. Frank was.

I tried to be involved with my children, who were now ten and thirteen years old, but the weight of physical pain and knowing I was failing them made it difficult to even hug them. How did I keep on working? I don't recall. How did I care for my children? I have no idea. Perhaps God wiped the slate clean to protect me from remembering the trauma of not being there for them. I believe God loves us enough to do that sometimes. Psychology calls it dissociation—I call it divine intervention.

Most days, I feigned sanity quite well, but one afternoon, I locked my office door because I had the oddest sensation that my body was trailing some inches behind me. A cold, gray energy began to enfold me, the kind you see in horror movies when the roaming spirits of the dead come to haunt unsuspecting souls. At one point, I thought a python was gripping my head, slowly moving down to my throat to strangle me. I pulled the curtains, curled up in a fetal position in the corner, and began rocking back and forth, worrying whether my rubber-band mind was about to break. I had visions of being institutionalized like Grandma Helen.

Heaven only knows how I managed to get home that evening. I lived only blocks away from the church. Under the dim street lamps, I figured only a few people would notice me staggering like a drunk. As the evening wore on, I sensed the Grim Reaper was closing in on me and I might lose the roll of the dice. The pain medications I was given for the migraines were no more effective than jelly beans. My doctor had scheduled an MRI for six a.m. the following morning due to the relentless headache I'd had all week, along with vomiting several times a day. Around nine o'clock that night, I begged to go to the hospital, but my husband refused to take me, saying he needed his sleep to teach the next day. Fr. Frank came to our apartment to pray with me. He always carried the spark of the galaxies in his eyes, listening with a deep prayerful reverence, wrapped in unconditional love. That evening he was worried beyond measure. My skin had a pea-green pallor to it, my breathing was shallow, and my bones protruded from the rapid weight loss. But I was concerned my husband would wake up and find Fr. Frank by my side, and there would be trouble. Reluctantly, I asked Fr. Frank to leave, hoping I could sleep and not die during the night.

About three in the morning, I called a cab to get to the emergency room. Once I was examined, the nurse said my pulse couldn't be found and I had the clammy skin of a person about to keel over. And yet, as on previous occasions, the attending physician said the pain "is not as bad as you think" and "you're just a bit stressed and dehydrated." Like an animal foaming at the mouth, I stood up on the gurney and let out a blood-curdling cry: "You idiots, I'm dying!" I then blacked out, collapsing half way off the gurney. A doctor told me later that I had flatlined and they had great difficulty reviving me. My husband was called to bring my insurance card, but given he was on his way to school, I waited until late afternoon in the hospital hallway to be admitted. It is a mystery to me that the only thing I remember from this near-death experience was the sensation of being pitched into a pure black hole of nothingness. There were no lights, no God, nothing. When I came to, I was unable to walk. It was as if I'd been drained of all blood and water, wrung out. I wondered what kind of transfusion I'd need this time to recover.

The psychiatrist, a cocky, self-assured middle-aged man, examined me briefly. He put a restraining order on my husband, barring him from visiting me for two weeks. The psychiatrist stated bluntly that my husband was dangerous to my mental health. "Seeing him is detrimental to your recovery. Only the priest will be allowed to visit." I was grateful to have been diagnosed as suffering from malnutrition and exhaustion versus anorexia and mental breakdown. The story that ran around the parish, like a delivery boy on roller skates, was that I had lost my mind.

Due to the fact that mental health services were not covered by my insurance, and I was allergic to anti-psychotic medications, I was sent to a nearby convent to recuperate and pray. My mother had been sent to an orphanage and later to a finishing school to be cared for, and here I was, going to a convent to deal with my unfinished business with her. Staying away from home, however, meant I could not see my children unless someone gave them a ride. What almost killed me was hearing from my husband that he told the children they were responsible for my illness—that, if they behaved better (and they were not misbehaving kids), my headaches would go away and I'd be "all better."

The convent I stayed in was very welcoming. For over a year, I'd been immersed in charismatic prayer meetings with the nuns there. During that year, I was often called upon to lead healing services, which made me feel that, in spite of my deficiencies, God still worked through me and brought about miracles for many people on whom I laid hands. In those moments, I knew people were enjoying the rainbows of God as I'd dreamed of as a child.

The main caretaker during my recovery was a sweet dumpling of a nun whose joy of the Lord was infectious. She appeared to float a few inches off the floor as she sang, "Thank you Jesus, praise you Jesus." I could hear her sing-song throughout the convent as she sliced and cooked the disgusting chicken livers my physician ordered to strengthen me up. I gagged and stayed in the bathroom as she sautéed. And I don't believe she knew that I sent Fr. Frank, in his black suit and roman collar, to the Jewish delicatessen to buy them. Some things are best unsaid.

Years later, a Cherokee woman told me that, in her tradition, the spirit animal for a radical mystical woman was the chicken! This certainly was a far more entertaining viewpoint than the diagnosis the psychiatrist labeled me with. I would much rather be a mystical chicken than be a person with intractable major depression.

I stayed in the convent for six weeks, gaining stamina to walk again, bringing back memories of doing the same thing following my childhood bout with rheumatic fever. I also had hours of spiritual direction to help me develop boundaries so I wouldn't be porous in picking up other people's negative energies. I was so psychic that I was slightly psychotic. When I wasn't sleeping, I was praying, ashamed that I was begging God to take my life so my children would be freed of their wretched mother. Just thinking of how absent I'd been from my sons' lives made me want to turn inside out. One day while sleeping on the floor, too weak to climb into bed, I was given a dream about my situation.

In the dream, a young mute Spanish Jewish boy cuts open my body. He makes simple hand gestures and spits on several internal organs, restoring them to wholeness. When he came to my liver, he kissed it and connected all the organs together with a silver string. Then the boy wrote in the sand, in Hebrew, "When will you ever know you are loved?" While there are layers of psychological and spiritual interpretation to this dream, the core message was clear. *You will not get out of life until you surrender to the power of knowing you are Beloved—and in your body.*

When it was time to return home, I had no doubt that I would ask for a divorce, although I agreed to go to marriage counseling with a priest counselor chosen by my husband. After a few weeks, the priest recommended we attend a Marriage Encounter weekend, a last-ditch effort to see if the marriage was salvageable. I was hesitant, in light of the priest's behavior in the previous session. He was so disgusted that he shook his fist in my husband's face: "Let this woman go . . . you don't deserve her . . . and I'm sick of listening to your shit and rationalizations." At least someone realized I wasn't the flaky biscuit on the menu.

We decided to attend the retreat, primarily because my husband refused to admit the marriage was over, and, if it were, he was quite determined to make others see that I was to blame. Halfway into the retreat, the facilitator, who also happened to be a priest, bluntly recommended that we divorce. "Honey, you are like a piñata swinging wildly in the air, waiting to burst open so you can taste the goodness of your life. Time to be broken open."

At the evening meal, small cards were placed on our plates, and mine was from the Gospel of John: "I came so that they might have life and have it more abundantly." Later, as I stared out into a blinding snowstorm, I realized my life was as barren as the trees, as frozen as the snow outside my window. And yet, there was a peace in this wintry scene that reminded me not to fear. Just as the light of the moon made everything glisten, I knew I also was wrapped in God's loving protection. Maybe I could believe in my own worth and break the shackles that were killing me: the lie of not being good enough. Just maybe I could set aside feeling like the white of an egg that was separated from its yolk and be whole once again. Before I went to sleep, I wrote a thirteen-page letter to my husband, releasing him from all guilt about our relationship, admitting that all of his behavior was a reflection of the negativity of my mind, of my mother's mind. The gift to me—which I didn't include in the letter—was that I woke up to the cruelty that had driven me to the brink of destruction, and realized now that I had to retrieve the essence of my own goodness—something he was not capable of giving me or even reflecting back to me.

Following the retreat, I called my parents and asked for a loan of $500. Admitting my failure cut me to the core, but I had no other option. The woman lawyer who had been recommended to me took this sum without question. After interviewing me for an hour and seeing how haggard and diminished I was, she had only these words for me: "Honey, you will die an early death if you don't do this." I was petrified I would lose custody of my children on the grounds of negligence because of my ill health, or that I'd be institutionalized like so many of Ma's family. The lawyer raised her voice to me: "Annette, stop your nonsense. You are not the crazy one here, believe me. You've been suffocated and ground down to pulp. Trust me. You will be free within six months."

I went through the process of separation and divorce as if I were wrapped in cellophane. Some details are crystal clear, others a blur. Telling the children was humiliating, the words sticking together in my mouth like tufts of cotton— barely coherent. I was ordered by the court to undergo psychological testing, which freaked me out. However, my lawyer demanded the same for my husband, and the results put me in first-class normalcy, while his grades indicated second-class pathology.

A week prior to the divorce, the court psychiatrist called in my husband and me. He interpreted the results of our psychological testing and gave his recommendations. Once again, an insightful man took me off the hook. "You are not crazy," he told me. My husband argued over every word the psychiatrist said, and, in utter exasperation, the shrink (who was about 5'5") stood on his immense mahogany desk and screamed out loud, "You are an idiot and I'm not about to take your illogical crap. She's not the insane one!"

"And you, Pickle," he said to me, "Run as far as you can, and get the hell away from him. Do you hear me, Pickle? Get a life. You are killing yourself. Now, one more time, you are not insane!" Why he called me "Pickle" is a mystery, but it certainly added comic relief.

On the day of the divorce, I dressed in gray polyester slacks I'd sewn for less than five dollars, along with a white turtleneck sweater from Goodwill. It was important that I make a good impression, so I stitched up a cherry-red wool jacket with silver buttons. They cost three dollars, which for me was a splurge. Interestingly, the colors were the colors of my high school uniform. As usual, an agonizing migraine accompanied me into the courtroom, and drove its claws into my skull when I was called to the stand unexpectedly. My husband's lawyer was adamant in maintaining I was an unfit mother. "I am asking the court that, if she gets out of control or has another breakdown, her children be removed immediately. She is a danger to them." I'm not sure what would have happened that morning without the intervention of the court psychiatrist's report and my lawyer. She told the judge that the relationship was "killing" me—the only real danger was my ex's emotionally abusive behavior toward me. At times, I still wonder at the depth of denial I lived with, in terms of the swamp of grief I tried to navigate. I recall a clairvoyant saying to me that, in the marriage, I'd literally been poisoned against myself—as if a hole had been burned through my power center and I lost any reserves to continue on. And yet, at the right time, at the right place, individuals came forth to offer their expertise, advice, and compassionate care, and I tapped into the courage to move forward.

My ex-husband next demanded we apply for an annulment through the Catholic Church, and I wished I'd had the court psychiatrist as my advocate for that process. During the first meeting with the tribunal, the assigned priest was stiff as an over-starched collar, his hands crossed over a stack of manila folders. There were no windows in the room, and the only light was from a spotlight in one corner of the room, which, of course, illuminated my head like an alien ship. He was already annoyed with me as, upon reviewing the annulment materials, I'd refused to complete the paperwork. I found it denigrating. While I was willing to discuss an annulment with the proper authorities, I was clear about one thing: I would not be browbeaten into submission by church officials.

When I inquired about the stack of papers in front of him, the priest pompously stated that all my mental health and medical records had been released to him for review—without my consent. I knew my ex-husband was behind it. For several hours I was grilled like a skewered chicken roasting over an open fire, only to be tossed aside as spoiled goods at the end. "You have a history of mental illness, psychotic behavior, and delusions about God. We have evidence that you are a negligent mother and a less-than-obedient wife. You are not a candidate for annulment."

I've always worried that, given the right conditions, I could erupt like a volcano. I was overwhelmed by the urge to knock the crap out of this man. But I had sense enough to simply bolt out of the chair, not fling it against the wall, and run for my life.

I walked along the lakefront for many miles, chilled by the biting wind, going to pieces by the thoughts racing in my mind. I worried that I would attack anything that dared cross my path. At one point, I tripped over the gnarled roots of a weathered oak tree, collapsed against its trunk, and I came to my senses. I found a wrinkled piece of paper in my coat pocket, straightened it out as best I could, and scribbled a suicide note to my sons. "I love you with all my heart, but I have nothing in me to keep on living, nothing to give you anymore. I'm so sorry. You deserve a better mother. Please forgive me. I promise to watch over you like an angel for the rest of your lives. Please don't hate me—you are better off without me. Love, Mom." I sprawled out over a large boulder resting against the tree and passed out. As the shades of evening dimmed in the orange and coral sky, I came to, huddled over my tear-stained jacket. In retrospect, I suspect many people would think that such a heinous act was pure selfishness. All I knew in those moments was death-defying despair. I was an empty, hopeless, shattered, desolate woman who only wanted peace, who only yearned to return to God.

That evening, even as I pondered the final details of my decision, an inner voice urged me to attend a concert at a Jewish synagogue where a friend was performing. Still in a trance-like state, I took several buses to get to my destination. Walking up the sidewalk, a light breeze embraced me, stopping me in my tracks. At eye level, I saw the words embedded in a magnificent mosaic: "I set before you life or death . . . choose life." My body spun and rocked like an unbalanced washing machine. As I choked on my sobs, in a flash, I knew God was rearranging my brain and kissing me back into existence. I could not snuff my light out.

I asked my ex if he could take the children for several days to give me time to think, and to begin searching for a job that would pay my bills. But my soul had other plans: there was an inner transformation I needed before I could move on. And so I succumbed to a brief—but powerful—private psychotic break. The breakthrough lasted three days and three nights. My companion during this experience was Fr. Frank. His kindness and nonjudgmental presence allowed me to re-experience the book of my life, its pages fluttering in my face, spinning and hissing all the lies I had internalized from my family history, my marriage, religion, culture, and even from psychology. During the second day without sleep and no food, I entered a dream state in which I spiraled downwards inside the body of a voracious cobra, encountering each layer of my psyche and of the collective soul of women. The images were so vivid, so intense, that I could only surrender to the energy carrying me. I realized many years later that I'd witnessed and lived through the experiences described in Dante's *Inferno* and in William Blake's illustrations for the book of Job.

The culmination of this psychosis, my descent into hell, was alarming. A very small, very black creature lunged from the ominous blackness and snarled, "So who do you think you are anyway—a woman? Well, let me tell you, that just ain't good enough." I remember fainting, engulfed by the viciousness of that voice. Surely, I experienced the dismemberment of my identity. It may have been minutes or hours later that I awoke, hearing the warmth in my priest friend's voice, and feeling the tenderness of his hand as he prayed with me. He took me to the psychiatrist who had been treating me after my previous collapse. He shook his head in disbelief and confirmed that I'd experienced a brief psychotic episode. He again advised anti-psychotic medications, but, given my past experiences with the severe side effects of these drugs, I knew I wasn't going to fill the prescriptions. I also knew I wasn't going to continue with the woman therapist who turned her back on me during sessions as she cleaned off her plants, wrote notes, or occasionally brushed her hair. One time I asked her if I was boring her, and she said, "Yes." I would find another method to heal.

> *The images were so vivid, so intense, that I could only surrender to the energy carrying me.*

The psychotic break was both a psychological and a mystical bowel movement. It was a grand dump that uprooted the falsehood of my unworthiness and cleared the way for my divinity to take root. And my head was killing me. I begged God to fill my empty life tank and somehow had the strength to welcome my sons home and return to work. The boys were self-supporting and were able to exist on macaroni and cheese and cold-cut sandwiches, with bread from the day-old bakery across the street. Their favorite sport was to buy stale pretzels, chew them into wads with their saliva, and, at night, plaster their bedroom ceiling with spitballs. I didn't care—at least they were having fun as I was throwing up in the bathroom.

Walking back into my office was a nightmare. My attempts to make a dent in the complexity of problems faced by the homeless seemed as hopeless as trying to stop the train wreck taking place in my daily life. I loved the people I served, and yet, I was inwardly tortured by the struggle to stay alive. I was acutely aware that the fragility of my mind could develop into a mental illness far worse than a three-day psychosis. In the midst of this turmoil, a prophet appeared, a schizophrenic man I'd served in my work at the parish. He'd disappeared for a few months, and I wondered what had happened to him. One morning at work, there was an insistent knock on my office door. When I opened it, a police officer introduced himself, and politely asked, "Pardon me, lady, but are you the Blessed Virgin Mary?"

I laughed. "Well, not the last time I checked."

He said, "Well, there's a man in the back of the paddy wagon who escaped from the local mental health facility. He refuses to go back until he delivers a message to you that he says he received from God. *And* he says you are the Blessed Mother." I knew the man he was referring to. He was forty years old, short, muscular, tough looking, and walked like he had a saddle between his legs. Following many years in the Marine Corps, he spent most of his life in and out of mental institutions. He thought I was one cool lady because I set him up with a daily meal at a local restaurant, where he could start his morning with a cup of coffee. Then he roamed the neighborhood until it was time to retreat to the streets to sleep. As the cop scratched his head in bemusement, I told him to bring my friend in. He was more agitated than usual, and he immediately started rambling about the message he'd received from God during his morning shower. "This is a matter of life and death, and I had to tell you in person."

"Okay," I said, "I'd love to hear this."

"Well," Joe said, "God says he has a man for you in your life."

My unspoken sentiments were "Good grief, I need another man in my life like I need a hole in my head." Instead of blurting that out, however, I smiled politely and asked, "Oh, and who does God have in mind?"

"Well, God said you won't believe this, but you have to believe it. It's Father Frank." Without giving me time to fall off my chair in shock, or even to say thank you, this supposedly deranged man left the office, mission accomplished.

Unfortunately, the pastor was sitting in the next room, heard everything, and took it for truth. The next day, after his daily bout of drinking, I was fired.

I was given strict orders not to open my mouth about why this occurred, and, in return, the parish would continue my medical benefits until I had other employment. Given the precariousness of my mental and physical health, I took the road most traveled—shutting up in order to get what you need to survive. I was a defenseless woman in the face of church hierarchy. I could have blackmailed him with evidence of his advances toward me while he was under the influence, but I chose not to. No one would have believed me. That was another day when I walked to the lake, thinking about ending it all. And yet, one of the priests, when he heard I'd been fired, looked at me in the eyes and said, "You couldn't make the decision to leave this unhealthy place, so God stepped in to save you. You are blessed, and God will care for you."

Had someone cut my knees off with a chain saw, I'm not sure I would have felt more defeated. Now what? After the divorce, I received a paltry thirty-five dollars a week for child support, and my paltry salary for eighty hours a week barely paid the rent and utilities. I had a college degree, a BA in English, with no teaching credentials and fat chance of getting a reference from a boss who fired me. I had zero confidence, and, honestly, I felt and looked like a pile of crap. Powerless, petrified, pathetic—that was how I perceived myself.

I found an opening for an office manager position in a western suburb, and Fr. Frank encouraged me to apply for it even though I had no typing skills and no experience with accounts receivable or dictation. I was at my wit's end, and so I lied my ass off. "It will take me a few weeks to polish up my typing. Have no doubt, I will be the best manager you've ever had." The truth was that Ma had refused to let me take typing classes in high school, as she felt it was beneath me—only for the dumb girls. I was determined not to repeat my childhood trauma of having to beg the neighbors for food, or having the electricity turned off for non-payment of a bill. It was bad enough that I had to sneak food from the parish food pantry at times to feed my sons.

God only knows why I was hired, but within two days I started a new routine: waking at five a.m., making lunches for the boys, riding on two different El Trains, transferring to a bus, and walking the next fifteen minutes to the work place. I returned home at nine p.m., having worked a ten- to twelve-hour day. My children had to fare for themselves part of the time, but they rode back and forth to school with their dad and had their evening meal with him. He lived in an apartment on the next block, directly across the alley from ours. This worked particularly well for my oldest son, whose relationship with me ruptured following the divorce. The fact that I was rarely home and, when home, was too exhausted to be mothering caused us to drift further and further away from each other.

About a month into this grueling schedule, I had a weird experience that made me think I either needed a different job or had to move closer to the workplace. I was on the El Train, about 6:30 a.m., seated next to the door because of my anxiety about missing my stop. As I was reading to stay awake, I suddenly felt a piece of cold metal push against the middle of my forehead. A young man was holding a pistol to my head. I said, "Oh for God's sake, it's too early in the morning for this—please sit down." Minutes later, luckily for me, the train came to a station, and when the car doors opened, half a dozen policemen tackled this man to the platform. As I walked in the cold rain a few minutes later, I marveled, *Wow, woman, you've got guts—guess you're not the "wuss" you think you are.*

More impactful than a gun to my head, however, was a growing dread I woke up with every morning—a dread I couldn't consciously account for, but one I couldn't will away. And then, one morning during my daily prayer time, I opened my Bible, asking for guidance, and was given a reading that would define my identity as much as my first near-death experience. The words from the prophet Ezekiel jumped off the page, a hidden trap that ensnared me like an unsuspecting animal. "Son of man, on the very day I deprive them of their sons and daughters who are their strength, their pride and glory, the delight of their eyes, the joy of their hearts . . . they will know I am God." Like a flash of lightning, I intuitively knew why this reading had come to me: I had to give up my sons. I felt like my skin was peeled away, and every nerve in my body was on fire. And yet, something inside of me saw the truth and whispered, *Trust God—it is the only way.* I had to choose: either surrender the delight of my eyes, or stay on death row, where they might well lose me another way—in a coffin. I had to surrender the care for my boys in order to be restored.

In truth, I didn't surrender elegantly—I screamed at God until I was hoarse. *Let go of my children, are you friggin' out of your mind?* I cried until my eyelids turned inside out. *Hand them over to the man I could not tolerate being with? Am I nuts?* And still, I said yes.

It helped that my older son wanted to live with his father, and it wasn't right to separate them as brothers. But I spent days heaving with guilt, wondering what people would say about my decision. I wasn't wrong about the deluge of negativity that came my way. "What kind of a mother does that? You must be mentally ill." "No God would ask that of a woman."

When the day came for the boys to move out, I put some wrapped Twinkies in between their white socks and t-shirts. Most of their belongings fit in small duffle bags—that is the upside of being poor. I was sure my heart had been cut out and was hiding under my feet, and yet, I couldn't do it anymore. I had given all I had. Nothing was clear, nothing was safe, nothing seemed important enough to live for—except the tenderness and anguish of hearing my youngest son say, "It's okay, Mom; I'll come see you soon. I love you."

The ultimate cost of my transformation was more than I bargained for. Like death, some losses are so unimaginable that all one can do is wake up each day, embracing the ache, trusting the Divine—and forgiving oneself for that which is unforgettable.

Shortly after the boys' departure, I rented a second-floor apartment near my new job. Public transportation was a God-send as I didn't have a car. The apartment was two blocks away from the high school that the boys attended, making it easier for me to go to school functions. At first, I secretly waited in the mornings to get a glimpse of them when they arrived with their dad in the school parking lot. After a few weeks of this self-inflicted painful activity, I decided to walk directly to work, which was about three miles away. I usually walked home also, conscious that every penny I saved would allow me to take my youngest son on a train ride or have an ice cream sundae when he'd come to visit on the weekends.

My oldest son rarely visited, not even on holidays or birthdays, and my attempts to reach out with cards or calls were met with silence. I wallowed in self-pity, praying that one day he'd remember I loved him and know that I wasn't the monster he thought I was. My youngest son was my lifeline. He would occasionally buy flowers from the grocery store and leave them on the piano bench with an "I love you forever" note propped in front of his favorite white teddy bear. He faithfully came on weekends, and I always dreaded the moment he'd wave goodbye from the El platform. He had the sweetest smile as he blew me a gentle kiss. I giggled to see his pants riding on the cuffs of his white socks. I'd be shouting from the street, "I love you—thanks for coming—see you soon," stifling hot tears. I knew this young boy loved me with all his heart. He never complained that the highlight of our dinners was only Velveeta cheese and macaroni shells, along with an occasional candy orange slice or spearmint leaf.

We had such joy in taking several buses to get to the mall to buy school clothes, just sitting quietly with each other, occasionally just smiling that all was well in that moment. He was a top-notch clarinet player in an amazing jazz band, and Fr. Frank made sure I had transportation to the band concerts that weren't at the school. I'd place a silly stuffed animal, called Tiggy, on my shoulder or on my head at some point during the concerts. We'd giggle. We also had a special bond through his white stuffed polar bear, a steady companion throughout our mutual pain. I still remember the day I did surgery on this decrepit creature, filling it so tenderly with polyester filling, sewing on new eyes, remembering that love continued to make all things new.

CHAPTER 11

Mr. Frank

For the first time in my life, I was alone. I'd lost everything. Being fired from a job I loved, failing in a marriage, losing an apartment that I'd called home—all was irrelevant. I'd been stripped of the flesh of my womb, blasting my identity to specks of dust. My sanity and physical health were precarious, leaving me vulnerable and anxious. Somehow, I had to create a different life from the ragged fragments that lay at my feet and afflicted my heart. Not being able to afford a car isolated me from everybody except Fr. Frank, who continued to be my best buddy. We called one another frequently, often talking way past midnight, sharing about everything, including dreams and our thoughts about where our personal journeys were taking us. Where our relationship with each other was headed was the proverbial elephant in the room, a conversation that neither of us was ready for. We cared for each other intensely, and yet, Fr. Frank was hooked to Mother Church, and I was unhooking from my prior life and the impact of my mother's scalding negativity. Fr. Frank was very committed to being a priest, and, honestly, never in a million years did I imagine being married again. Just the idea made me gag.

However, there had been moments when a glimpse of the elephant caught me by surprise. It happened one time when I was going to him for confession. I was droning on and on about what a hideous person I was for wanting a divorce, for being a deplorable mother and being a wretched ingrate for not wanting to be alive. When I stopped, I noticed that Fr. Frank was snoozing on the job! At first I was embarrassed that I'd been so damn boring, but then my sense of humor saw an opportunity. I decided to tie his shoelaces together and tie his alb—the long vestment priests wear around their necks—in a big bow under his chin. As I left the confessional, which was in an open room, I felt uneasy and turned to the Bible for guidance. As a charismatic, it was normal to take the Bible in my hands, close my eyes, and reverently pray to the Holy Spirit to lead my fingers to a passage for inspiration. I always felt heat in my hands as I touched the pages. I irreverently called this "Bible roulette"! This time I gasped as I stared at the words before me. "Untie the ass and bring it here." The passage refers to the time Jesus was entering Jerusalem, just days before his crucifixion, and he needed a donkey to ride on. "Oh, sweet Jesus," I thought, "I am in trouble." Yes, the obvious meaning of this passage for me was *untie his shoes and quit being silly and stupid*. But instead, I had an intuitive flash that Fr. Frank was on the road to his own unraveling and that I'd fallen in love with one of God's untouchable souls. As a solid ice maiden, I wasn't ready to be melted away by this handsome cleric with the smiling eyes.

In retrospect, all signs indicated we were meant to be together. For months, we walked around each other like two abandoned mutts wondering how to get the leashes off our necks. We didn't understand this at that time, but over the course of the year we began asking the question: Could we be together? Our relationship was forbidden by the Church and was scandalous to the people we knew. My prior marriage was not annulled by the Catholic Church, so in their eyes I was not free to marry. Fr. Frank had made a solemn vow to God and wasn't free to marry. Both Fr. Frank and I were raised in families and social circles that would treat our relationship as completely taboo.

And yet, within our hearts and souls, this love didn't feel wrong—it felt life-giving, a blessing beyond description. We both had to wrestle with the issue of whether we could trust the voice of our soul, our God-self, when it ran counter to our religious traditions and the beliefs of people we respected. Fr. Frank struggled for two years, discerning God's will for him, given that twenty years prior he made a vow to God in good faith. Could he be true to the person he had evolved into and trust the path that God and his soul were leading him on now? Was he being deceived? My question was a bit simpler, I believe. Could I trust that my Spirit-filled soul was leading me to living in the wonder and fullness of love? Was I being called to relinquish the desire for death and receive life?

My question was resolved in a prophetic dream. In it, I am in an old Victorian frame house that has a beautiful library, with floor-to-ceiling books hidden behind finely lacquered wood doors. Jesus is sitting at a polished desk and appears in his transfigured form. His robes are ivory color, his face a radiant white ball of light. I tell him how bothered I am and ask, "Is it right for me to marry Fr. Frank?" I have to repeat the question three times. Three times Jesus looks to the ceiling and asks, "Father, shall I tell her now?" Then Jesus takes my hand and leads me into a kitchen. His face changes into the face of the cab driver who has consistently shown up in my dreams at pivotal points of my life. In those dreams, I'm usually walking down an unlit road, and, suddenly, a yellow cab comes from behind and stops. Jesus is the cabbie, and he takes me to my destination and never charges for the ride. I know him through his starry, twinkling eyes. In the present dream, he sits across from me at the kitchen table, holding my hands ever so kindly, his eyes keenly meeting mine and says, "Annette, the issue is not whether you marry Fr. Frank—just don't abort the baby."

At my age, it was clear that the dream was not about biological or moral issues. It took me months to realize what Jesus wanted me to understand: that, in our relationship, I was to preserve the memory of divinity that was growing in my bodily reality. I was not to let it be dissolved by the power of Frank's highly evolved spirit. I had to avoid trying to be like him. I'd followed that path with Jesus, trying to *be* Him, but I'd come to see that this was a distorted interpretation of God's message. I had to live as the woman I'd been ordained to be according to the divine blueprint imprinted on my soul. I had to claim the "I am who I am" song that was in the depths of my heart. In so many ways, Frank and I had both been seduced by the fierceness of oneness with God, but it was separated from our human selves. Now we had to live and integrate our divinity with our humanity.

Fr. Frank's answer came more slowly. It began when his spiritual director suggested that Fr. Frank go to counseling to face the struggles he experienced living as a priest. This had been suggested to him many years prior, but this time Fr. Frank agreed and began a year of self-discovery: listening to his dreams, paying attention when something moved him, getting in touch with his feelings, and re-evaluating some deeply rooted and sacred belief systems. Slowly, he was set free from a way of life that, as he came to see it, "was making me what I hate." In all honesty, I didn't believe Fr. Frank would break away from his marriage to God. He was so out of touch with his own soul's knowing. Several times I threw up my hands in frustration, wondering why in hell it was so hard for him. I wanted to shout, "Get a life—for God's sake, Frank, wake up!"

And then he had a dream that seemed quite obvious about what decision he was to make: In the dream, he is in a tall building, a prisoner of the Nazis, and is going to be tortured. He sees an open window and jumps out, even though he knows it will be fatal. Neither of us had to be rocket scientist to interpret the dream: to leave the imprisonment of the priesthood even though he'd lose his life as he knew it.

On February 14, 1981, at the stroke of midnight, the phone rang. From my experience, a call that late at night meant only one thing—someone died. I answered with a fluttering heart to hear: "Bunny (my nickname), this is Frank, and I've decided to leave the priesthood." (A brief pause.) "Will you marry me?" Ever the romantic, I quipped, "Oh for God's sake, it's too late for me to think about that—call me in the morning." And I hung up. At precisely seven a.m., he called again, and asked me to marry him. Taking a deep breath, I said, "Yes," and hung up. Since then we faithfully re-enact those two calls every Valentine's Day. Before the invention of cell phones, Frank found a pay phone to make the midnight and early-morning calls. He asks the same question, I give the same answers, and we laugh uproariously.

Fr. Frank met with his parents, five brothers, one sister, and their spouses to tell them about his decision. He respected and honored these gentle, deeply religious, and loving people. He'd married some of his siblings and baptized several of their children. No doubt, Fr. Frank walked in God's shoes in that encounter. As expected, Frank's mom and dad were devastated beyond words. His mother was sure that Frank would end up committing suicide, as happened to one of his classmates after leaving the Jesuits. His father took Frank aside and confided his anxiety to his son: surely Frank would be eternally damned, forever exiled from God's grace. The sanctified image they had of their son, and their pride in his vocation, disintegrated into a sea of confusion. Then there were practical questions such as how Frank would be able to support himself and a wife once he left the safety of the Church that provided for all his needs. What hurt them the most, however, was *how he could do this*—break his vows to God as a priest in order to marry a divorced woman with a troubled past!

Frank's family didn't understand that, although he and I were breaking our original vows to God, we were finally entering into a covenant with life itself, living within divine inspiration and love. Frank's family's religion focused on being faithful to the teachings of the Church, and they accepted what Church authority declared to be truth. Being led by God in inner experience was a foreign concept for them. And yet, their deeply held beliefs didn't keep them from embracing us as a couple, which was a profound blessing. Their son was a man of tremendous integrity, a gentle soul who radiated love and kindness. Little did anyone in the family suspect the cavernous loneliness this vessel of God carried within him underneath the stiff white collar resting on the unwrinkled black shirt. They knew he was a man of love, a man of incredible depth and devotion to God, and yet, he was a man whose heart wept as he raised his silver-and-gold chalice during the consecration of Mass.

In spite of having no immediate career, no social status, and no financial security, Frank trusted that God would lead him and provide. And no one of his family, or anyone who knew Frank, could deny the depth of the love he had for me—and still has to this day. I've been healed into life by God through Frank's presence. Simple but true. His love is as profound as a starry night, sustaining as the morning star. I've come to believe that part of my mission, and his, was to receive and integrate the Divine through this evolved relationship. My gratitude is beyond words.

Frank asked permission to share with the parishioners his reason for leaving his vocation, but his request was turned down with a resounding "No" by the pastor. He was to borrow a car, pack it with all his possessions (thirteen brown boxes accumulated over twenty years of service), and leave through the alley, at midnight, to avoid meeting anyone who'd attended his masses. He was a scandal, and I was the scarlet "A" hanging over his heart. Given the cloud of shame that hovered over us, we decided not to live together until our marriage. Some friends from my new church community found rooms in people's homes or condos he could rent while they vacationed.

We were married on September 5, 1981, in a Fiddler-on-the-Roof kind of ceremony. We couldn't be married in church, so the wedding took place in a dear friend's backyard. She and I had been in group therapy together, and we bonded through our childhood dramas and our spiritual transformations. Her neighbor sent a cleaning woman to tidy up her home, and other friends went to the local funeral homes, gathering up leftover flowers to decorate the backyard fences. Frank and I had little money, and all we could spare for the entire ceremony, including food, was $200. Thank goodness for the generosity of our faith community, who baked untold pans of chicken tetrazzini for the occasion! Although Frank and I saw ourselves as ordinary bumpkins blessed by love, our new faith community embraced us as beacons of light, of the holiness within ordinary life.

On the way to the wedding, we were driven through the town that day in our special limousine, my friend's slightly dented van, chauffeured by her husband, who was dressed in jeans, a tuxedo jacket, and a black top hat. Her three sons made delightful posters that were pasted on the back of the van reading,

"Congratulations Baer (Bear) and Bunny! We luv you."

I rode in the front seat, smiling and waving like Princess Diana, pretending I was royalty in my long pink-flowered cotton dress that cost ten dollars on the sale rack. Our celebration was performed by a Basque priest stationed at our former parish. He was studying in the US after spending many years as a missionary in Africa. On the day I was fired, he came to my office, closed the door, knelt down in front of my desk, and began to weep. He said he'd never met anyone so attuned to God's needy people, and he was ashamed how badly I'd been treated by the pastor. "You are blessed among women, and God will restore you." At our wedding, he proclaimed to the standing-room-only backyard, "I am so sad today for my Church which will not recognize two of the most beautiful, godly people I have ever met. I cannot officially marry them, but I will celebrate their love and bless them with all my heart."

We hadn't told our priest friend what had transpired the day before at the courthouse. Just before officially pronouncing us man and wife, the judge asked, "Is there any reason why this marriage should not take place?" In that moment, lightning struck a power line outside the courthouse, and all the lights went out. The eyebrows of the judge shot up in shock, but he regained his composure in an instant, and pronounced us man and wife, muttering, "I really don't want to know what *that* was all about!"

During the wedding ceremony at our friend's home, Frank accepted the fact that he'd never be a sacramental minister again, having exchanged his priestly collar for a wedding ring. In divorcing himself from his vows as a Jesuit priest, he had to face the fear of not being worthy in the eyes of God. As for me, I exchanged my ring of darkness and unworthiness to remember the words etched on my heart—I am beloved of God. We wrote our own vows, mine scribbled on a crumpled piece of paper and his perched on his heart, waiting like an innocent sparrow to sing his undying love for me. His words were simple and humble, eloquent and profound, and left me dumbfounded. My mouth dropped open, and I blurted out, "How the hell do I follow that!" which brought our guests to howling laughter and clapping.

Frank has continued to be a golden mouthpiece for God's unconditional love. There are times I've heard him speak about the Divine where I am brought to my knees. It is clear that in his ability to empty his mind, the Spirit of God rushes through his being like a pure mountain stream.

Mr. Frank

Living with Frank is easier than breathing. For a long time, I waited for the proverbial shoe to fall, fearing he'd transmute into a poisonous snake or something worse. It never happened—never. In thirty-seven years, Frank has never spoken an unkind word to me. He is a man of Scripture—a man without guile—totally incapable of unkindness or an unloving heart. Nothing more needs to be added.

Two days after our wedding, I attended my first class in graduate school, studying social work, and Frank took his first real job as a computer programmer. At the age of forty-three, Frank entered a world stripped of daily Mass, confessions, long nights of prayer, and isolation—a colorless slate turned into a painting waiting to be filled with hues of love and fulfillment. As part of Frank's search for a career that would support us, he had taken two courses at a local college to see if he had an aptitude for programming. He found a company that would hire people as computer trainees and took a four-hour test to see if he qualified for the position. He did well—only one error in logic—and he was accepted. Rather impressive for someone who studied mainly philosophy and theology for twenty years! We lived in a modest first-floor apartment with a rather nosey landlady. Our mail was dropped on the floor of the building's foyer, and she apparently looked through it and saw mail was addressed to "Rev. Frank Hulefeld." She stopped Frank one day and asked, "Who are you?" He gently told her he worked at Time Inc. and was in love with his beautiful lady. The answer didn't satisfy her, so she persisted. "Who are you, *really?*" When Frank told her about leaving the priesthood and marrying me, she grinned from ear to ear. "That is the most romantic thing I've ever heard." We lived there for six years, and she never raised our rent.

My internships in social work validated my proficiency and gift in dealing with the misfits of the world. My first assigned client was a fifteen-year-old boy in a locked psychiatric ward. He had the same first name and birthday as my older son, and his mother had the same first name and birthday as me. Mother and son. I laughed at our bizarre connection, and I told no one the inside joke: but for the grace of God, I could have been the one locked up.

My supervisor had an amazing sense of humor and one day sent me to do an evaluation on a very disturbed woman whom no one could console. This always seemed to be my role in life: *you go—you'll understand—and they'll love you.* I peered through the barred window and wondered what was causing this woman so much angst. She went from babbling gibberish to screaming and pacing to clutching her heart to madly smoking. I decided to walk in while humming a soothing lullaby, recalling how that always soothed Grandma when she felt abandoned. I first had to get through the cloud of cigarette smoke hanging in stale silence. As soon as she heard the sound purring in my throat, her head pivoted like a bobble doll, and her hands grabbed onto a table leg.

Like a clasped locket opening, her mouth broke open, and the treasures of her broken life poured into my listening ears. Her life had similar trinkets to mine, but when she wailed about having fallen in love with her local parish priest, and how he chose to erase her from his heart rather than leave the priesthood, I wasn't sure I was going to be able to contain this bombshell. My supervisor knew I'd married an ex-priest, and he'd deliberately assigned this woman to me! Looking into this woman's eyes, I stepped into her torment, one that could have been mine—the devastation when love is ruptured. I'd rarely entertained thoughts of what my life would have been had Frank chosen to remain bound by the clerical cloth.

My second placement, which became a permanent position following graduation, was in a shelter for abused women. This was unbelievably difficult for me. The on-call schedules at the shelter were erratic, angry abusers slashed my tires, and my headaches were consistently an 8 or 9 on the pain scale. Listening to the women's horrifying stories, and seeing their battered bodies, stretched my sanity. The layers of childhood abuse and the marital diminishment that I'd sustained for years surfaced and demanded my attention. The dried glue of my denial, which had kept the layers of dispossession in one undefined clump, now gave way. In the safety of Frank's love, I could now face the remnants of destructive beliefs that continued to hold the feminine spirit within me as hostage. I dreaded this prospect, fearful I'd destroy the one relationship that confirmed my goodness. I trusted Frank would always be my faithful companion.

CHAPTER 12

What's It All About?

Happiness can be found in the darkest of times if one only remembers to turn on the light.

—J.K. ROWLING

When I married Frank—my man of God—my friends, healthcare practitioners, and I all anticipated a steady improvement in my physical health. I imagined that his kindness and unconditional love would be the magic elixir I could drink to bring back the skip in my step. Ha. As the murderous migraines and mysterious undiagnosed illnesses continued, and sank their teeth ever deeper into my existence, I again slid down the familiar rabbit hole of smothering depression, just as I had when I was sent back to earth after my first near-death experience.

At age thirty-nine, I was beginning to realize that the stress of emotional and sexual abuse was not the main ingredient for my failing health. I was homesick for God and I believed that dying would stop the pain. I was still resisting being human. I was not aware that what had to die was the belief that I was separate from the Divine Soul that was determined to be me in a female body. Spiritually, I was one with this truth, but I didn't have the psychological maturity or awareness to embrace it at this time. Remembering that I was/am one with divinity required a slow, methodical churning and stripping away of generational and institutional sludge I'd accepted as truth. Something like the process of chiseling away layers of rock to reveal the beauty of a diamond.

Although I had reservations about seeking help for all the internal baggage I carried around, with Frank's encouragement, I pursued every imaginable and unimaginable modality, seeking answers, a cure, or at least some relief for my issues. During social work school and post-graduate work in the mid-eighties, I plunged into traditional psychological therapy, exploring every crevice of my past, chipping away at the barnacles I'd acquired from all my relationships. I relied heavily on journal writing and art therapy and resorted at times to primal scream-ing and biting my nails down to raw skin—anything to be set free.

In talk therapy, I could have won an Oscar for best screenplay as I faced my emotional torment. Just like Ma, who woke up each morning with a can of Comet cleanser in her hand, I carried the torch of "cleanliness is next to godliness" in my jackhammer attempts to break open the cesspool within me. And just like Ma, who relentlessly cleansed the surfaces of toilets, sinks, and floors, I obses-sively scrubbed away at my "what is wrong with me" and "let's get to the bottom of the suffering" mentality. *Damn it—there has to be an answer to these migraines and bodily weakness—somewhere in the midst of all this shit, there has to be a golden nugget.* Yet, my obsession with taming the demons of my mind didn't break the grip of amnesia about the Divine Feminine.

As each treatment modality fell short of what I needed, I decided to seek guidance through working with my dreams. Dreams were the primary source of direction for my life, but I'd hesitated to reveal this to therapists or friends. The few times I did, the response usually was I had a vivid imagination and I had to be more realistic. Imagine the comfort when a woman I met during a lecture series on the hidden language of God in dreams agreed to be my spiritual director. I was fascinated by her approach to dreaming as a spiritual discipline, an approach that went beyond a personal psychological analysis of images. I can never forget her glowing wavy copper-red hair that was as graceful as her accepting presence. Maybe she was a female angel like Sister Elizabeth, or, given her height (six feet tall), she could have been a white version of Auntie from Harlem. Like those two women, she recognized my authentic self and saw the beauty of the light from within me. "Annette, God speaks to you directly in your dreams. You carry a gift in your connection with Source, and your dreams and visions are the roadmaps, the revelations to remembering who you are. Listen. Believe. Trust."

Spiritually, I continued with charismatic prayer to sustain my relationship with Jesus although, in retrospect, looking to Jesus to save me was a major stumbling block in my evolutionary process. The issue wasn't about being saved. It was remembering and embracing my divine humanity. Without conscious knowledge of this, I was driven to a desperate quest for healing: meditation, shamanism, acupuncture, color and light therapies, trance dance, colonics, flow-er essences and oils—you name it, I tried it. I once bought a $50,000 machine that purportedly claimed would restore me to health by safe jolts of electricity.

Thankfully, I never fried to death.

To detoxify my body, I subjected myself to restrictive diets, sometimes eating only fruit and vegetables, sometimes only various types of beans with small portions of dried fish, along with fistfuls of supplements. The bean diet was the most hysterical, as I turned into a human fart machine. I must have blown enough wind to single-handedly clear a sidewalk of its autumn leaves. Poor Frank. He giggled with me when I turned into a human repellant machine, wrapping others in a fog of noxious gas. Along with the diets, and because I reacted negatively to most medications, I turned to Chinese herbs. Oh my, I spent thousands of dollars on nasty-tasting herbal concoctions. Once brewed, the pungent odor made me gag, but I held my nose, prayed to Jesus, gulped it all down, and busted a gut laughing with Frank over the foul smell. These alternative treatments were not covered by our health insurance, but Frank never complained about the drain on our finances.

One of the most compassionate clinicians I went to was an environmental physician who, after hours of allergy testing, said to me, "I am so sorry, but you are in the one percent of the population that is allergic to everything. You ought to be living in a bubble, and then you'd feel decent. I am so sorry." This physician recommended that I be placed in a special hospital for six weeks or longer, with no contact with the outside world, and follow a protocol he'd designed for people like me. But he admitted, "There is no assurance that when you leave the hospital your severe reactions won't return." He was acutely aware that I worried about everything I put in my mouth and was hyperalert to environmental toxins. Medical tests that included iodine immediately produced an anaphylactic shock reaction, as did shellfish. Exhaust fumes from cars and trucks brought on dizziness and severe fatigue, making it nearly impossible to drive. Tears slipped from his eyes, resting for a second in the deep wrinkles of his face. What was I going to do? There were opposing voices in my head: *Why bother? Nothing ever works* versus *There has to be another way.* Insurance wouldn't cover the steep cost of treatments, and I also balked at seeing myself as a freak of nature. The suffering was horrific, and yet I didn't want to accept living with such severe limitations. I chose not to pursue the treatment.

Several professionals I sought help from became frustrated with me. When their treatments failed, they concluded that my headaches and illnesses were psychologically based—due to my mother's abuse, or my ex-husband's rage, or me wanting to be a victim. One traditional therapist interpreted my unrelenting physical pain in the following way: "You have this magnet of darkness in your soul that you are unconsciously attached to—like being a bad seed but pretending to be a good seed."

The most damaging comment came from an alternative therapist who blasted me: "You don't want to get well." While I believe these highly trained clinicians meant no harm, their human disappointment in not being able to fix me led them to condemn me, thereby validating and augmenting the sense of powerlessness and disgust I already had with myself. Their comments, like my ex-husband's and Ma's, were a megaphone for my own thoughts.

I respect the scientific brilliance of both Western and Eastern medicine, and I applaud each specialist I met, even the one who scratched his head and said, "You are a conundrum to say the least. No one can figure you out." I even find it humorous that I was told everything was in my head. There is truth to this, and yet it was ultimately myopic. There was always the missing piece. I've come to believe that these modalities failed to grasp that there is a divine configuration of energy behind every pain, a divine "this is me" particle that consistently and lovingly kept trying to break through the human trauma so that I could be a unique expression of the Divine on the earth. In other words, there was an as yet unnamed evolving wisdom birthing through me, and the delivery was fraught with personal and generational lesions from the past.

Women like me—who react negatively to medications, and are not always helped by alternative treatments or traditional psychological therapy—challenge the way we make sense of mental illness, physical pain, and spirituality. How many of us are "conundrums" written off as crazy when, in truth, we are the bearers of divine energy, an evolving consciousness of an embodied feminine mysticism. Granted, we cannot dismiss the hard work of cleansing our distorted ego beliefs and past traumas. But there is so much more. How many women compulsively claw away at their flaws and weaknesses, despise their bodies, and forget that being an accomplished woman is not the purpose of life? How many women forget to listen to the murmur of the divine God-ness that yearns to claim its voice through them? None of the doctors or practitioners who treated me had the tools to figure this out, so it was not possible for them to fix the root of the loneliness I cradled in my heart—the perceived separation from the divine nature that was/is mine. Behind the voice of pain was the song, the yearning of the Divine to experience life through the holy ground of my humanity, my body.

Long before I could wrap my head around these insights, a crisis occurred that resurrected old memories I had tried to blot out. They were memories, as it turned out, that contained the exact elements needed for a radical shift in the way I judged myself as a mother. In January 1986, I received a phone call from my oldest son. "Mom, I don't feel well. Can you get me a doctor's appointment?" Just two short sentences, but they triggered a full-blown panic attack. I'd been estranged from him since he was fourteen years old, eight years ago. I was convinced that he dismissed me as "the bad parent" who abandoned him by divorcing his dad. That wasn't the first time that he felt I had ruined his life. When I brought his baby brother home from the hospital, he shunned me for several weeks. He'd take his favorite blanket and pillow and sit forlornly in the dimly lit hallway of our apartment. He kept his back toward me even when I slid plates of food to him so he wouldn't go hungry. I guess he thought that a "good mom" would know better than to bring home a blob from another planet!

Aside from me attending his high school graduation, and him attending my wedding, we rarely saw one another. He didn't answer my phone calls, respond to cards I sent, or visit me. Once, when he was nineteen, I was startled to receive a sweet card from him that had three simple words printed on the inside: I love you. I burst into tears. I was sure he was going to commit suicide. Only a guilt-ridden mother can understand that kind of reaction.

Given our estrangement, his call for help translated into *Please help me. I think I am dying.* Within an hour, he was examined by one of the physicians at the health center where I worked. The doctor initially diagnosed his breathing difficulty as some kind of stress response. I heard Ma's "that is stupid" mantra in my head, but who was I to contradict a doctor I trusted? Reluctantly, I drove my son back to his dad's house, feeling grateful for the reconnection.

Two days later, in the evening, he called again and asked me to pick him up. His voice was barely audible: "I'm really sick, and Dad doesn't believe me." I couldn't get into the car fast enough, and I willed my body to stop shaking so I could place my hands on the steering wheel. Although my son was very pale, visibly frightened, and very silent, I failed to appreciate the seriousness of this situation. What other explanation for my decision to pick up a movie *I Heard the Owl Call My Name* on the way home? When we arrived at our townhouse, I popped the movie in, hoping it might buffer the unease between him and me. I was clueless as to what the movie was about and certainly was not prepared for the opening scene—a mother burying her young son. As the scene continued to unfold, my own son grabbed his heart, and whispered, "I am dying. Please take me to the hospital."

In complete shock, Frank and I drove him to the ER, never thinking a call to 911 might have been better. He was quickly diagnosed with pericarditis (an inflammation of the sack surrounding the heart). He had a massive bacterial infection, and his pericardium was filled with so much fluid that his heart could barely function. All I could imagine was a boa constrictor wrapping itself around his heart, each move squeezing the life out of him. He was admitted to our local hospital and transferred to a major teaching hospital twenty-four hours later. He was placed in intensive care, where he remained for one month.

I obeyed the medical staff who advised that I not stay at his bedside. "Don't worry, we'll call you if you need to be here." However, several times I received calls at work: "Your son is failing rapidly. He may not make it until you arrive. We are so sorry—please come immediately." Miraculously, each time I arrived, his heart and vitals had stabilized, and he'd return to a conscious state. I could only describe my situation as being like a human yo-yo.

Three surgeries were performed on him during those thirty days. The last one took place on what would have been on my twenty-fifth wedding anniversary, had I remained married to his dad. That day, the pericardium around his heart was removed. The surgeons said if this surgery failed to stop the infection, he wouldn't be expected to live. Looking into the surgeon's eyes, all I could see was an image of a scalpel in the Grim Reaper's manicured fingers. The palms of my hands were gouged with marks of desperate prayer and alarmed torment. As the nurses wheeled my son past me from the operating room, he cried out in a muffled child's voice: "Mommy help me—mommy help me." Frank caught me as my legs folded under me like I'd been standing on rotting boards.

When the doctor came out to give the details of the operation, I begged to be at my son's side, but my ex-husband apparently had told this physician that I was an "irritant" to my son. "It's best you stay away from him for now," he told me. My mind spun in frenzied panic. *Let me die, not him—nothing was his fault—he didn't ask to have such a rotten mother.* I felt like I had only been a demolition ball wrecking this young man's life. It was as if his feelings about the divorce, his feelings of being unloved and uncared for, had turned the lining of his broken heart into a thick Rubbermaid sack.

A few days later, when the surgeon returned my call, his steel-tongued message sliced me like a crisp green apple. "It's your fault for not getting the braces off your son's teeth years ago. Your neglect is why he's in this mess." Frank was in the room when I slammed the phone down and let out a blood-curdling scream. A cascade of vomit exploded all over my clothes and bedroom, relieving the migraine headache. This doctor had no clue how I had pleaded with his father to have those braces removed. Now I was being humiliated, accused of nearly killing my son because I wasn't able to physically make him go to the dentist when he was a teenager. I know my ex didn't get the same call as I did. I was repulsed by a belief I'd subconsciously bought into: Everything that goes wrong is the fault of the mother. Frank cried, gently holding me as I bawled until my eyelids were swollen shut.

The good news was my son was given a new lease on life. His braces were removed, the infection was cured with antibiotics and surgery, and in six months he was fully recovered. He was given only two limitations: don't ski and don't let anyone punch you in the chest. The miracle was more than physical. Frank and I had visited my son every day in the hospital, and he came to realize that I loved him. In many ways we cracked open the damaging spell we'd woven between us: I wasn't a good-enough mother and he wasn't a good-enough son. In the midst of this illness, the spirit of Life conspired with the spirit within us to heal both of our hearts. A relationship that both of us had given up on was reborn.

Seeking the Divine Feminine

CHAPTER 13

Entering the World of Shamanism

If your heart is truly open, then all of nature, Life,
and experience is the mystery of interconnection and
opportunity for communion.

—ANONYMOUS

From the smoldering rubble of confusing and unrelenting pain, I discovered an unexpected joy: writing. It was as if an angel, maybe the spirit of my friend Sister Elizabeth, turned my fingers into faucets, which, once turned on, poured my life's pain into poetry. One day in a bookstore, I saw an advertisement for a writer's workshop at a prestigious college, and as I read the flyer, I muttered to myself, *What do I have to lose but a week of work? Go for it.* At the workshop, two well-known authors gushed over the pieces I presented, urging me to get published and pursue a career in writing. I was overwhelmed by their praise, but I filed their business cards away, thinking I wasn't ready for public recognition. Deep down, I didn't trust a word of their praise. Their only critique of my style was that I wrote "from the bone," meaning I wrote with a starkness that could potentially make a reader uncomfortable. But I understand now that this was also a compliment about the power and purity of what I communicated. "You need to put meat on the bone so people won't shudder at the rawness of your words."

Shortly after that, Frank, buoyed at the news of praises my writing received, encouraged me to attend another weekend conference, this one in the Southwest. "They wouldn't encourage a dud to keep writing," he told me. Once again, I arrived at a strange place, wondering how I'd manage the events, given my headaches.

Once I was settled in my room, I visited the workshop's lounge and was drawn to a dog-eared magazine lying on an end table. My eyes saw the words "soul retrieval" on the cover, and I thought to myself, *Really, that's crazy. If you lose your soul, you're dead.* But as I began reading, the words sucked me in, quickening my spirit with curiosity and hope. What if a trained person, who worked with spirit guides, could actually find where part of my soul was hiding and return it to me? What if this was the magic bullet I'd been searching for to put an end to my pain? I then recalled a dream I'd had the previous night. I was a small child walking through very dark and dense bushes, as if I were searching for lost treasure. I found clusters of small lights, and I gathered them into a lovely woven basket. The more light I gathered, the bigger I became. I could see spooky, ominous caves in the background. They vibrated with some unknown danger that could only be handled by an adult. I felt a chill go down my spine. Was the dream telling me that parts of my soul were missing in those caves?

The article stated that, according to ancient shamanic traditions, soul loss occurs during times of trauma, such as near-death, accidents, sexual abuse, fighting in a war, death of a spouse or child, surgery, and other conditions of loss. It's as if some part of the soul, when it undergoes a traumatic experience, slips away unnoticed, seeking protection in a safe space in the unseen realms. The result of this dissociative condition can lead to serious consequences such as severe depression and anxiety, chronic illness, fatigue, intractable pain syndromes, and a feeling of walking around like a zombie. Memory after memory bounced against my mind like I was a pinball machine. This article was describing my life!

I found it hard to sleep that night. It occurred to me that, prior to abuse, I compared my essence as bubbles of possibility inside a bottle of champagne. With so many incidents of abuse popping the cork, the effervescence slowly fizzled out. When I nearly died, the remaining bubbles of joy flew from the bottle,

Was the dream telling me that parts of my soul were missing in those caves?

eager to return into God's essence. When medical intervention put the cork back on my life, therapy focused on the liquid that was still in the bottle. No one realized this approach was ass-backward. The liquid of my soul's champagne wasn't the issue. It was the absence of the bubbles, the separation from the joy of life that made everything flat and tasteless. I pondered all night if the bubbles were parts of my life force that could be invited back home through the gift of a shaman.

Upon returning home to Chicago from the conference, I wrote a letter to the author of the article. I was upset with myself when I realized that she lived in Santa Fe where I had just been. I wasn't sure how I'd pay for another airline ticket, but I had to trust that the resources would be available. My wounded self wasn't sure that I wanted my life back, but I certainly could do this for Frank. He loved me to the moon and back, and he'd prefer me to be on the earth. The author called me within two days of receiving my note and referred me to someone nearby who was trained in soul retrieval work. The tone of caring in her voice soothed any fears I had about the process. The prompt response of the shaman she asked me to call was an equally reassuring sign: this was a good time to be retrieved.

A few days later, I traveled to the shaman's office, which was about two hours from my home. I had no idea what a shaman was. I figured he was like a Catholic priest who used drums and rattles instead of bells and pipe organs. He could have been Bozo the Clown or Jesus in modern clothing—I didn't care. I was depleted from the migraines and the profound depression in my bones. Frank offered to go with me, but I knew I had to go solo. I gulped with unrestrained guilt as I saw the worry shadow in his eyes, and I wept as he gently gave me his signature bear-paw wave as I got into the car.

Later, Frank told me he came to peace about the trip when he "saw" a seven-foot Indian sitting in the front seat with me—his legs cramped up against the dashboard. This was a matter-of-fact situation for Frank as he often experienced Jesus as a Native American Brave. He felt his lady, as he liked to call me, was in fine hands that day. Frank had written out detailed directions for my journey, because I could get lost in a paper bag. When I arrived at my destination, voila, a parking space appeared, and I was in front of the address I was looking for.

The brick building I entered was narrow, and, as I walked up to the second floor, each step of the old stairs creaked. At the top of the stairs, I became flustered as I peered down the dimly lit hallway. *Oh crap, what now? Is this a setup to be abducted by alien spirits?* There was no public telephone to call Frank, so I breathed down to my toes and sent telepathic vibes to him. *Hey, this is creepy and I am freaking out. Send a prayer. Hope I stay alive. If I don't, remember I love you forever, and we'll meet again.*

Where was the shaman? And then, with only the soft footsteps, wrapped in leather moccasins, he appeared. He motioned for me to follow him into his office, which could have passed for a renovated cardboard box. There were no pictures on the graying plaster walls, and no chairs to sit in. The faded yellow shade on the window was pulled halfway down, allowing just a hint of color over the surface of the dingy gray, worn-out carpeting that cried out for the service of a Merry Maids cleaning crew. Embarrassed at my rudeness in not greeting the shaman, I turned and simply nodded. He was balding, wore faded denim jeans and an ugly plaid short-sleeved shirt. But when he smiled, the glint in his eyes melted all my anxiety, and I saw a web of light start to form around my body. He introduced himself and nonchalantly asked if I was aware of the seven-foot Indian walking behind me! I giggled: "Yes, he drove here with me!"

He invited me to sit on the floor of his healing room and encouraged me to tell whatever part of my story I wanted to. He listened so reverently, his head occasionally dropping forward, his baldness radiating like an orb of compassion. I told him of my physical ailments, a bit of my history, the article on soul retrieval I had encountered, and my deep desire to see if this ritual could bring me some relief. He spoke little but nodded occasionally to assure me that he understood.

When I paused to indicate I was done, he invited me to lie down on the rug, all the while walking me through the steps of the retrieval. After I was lying down, he placed a faded red farmer's kerchief over my eyes. "I'm going to drum for a little while. Let yourself float on the rhythm of the drum. I don't want you to be startled, but I will lie down by your side at some point." I had a fleeting thought that all of this was bullshit, but I knew Jesus would not lead me astray. "Now, as I travel into the unseen realms, I will not speak to you at all. You will probably also see things during this time. I have a feeling you'll be traveling with me." I shivered, knowing he was right—I'd been traveling in the spirit world all my life, without the use of a drum. "The final thing is that, after I find all your lost soul pieces, I will bend over you and blow them all back through the top of your head. Don't be frightened. I will not harm you. My breath may feel warm, so, again, just relax and welcome yourself back home into your body. Okay?" While he was speaking, I had already begun seeing visions and could barely whisper, "Yes, I am ready."

The shaman sang to the helping ancestors to guide the journey, and I almost burst out laughing. He sang so off tune and in a language that was gibberish to my ears, yet not unlike when I would speak in tongues during charismatic prayer.

With the first drumbeats, my spirit heard the voice of the Divine, and I leapt through the veil between this world and what we cannot see. Several spirit helpers, including Jesus, carried me into familiar realms I had lived in for years as a child—I was home. I saw animals walking freely amidst swaying trees and plants that sang musicals. Like a photograph album, pages of my life flipped open. As I found out later, I was seeing what the shaman was seeing. There were several times when I felt disoriented, as if I was tumbling upside down, or flying like a saucer through the night sky. At one point, I was inside a dark cave with little children reaching out their hands, trying to grab my hand, their faces gaunt and forlorn. Remembering their profound loneliness still brings me to tears. One image in particular was of a little girl, with long curly hair and very dark circles under her eyes. She never moved, never said a peep. I had no doubt that I was seeing myself as a four-year-old. As the journey was coming to a close, I sensed an electrifying current waking up my body. The magnificent mystery I'd come from, a home I could not describe, were one with me.

Then the shaman sat up very slowly, knelt at my head, and returned my re-trieved parts through his breath. As he predicted, an energy of the most exquisite warmth washed through my body, a lavish immersion of pure love. I'd always wanted to experience what the apostles did when Jesus breathed the power of the Holy Spirit into them—and this was it! How funny that my Jesus showed up as a balding Russian Jewish shaman.

He sat with me in silence for several minutes, then said, "I never bring back as many soul parts as I just did for you (seven parts), but the helping Spirits said, 'She is one of us—she can handle this.'" The shaman told me that the cave I saw was called the Cave of the Lost Children, a space within the spirit world where the soul parts of traumatized children hide out until they are found. This unas-suming holy man then reframed the pain of my life as an initiation, a process whereby the spirit world was helping me reclaim the shamanic, mystic skin that I'd stepped out of during trauma. He shared with me several examples, including events in his own life, illustrating that healers traditionally faced life-threaten-ing challenges—even death, as in my case—before they became healers for their communities. Although I hadn't revealed the abuse by my mother, the shaman affirmed it all, including the abuse by several members of Ma's family.

What startled me was his comment that my path wasn't a personal one. He sensed that I'd agreed to transform the resonance fields of seven generations of crazy, abused, and spiritual women in my family. With a twinkle in his eye, he stated that I'd agreed with God to be born, as an act of Love, for this task . . . some-thing I'd never stated out loud, for fear of being labeled whacky and grandiose. My heart also skipped a beat when he mentioned I had a gift for writing and that my words would bring healing to other diminished and dispossessed women. "You have a natural ability to travel between the worlds, and this gift will bring healing to others." His final question focused on how my body felt, now that so much of me was returned. "Well, I do feel heavier, like a few bags of sand landed in my legs and tummy." When I stepped on the scale a day later, I was five pounds heavier!

While it took me two hours to travel to see the shaman, it took me eight hours to get home. My initial feeling of being so alive quickly shifted into feelings of disorientation, bewilderment, and an unbelievable desire to sleep. I could barely keep my eyelids open against a fatigue that felt heavier than a sleeping child with sopping wet clothes. I didn't have my knight in shining armor, Frank, to drive me home, so I drank a large cup of black coffee to jump-start me, followed by two large Diet Cokes. As a security measure, I pulled into a gas station at every exit along the interstate highway, called Frank on a pay phone, and began each conversation blubbering like a drowning whale. He must have been nervous as hell, but he kept reassuring me I would be fine: "Drive carefully, and keep the calls coming." He suggested at one point that I get a hotel room, or he could rent a car to come get me. Although my body was tumbling with nausea and near-explosive diarrhea, my answer was the same: "I'm going to be fine—just keep praying. I'll get home safely. I didn't come all this way to die. I love you."

The shaman forewarned me that, after soul retrieval work, traumatic memories often come back, bringing waves of feelings and images. This was very helpful as I drove home, because I felt like both a woman carefully driving her car and a child looking for her dolly as she trembled in her bed, praying that mommy would stop treating her like *her* favorite baby doll. I was a woman calling the love of her life on the phone, begging him to keep her grounded, and, at the same time, I was a twenty-year-old woman begging to die, hoping someone would care for her baby. With the grace of God, Frank's prayers, and the seven-foot Indian who accompanied me, I arrived home safely. I collapsed into Frank's arms and was asleep before my head touched the pillow.

In the days following this experience, I slept more than I talked and wept more than I smiled. The energy of seven parts of my early childhood had come back home to me, and I didn't know what to do. It was like having three sets of twins and one other child all in one birth. The fact that Frank and I can be a loving presence to each other without words was a tremendous gift during this reintegration process. I cuddled up like a caterpillar dreaming of butterfly wings, and he listened.

The shaman took me under his wing, referring me to several training opportunities by the woman shaman who wrote the article on soul retrieval. I resonated with the truth of his statement, "You are one of us," and I certainly wasn't going to deny the seriousness in his voice when he said I had a difficult path. The intensity of my spiritual call would leave little wiggle room for ego distractions and fluff. I had no intention of accepting the title "shaman" for myself—I just wanted to be a woman of God.

While each shamanic workshop helped me learn basic skills, it felt as though I was in a refresher course instead of an initiate's training. Shamanism was like treasure folded in layers of golden velour; all I needed was help with unfolding the tapestry of this ancient spiritual tradition. I was less fearful of the invisible spirit realms than the visible realities of life. After all my attempts to find healing through Western medicine, alternative therapies, counseling, and Christian prayer, it came as a complete surprise that shamanism brought such restorative healing to my soul and body. Therapy had certainly strengthened my ego's ability to function in the world with a degree of security, but it was the spirit world that birthed my voice and enabled me to say yes to life. Working spiritually helped me stop regurgitating and analyzing the incessant chatter in my mind. I came to realize that my trust in the spirit world, including trusting my intuition, was a direct gift from the Soul.

CHAPTER 14

Christianity and Shamanism: Strange Bedfellows

A new culture will have to develop, in which neither humans nor their inventions nor God is at the center of the universe. What should be the center is a hollow place, an empty place where both God and humans can sing and weep together.

—MARTÍN PRECHTEL

Even though I remained on the fringe of most social groups, Frank and I were quite active in a lay-based faith community. After my soul retrieval experience, several friends remarked that I seemed to be getting healthier and I looked more relaxed. I was conflicted as to how to respond. It was one thing to be a liberal-minded Christian, and another to understand how shamanism, a nature-based spirituality, could be embraced into one's faith practices. At the time, Frank was a volunteer pastoral minister in the community, and I didn't want his good name tarnished because of my unconventional spiritual adventures. I decided to take on the Cheshire cat's appearance for a time, and merely said, "Thank you. Yes, I am doing better."

As I gained courage in sharing my experiences with shamanism, some of my religious friends expressed concern. They saw me as betraying my Christianity. "How can you subscribe to primitive, pagan practices?" "Aren't you afraid the evil one is deceiving you with a false light?" From my point of view, such comments stemmed from misconceptions and fears. Because my faith in the unseen realms was so strong, I'd reply: "It's the best I know and it's what keeps me alive." Some people shook their heads at this and suspected me of being a heretic. "How can you trust your personal relationship with God, and teachings you receive from the spirit world, more than the long-established traditions of your faith?" I respected my Catholic faith tradition and, in fact, continued to be more secure in following external wisdom and religious traditions versus trusting my inner voice. I wasn't ready to admit I'd unbound myself from traditions that were rooted in patriarchal beliefs, especially those that diminished the feminine spirit or set aside the mystic.

The truth was that the spiritual practice of shamanic journeying awakened and strengthened the mystic in me. It was a vehicle whereby I could have a direct experience of the Divine, where I could deepen my communion with God, the spirit world, life, and the divinity within my soul. It affirmed what the dream teacher had said to me after my breakdown. "You have a gift to receive revelation, and Jesus is your teacher, not other people." Granted, this kind of unmediated spirituality demanded intense discernment, but the results shifted my consciousness and unearthed a divine memory that lived in my bones—a call to be a co-creator with all of Life. For these reasons, integrating shamanism with my Christian faith was not a problem—it was fulfilling and grace-filled.

My reticence in sharing about the shamanic healing workshops changed dramatically in September, 1993. Our dear friend, the one who had generously offered her home and backyard for our wedding, called to say that her breast cancer had metastasized. "The doctor says I have 'hot spots' on my bones." I blurted out that if she wanted a prayer ritual, I'd do it. I asked whether she'd be offended if I drummed and journeyed on her behalf. I had no intention of foisting my beliefs on her. I merely volunteered to work directly with the spirit of the cancer, something foreign to our traditional prayer services. My love for her was stronger than my fear of what the members of our mutual faith community might think of me.

On the day of the ritual in our home, I woke up with one of my "killer" headaches, but it had a unique quality that day. It seemed as if a dark fog enveloped my whole body in a pain that went beyond my throbbing head. I connected with Mary and Jesus, my spirit guides, and they made it clear to me that all I had to do was "show up in love" and surrender myself to their guidance. That afternoon, I slept in a darkened room, waking only when thirty-plus people arrived that evening, filling the ground floor of our home wall-to-wall. I waited until everyone was quiet, seated in soft candlelight. Then I asked my friend to lie down on my healing blanket—a blanket woven by Native Americans, a precious gift from Frank.

I lay down next to my friend, gently holding her hand while Frank and several community members drummed. We chuckled at how silly we must have looked, lying like dummies on the floor. I muttered to my friend, *Just relax,* even as I wondered what in the hell I had gotten myself into. Usually, my journeys are vivid and detailed, sometimes bordering on Spielberg intensity. But something strange occurred that night. Although I was blindfolded to reduce all external distractions and light, my internal sight was also pitch dark. For a moment, I freaked out: *Have I gone blind?* But my trust in Spirit quickly erased this thought. Then, the voice of Jesus directed me where to put my index finger on my friend's body. If I placed it even half of an inch off, Jesus gently moved my finger to *the* spot, and heat poured into her body. I had no consciousness of the drumming, no awareness of anything except a burning laser beam of Love moving through my fingers. My friend later reported that the time on the rug was unconscious for her, as if she'd been taken somewhere else.

When I finished, every person in the room came forward and blessed our friend, promising prayers for the week until she received the results from her next CAT scan. In that moment, I was grateful that she felt so loved and had settled into a peaceful state of mind. I was so relieved when people left, as I needed to puke—and I did, several times. Later when I slipped under the bedcovers, I told Jesus I hoped he'd done his job, as I certainly wasn't much help. While I understood that prayer involved a willingness to let go of the outcome I hoped for, I struggled mightily as I so loved this friend.

Four days later, as I sat praying in my favorite recliner, I heard the familiar lilting voice of the Blessed Mother say to me, *This will be a miracle.* Ten minutes later, my friend called to report that the scan showed no cancer in the bone. As she gave me specifics about the spots, I realized they were exactly where Jesus had placed my fingers. When my friend's oncologist was notified, he was stunned— and my friend was numb. "Doc, are you sure?" "Yes, I am sure—someone must have been praying for you, young lady." Unlike others who may have believed this was a coincidence or a misreading of the test results, my friend accepted that she'd been healed, as did her specialist. She is vibrantly alive twenty-four years later, still profoundly grateful to the Divine Mother for such a blessing.

I'm not sure what others thought of my friend's healing, with the exception of one woman who was not a Catholic, just a faith-filled Christian. "Well, I felt *something* that night, and all I can say is that it was a miracle, that's for sure." My impression is that many people found it easier to believe in the power of modern medicine and were more skeptical when it comes to unseen interventions from the mysterious and unseen spirit dimensions. To me, neither world is mutually exclusive to the other, each weaving their magic and skill together for the possibility of the miraculous. And, granted, not every healing ceremony results in a cure—and that is not for us to judge or try to control. There is a mystery about each person's life, an agreement between the Soul and the human being that we are not privy to—and are not to interfere with. The Divine energies will complete their mission in ways we cannot imagine—and which we are to be witness to, with awe and reverence.

Shortly after this prayer ritual, a friendly and charming priest I knew called and asked if he could come talk with me. I was a bit nervous about this because he was strong-willed and very Catholic (of course!). I'd also been told that he was upset by my particular form of spirituality. I invited him to our home, thinking a personal conversation would relieve his fears.

He was his gregarious self at the beginning of our meeting, but he quickly became confrontational when I tried to answer his questions about my shamanic beliefs. He couldn't believe I called myself a Christian, in light of my trainings with native people and their ancient traditions. Even more, according to him, I'd betrayed the name of Jesus by conducting healing services with drumming and strange, wordless songs. Why didn't I use traditional prayers and scripture readings? "How can you be sure you aren't being led by the Devil? You could be doing miracles under the power of evil spirits." I was dumbfounded. "These beliefs are not from God but from paganism—not Christ. And who gives you the authority to heal?" He went on. "Animal spirits? You are falling away from the Church and walking in dangerous territory." I could feel the anger rising up my spine like a snake of fire. *Buddy, don't push your luck. I may just tell you to shut up. You have no right—no right to judge me.* I didn't say this aloud, but Ma's voice was a spiked burr in my throat. I sat on my hands to control my trembling emotions. I was not about to cover things up, or crawl on my hands and knees, to prove that I was a good woman.

And then the rascally spirit I'd had all my life decided to take center stage, and I laughed out loud. That was not the "Christian" thing to do in front of an upset, deeply religious priest. I apologized for my outburst, but then I challenged him: "Why is it okay for a male ordained priest to dress up in robes, ring bells at sacred holy day rituals, throw holy water over people, and pray to dead people, and yet it is heresy or sinful for a woman, ordained by the Spirit, to sing to the Spirits, use a drum and rattles, and invoke the power of God to heal those who suffer?"

Trying to explain to him that shamanism brought me into direct communion with Jesus fell on deaf ears. The Church didn't call forth this kind of Christian, particularly if you were an ordinary woman. I could have pursued the mystical path in the convent—as a virgin, as a subservient and obedient woman. In shamanism, my calling to the priesthood was validated. I was blessed to be a woman priestess, a woman whose fire for Spirit could flare forth rather than be extinguished.

Not one to back down from spiritual controversies, I told the priest I was amazed at his distress that I communicated with people who had died. "You talk about them, you believe in the communion of saints, so why am I demented for seeing them and hearing what they have to say to us?" I didn't zip my mouth quickly enough to prevent heresy from slipping out. "I believe Jesus was a shaman." I continued: "He lived in union with God, and the Spirit moved him to serve the disenfranchised, the poor, and the sick." This describes the life of a shaman in a nutshell: being a hollow bone, a channel through which Spirit works to bring healing to the greater community. I admitted to the priest that I couldn't deny the power of Spirit while in this state of divine union, nor could I dismiss the healing of people's spirits and physical ailments through this process. God had found a way for me to answer my deepest calling. I could tell by his facial expression, he wasn't pleased with what I was saying, and yet, he restrained himself from further comment. We parted cordially, and I was at peace knowing we would not see eye-to-eye on this matter. I wanted to at least agree to disagree, but somehow felt even that was too much for him.

After several years of training with outstanding shamans and practitioners, I decided to offer soul retrievals and community rituals based on ancient traditions. Overall, the impact of soul retrieval work was miraculous. I could see the color come back into people's faces as they embraced the different parts I returned to them. I saw the change it made in their everyday lives.

The dilemma for me was with the small number of people who, for various reasons, were not able, or were too fearful, to receive the gifts from the spirit guides. I know that, for our modern mentality, saying yes to the reality and impact of the unseen realms can seem intellectually and scientifically ludicrous. And yet, to me, if you were open-minded enough to ask for shamanic work, why would you then dissect the information returned to you as if it were a frog in a biology lab? It was difficult for me to accept that most people were not as trusting as I was about the spirit world.

One of the most unnerving situations involved people who were upset that I was able to connect to their deceased relatives. "What's the matter with me that my dead spouse talks to you and not to me? Am I chopped liver or something?" I didn't take the comment personally, as I could hear what they weren't saying. *What's wrong with me? Don't they love me anymore? Did I do something wrong that they don't want to appear to me?* At times, the challenge came in questions such as, "Why did you see them in that color dress? How did you know that was their favorite color? Did you make this up, or was it a good guess?" I was prone to feeling like a failure when people were too pushy about details. I wanted to scream, *For God's sake, you've just been brought back to life, and you have to bitch and moan? Really!* But I was hearing Ma's voice in their complaints, and I admitted that to myself. Ma took apart any gift we gave her. It was never the right color, the right size, the right anything. Some people treated journeys with the same attitude.

I really understood the challenge of receiving something that most people felt was "woo-woo." Working with the spirit world is a mysterious business, and the results may not be the magic bullet people expect. Prior to any journey, I made it crystal clear that my role as "shaman" wasn't to be the healer—I was the awakener of the divinity that yearned to express itself through their humanity. The flame of God within us, what we call the soul, knows our mission for this lifetime, and delivers healing for *that* purpose, which is not necessarily what our human nature desires.

For example, sometimes people begged Spirit to cure a terminal illness, but the Spirit chose to release them from attachments to past trauma, catapulting them into deep grief work. Sometimes this produced a cure or improvement in their health, and sometimes not. I wasn't any different. *If I change my diet to all organic, if I leave an abusive relationship, I will be cured.* Or: *If I just resolve my childhood abuse, golly, I will be sailing through life like a bird with silver-tipped wings.* Other uncomfortable situations occurred when the Spirit's guidance called for family members to withdraw from contentious legal proceedings, or some were directed to forgive an enemy, or forgive themselves. Many times, such guidance was not acceptable to people.

For individuals who wanted me to connect with spirits of the dead, the information, the words, and messages I was given were unique and profoundly healing. One of my greatest joys was the time I told a person that I'd seen her son, skipping down a forest path, singing, "Zip-A-Dee-Doo-Dah, Zip-A-Dee-Ay, my oh my, what a wonderful day." She stared at me in utter disbelief, as this was the song she had sung to him as a child. I had no prior knowledge of this. But this one phrase gave her the gift of hope that her son was not lost in the afterlife, that he was not damned, despite the horrific circumstances of his tragic death. In such moments, I wept with the people, humbled by the power of the Spirit's Love.

I also recall the story of a woman whose dream-come-true fiancé had a fatal heart attack the very day she sent out their wedding invitations. She was spiritually attuned and believed they would one day be reunited, that he would always be with her. She confessed he wasn't a believer and asked if I could retrieve any information to console her about him. The journey was simple, and it moved both of us deeply. I saw her dead fiancé sitting on his grave, with a hand-written note and an artificial foot perched on his shoe. The note had details for his funeral and indicated he was going to stay close to the earth until after the service. In recounting the journey, I was hesitant to share about the foot, wondering if I'd just picked up some random image. However, I shared the image and she wept, relating how her fiancé had lost a foot in an accident during the war, which made walking excruciating for him. She still had a great sense of humor in the midst of her pain, saying she had no doubt he'd never walk away from her—alive or dead!

So, while uniting with Spirit was effortless—and I trusted my ability to communicate what I so clearly saw from the world of the spirits—my vulnerability and my downfall was being invested in people receiving God's gifts. The Spirit child inside of me, who woke up every morning with her brushes to paint rainbows of love, found it very difficult when people questioned, doubted, and set aside what the Divine had given them. And while I understand that some of this disappointment was rooted in a need to be affirmed, I also believe there was another kind of pain—I remembered the power of God's generosity, carried it in my spirit and heart, and it hurt when I delivered divine groceries and the produce was left on the counter to die.

CHAPTER 15

Our Lady of Guadalupe

I am your merciful Mother, the Mother of all who love me,
of those who cry to me . . .
Do not be troubled or weighed down with grief.
Do not fear any illness . . . anxiety or pain.
Am I not . . . your Mother?

—WORDS OF THE VIRGIN
SPOKEN TO JUAN DIEGO, 1531

While I had no difficulty in becoming one with Spirit, I was still clueless as to how deeply wounded I was in my relationship with the Divine Mother. For all practical purposes, I was a motherless child with the Mother's power. The Blessed Mother often worked through me in my healing work, bringing great comfort to others. I didn't absorb her love for myself. I could only pour it out to others.

In 1994, I had a startling dream in which Mary, the Mother of God, clearly instructed me to visit the shrine of Our Lady of Guadalupe in Mexico City. She said I was to travel there by myself, without Frank as my protector. I had a devotion to Our Lady, and the story of her shrine was familiar to me. In 1531, Our Lady appeared to a humble Aztec peasant, Juan Diego, and sent him to ask the bishop of Mexico City to have a church built in her honor. The skeptical bishop demanded that Mary send him a sign. It always stirs me to imagine the scene when Juan returned and opened his cloak, and cascades of Castilian roses tumbled out. The bishop fell to his knees before the image of Mary miraculously imprinted on the cloak. Frank bought me an exact replica of this image, and it hangs above our fireplace.

Following the dream, I took several hours to pray for discernment, and, with Frank's encouragement, I packed my bags for the journey. I just took the bare necessities: a journal, two pens, one pair of black knit pants, two cotton shirts, Imodium for diarrhea, and a pair of walking shoes. In essence, I was prepared for nothing!

Once in Mexico City, I found myself wrapping my arms around my stomach, reaching up to clutch my ribs. I walked the noisy streets bulging with peasant women, watching them wasting away on the sidewalks like mounds of garbage. Their dirty faces were gaunt, as lifeless as their mechanical arms that swayed limply in the dusty air, begging for loose change. They nursed their bone-thin babies on the sidewalks, hiding their faces under blankets stiff with urine and sweat. I could hardly breathe, uniting myself with the women and wondering what it was like to be sucking for life with hundreds of feet trampling by your head, threatening at any moment to accidentally squash out your existence. My mind and heart were stretched to the breaking point as I envisioned us walking upon a living cosmic crucified woman. The milk of the mother was sour under my feet.

I muttered anxious prayers to the Blessed Mother, wondering if I had mis-interpreted the intent of her dream. I'd anticipated spiritual wonder and miracles but instead was faced with nightmare images of women's degradation. I gasped to see a ghost of a woman propped against iron rails, her eyes gray and milky, her mouth toothless, dribbling. It sent shockwaves through my body, with memories of Grandma and Anna during their solitary confinement in the asylum. I began having dry heaves of agony that both Grandma and these women were scape-goats, bearing society's hatred and fear of the feminine spirit. I could taste the bitterness of what had pushed these women into the graves of their dispossessed lives, could hear the taunting voices of *You slut, you are not worthy*. The pathos of these women's shrunken bodies and wasted minds sent me reeling with memories of the separation from my children after divorce and illness. Without Frank by my side, I feared disintegrating into this old vortex of insanity.

It didn't help that I spoke no Spanish, and I had no sense of direction. *God help me* was all I could think. Navigating the streets had me quivering like a black light filament. I constantly expected a Volkswagen Beetle to suddenly drive up my leg and over my back and onto my head before I got to the next stoplight. When the traffic lights turned green, cars appeared around the corners like cockroaches when the lights are suddenly turned on. I really missed Frank by my side! It's great to trust in God, but holding air instead of a hand was not very consoling.

In the subway, I felt like a hamster caught in a maze with no exit. No one spoke English, or if they did, they weren't about to let me in on the secret. I was gulping back tears so intensely I almost missed the *tap, tap* on my right shoulder. A young woman, dressed in tight black leather, with glaring red lipstick and black spiked hair, sweetly asked if I needed help. In perfect English, winking with delight, she gave me directions to the Shrine of Our Lady. I reached into my purse to tip her, but when I looked up, she'd disappeared into the crowd. I thought to myself, *If that was the Holy Mother, she sure has changed! . . . Oh well . . . hey, thanks!*

Finally, I arrived at the courtyard of the new basilica, built in 1976. The words of the inscription carved over the door of the church were incredibly soothing. They promised that our sorrows are always heard and that we have no reason to fear illness or pain. We are always in the arms of the Loving Mother. Immediately, images of childhood ordeals tumbled over the lenses of my eyes like an out-of-control Rolodex machine. I gagged. "My mother? My Mother?"

As I stood there trembling, an impish-looking young boy began dancing erratically around my legs, black ringlets bouncing on his head like coiled springs. I clumsily looked for coins, wondering if he was the child of one of the exhausted women on the streets. As I reached to hand him the coins, I recoiled. Instead of fingers, he had only one sharp fingernail jutting out of his third knuckle. I shut my eyes for a moment, and in that second, he vanished, like the young woman in the subway.

I was usually astute at interpreting what I saw as signs from the spirit world. But this? I whispered to Mary my Mother: *I'm really feeling stupid for having believed in your dream. I'm scared out of my mind, and I'm about to poop in my pants. Your mission will have to wait for another day.* The Divine Mother was not about to be deterred by my whining, however. A gentle breeze swept through my hair, and the veils of uncertainty began to lift. Tears welled up in my eyes as the recognition dawned on me that I, too, was tap-dancing. I was tap-dancing around life because of a deeply embedded lie at my core: I had unconsciously accepted my suffering as punishment for having accepted abuse, for having failed my children, and for betraying my friend Jesus. Aside from Frank, no one would have guessed the presence of this diminished, desperado spirit that stalked me in the darkness of the night and the shadows of the day. In encountering the woman and the boy, I noticed they were not ashamed of their bodies. They were full of passion and vitality, not sheepish about wearing sexy clothes in public or of begging with full abandon, disfigurement and all. I didn't know how to integrate such disparate images of being a body: I related to the empty shells of the begging women, and I shied away from the sensual woman dressed in black, walking proudly in stiletto heels. And the young fingerless boy dancing circles around me? A potent reminder that, in my single-minded drive to live as a spirit walking alongside my body, I was like a single fingernail jutting from crippled hands.

As much as I wanted to go inside the church that it had taken me all day to find, I returned to the hotel. As luck went that day, it took me two hours to find it after leaving the courtyard of the basilica. I got off the train at the wrong stop and ended up walking through winding, narrow streets, tripping over garbage, startled by the big rats that occasionally crossed the streets before me. I had a map in my hand but had no idea how to read it. I wanted to pray for help but was too panicked, so I swore instead, apologizing to God with every step. When I finally arrived at my destination, I found an announcement under my door about a bus trip that was available in the morning to visit Teotihuacan, site of the famous Sun and Moon pyramids. I figured this was God's way of bringing me relief from the harrowing events of the day. The shrine would wait.

My recall of the bus ride to Teotihuacan is vague, except that the bus driver went faster than a roadrunner in the desert. This helped to diminish my shock as we flashed past dilapidated slum houses, barely visible through clouds of smog. We had to leave the windows open for air, and the sweltering heat soon had us coated in layers of smelly sweat, attracting road dirt and people's sneezes. When we reached the Plaza of Quetzalcoatl, I felt verbally clobbered by male vendors hawking their wares. They swarmed around me like horseflies on a muggy day, and, as so often in my life, they refused to listen to me as I tried desperately to stop their persistent attempts to get money from me. I kept thinking of the silent, famished women I'd encountered on the street the day before. Finally, in frustration, I shrieked at the men like a banshee. They retreated quickly. *Come on, Mother Mary, this is not funny. All my life, I get heard only when I cry or act idiotic. Do something!*

As if Mary heard me, I remembered the brochure I had in my pocket. In it was a fascinating story about the male and female Toltec masters who once lived in the Palace of the Butterfly. Apparently, these masters were able to go beyond their physical nature and be sustained by their spirituality. I was intrigued by any spiritual discipline that focused on transcendence—rising above the body. I was even more fascinated by the story that, after their spiritual initiations were completed, they climbed the Pyramid of the Sun, their bodies disintegrating as they ascended into the sun. I thought, *What an elegant way to go—how do I sign up for this program!* But, given my adventures to this point, I suspected enlightenment for me wasn't going to come with instructions on how to vanish into thin air.

As I looked up to the top of the Pyramid of the Sun, the pain in my head screamed through my entire body, *No way can you make that climb*, but my spirit leapt forward. It didn't take long before I was huffing and puffing up every step like a rusty old train engine, with sweat forming little rivulets dripping from my nose and chin. I must have muttered a million times: *Sweet Mother of God, you must be kidding me.* Once at the top of the pyramid, I became aware of the wind, my spirit friend. It was soft at first, and then it seemed to come to a standstill, as if anticipating a holy moment. As the sun sharpened my vision, a velvet black butterfly appeared at the bridge of my nose, its dazzling wings edged in liquid sunlight. Then there were two. Then there were three. My knees buckled, as I sank in adoration. The three butterflies swirled around in a circle, coming together in oneness, separating out, forming a cross, coming back together into one body, one wing. Several people gathered, equally stunned, as the butterflies vibrated, dancing in ecstasy for several seconds around my head. I sensed I would faint, but a stronger wind arose and held me up. Several minutes later, I wobbled down the stairs to be greeted by two white butterflies flitting around me, delicate as whispers of angel lace.

This encounter with God left me breathless. At the time, I had no frame of reference with which to understand it. Looking back on it, what an exquisite reflection of the meaning of the Cross, of the integration of heaven and earth, and the grandeur and interconnectedness of the Spirit within all of Life. The black butterfly reminded me that I experienced wholeness only as a spirit rooted in the memory of God, and that I'd forgotten the union of all parts of me within an embodied consciousness. I can now see that the magnificence, the fluidity of the black butterfly's movement helped soften my rigid concepts of God. At the time, I was convinced that ascetic spiritual practices and cleansing myself of all sin and imperfection were the path to enlightenment and union with the Divine. For years my spirituality and mental life were ponderous, preoccupied with shadow material and esoteric complexities. Such heaviness and examination of every detail of myself, while necessary on many levels, left me with a shriveled life. I hadn't appreciated that holiness involves both messiness and brilliance. That is what the Divine Mother showed me, both in the emptiness of the women's breasts that seemed to lap crumbs from the curbside, and in the radiance of the sun on fragile butterfly wings.

Of utmost joy was the appearance of the white butterflies that reminded me of Frank and I. It was a blessed invitation to be "light," to be the expression of God's soul that was imprinted on us at birth, before cultural and family restrictions. It was time to return to the mystical innocence of the child who loved bubbles, fairy dust, and painting rainbows in the sky. And with Frank, that was the promise. I recalled how one person at our wedding described us as two lightning bugs whose light never dulled, just glowed for everyone to delight in.

The next day I returned to the Basilica of Our Lady of Guadalupe and stayed there for approximately seven hours. I was numbed by the sight of hundreds of peasants crawling on their knees to the inside altar, praying silently with trembling lips, their weathered hands clenching black, brown, yellow, red, or white rosary beads. Many labored under huge, glorious bouquets of flowers, along with banners, balloons, and handmade artifacts all lovingly prepared for the Virgin. As they entered the church, they lifted their children as precious offerings to the Mother, holding them high above their humble bowed faces. The priests said Mass and distributed communion like robots with rusty joints.

To catch a glimpse of the Virgin's famous cloak, we had to step onto a conveyor belt that took us past the icon. It was suspended, halfway to the ceiling, protected behind bulletproof glass. Surely, there were more creative ways to protect the image of Mary without all of us needing chiropractic adjustments from twisting our necks upward to see Her. As I stepped on the conveyor belt, a familiar migraine aura crept into my peripheral vision, while a sense of awe enfolded me like a soft baby blanket. As I looked at the icon, the Mother's robes came alive, and blood poured out of her heart onto her right side, forming a shape like the opening of her womb. The Shroud of Jesus appeared on her left knee, and her left shoulder turned deep blue. She smiled and said, *Annette, welcome. I have so much to tell you, so much for you to speak of later.* I was too dumbfounded, too shaken to comprehend these words, so I ran to the bathroom. I remember forgetting to sit on the toilet and, instead, sank against the cold cement wall by one of the sinks. As if impaled by a sword, I thought, *Am I being asked to leave the suffering of Jesus, get off the cross, and enter the womb of His Mother?*

To this day, I am not comfortable sharing all the details of the visions that followed. Many involved teachings on the meaning of the life and death of Jesus, teachings that are not traditionally accepted. Others involved an awakening of the feminine consciousness that lay waiting in the marrow of my bones, trapped under the wreckage of my mind. I believe this is what Mary was trying to communicate to me when she appeared with a bridge of colored light across her womb, reminding me that the rainbows I desired to paint in the sky as a child needed to be more than colors admired from a distance. I would become a rainbow of color following the storms of my life, once I embraced my feminine nature. *Annette, say "Yes" to life, say "Yes" to my mysteries.* When I heard these words from Mary, I felt I was also being asked to help other women awaken to their essence, but *how* that would be done wasn't something I'd be told at that time.

Oftentimes after an ecstatic experience, I encountered things that were jarring and radically disruptive to my spirit. The visit to the Chapel of Tepeyac, the site of the first apparition of Our Lady to Juan Diego, was no exception. The local peasants and tourists jostled their perspiring bodies up the stairs to the chapel, where they offered their candles to Mary, singing and praying with great devotion. I slowly worked my way to the front of the chapel, bumping into a disgruntled short priest whose face resembled an injured stray dog. He'd come from behind a closed door, holding a large piece of stiff cardboard. Without hesitation, and at breakneck speed, he waved the cardboard, snuffing out all the candles on the long, narrow table. His final insult was to pitch the candles into a metal bucket. Anger surged through my blood, and I glared at the priest with an intensity Joan of Arc would have been proud of. I bellowed, "You cannot do that! How *dare* you? These people have sacrificed so much to buy these candles as a sign of love for the Virgin. How *dare* you? This is a *sin!*" I was quaking in my sandals, but it didn't stop me from picking up each discarded candle and placing it back onto the table. The priest's eyes registered gunfire, but he walked away. One very distressed peasant man grabbed a chair, started pulling his hair by the roots, and prayed the Ave Maria as if he were about to ascend to another dimension. I suspect my words were unintelligible, but the message was clear. Don't mess with a daughter of the Blessed Mother.

In retrospect, my fury wasn't just about these peasants and their candles. Minutes prior to this incident, I'd been infused with Mary's messages of how *beloved* women are, and how I was to be an ambassador on behalf of Her blessed, godly daughters—and here was this arrogant clergyman metaphorically extinguishing the light of these indigent, holy peasants. The cesspool of dispossession I came to Mexico with exploded like a giant bowel movement. I was one pissed-off woman, pissed off by the church's centuries-old attitude toward women as second-class people; I was pissed off at clergymen who strutted their power through control and superiority. I could no longer be still. How many women have struggled to be Light within the Church, and to embrace their dignity, only to be oppressed, diminished, pulverized like fine coffee grounds—all because they were women. The Divine Soul showed its outrage in that moment, and I gave it voice for everyone to hear. The sight of women furtively wiping tears from their eyes was a sign that they understood, and that I was forgiven for my rudeness and disrespect for the clergy. I wonder if my mother would have been proud of me.

My final irrational act of protest against the Church for its mistreatment of women was to kick the twenty-foot-high brass statue of the Pope that stood outside the original basilica. The words that came out of my mouth, as I crushed my toe against the metal, would have liquefied the wax in anyone's ears. As in real life, I was the loser in this confrontation with Church authority. I fractured my big toe and had to hobble around for the rest of my trip. That was one time I didn't regret pain.

In the back courtyard of the basilica were racks of pornographic magazines within thirty feet of other tables overflowing with tacky, gold and plastic images of the Mother and her Son. Milling about the courtyard were young men sporting white t-shirts, glaringly depicting nude couples making love. I was shocked by the contrast: inside the church, the Lady was concealed and untouchable, revealing only her hands and face; outside, her disowned and disrespected daughters were available prey for wandering, groping hands. No wonder I felt dispossessed and disempowered over being a woman:

Your purpose is not bigger than life. It is Life.

either you were an untouchable porcelain doll sheltered by God, or you were an object to be exploited, never valued for who you are. I had no model, no image for being a spiritual, emotional, embodied powerful woman. Before the visions, I was full of resentment and grief, loathing my womanhood. The Divine Mother now wanted me to unite with her so that her Love could revive the softness in my heart, a softness I thought was dead. She cautioned me not to look for some grand plan for my life. *Your purpose is not bigger than life. It is Life.* This message resounded like pure crystal, ringing with the consciousness that was evolving in me.

I decided to check in with Jesus in a remote corner of the basilica following this penetrating wisdom from His Mother. After some undetermined time of contemplation, Jesus appeared in front of me. From within a ball of glowing light, I heard him say, *Women have been silenced in their strength, humiliated into submission, and ridiculed for coming forth with their voice. No more, my friend, no more. You are Beloved. All women are Beloved. I have set you free. I have set them free. My death broke open this consciousness.*

Later that evening, I wept profusely as my heart and mind swirled with the messages I received, most of which I didn't understand. I believed Jesus's words were a promise that the feminine consciousness was coming out of exile, and that I, and others, would be restored as embodied, good-enough women and mystics. I laughed aloud about my path as a mystic, not as someone who prayed all day and baked bread in a monastery, but as a divorced, rather emotionally rocky woman, living in the world, married to an ex-priest. Maybe Frank was my black butterfly, and I'd have to put on the black leather jacket to complete my earthly mission!

· · · · ·

A year later, the Divine Mother and the Black Butterfly, my dynamic duo, called me once again into their presence during an intensive shamanic training in the Catskill Mountains. This was not the arid, poverty-stricken environment of Mexico. The landscape was lush with greenery, majestic mountains and hills, and cascading streams. Several days into the training, we were directed to connect to the spirit of an element of nature and, with that spirit, create a ritual to help release the psychological stories that clouded our energy fields and blocked our essence from flowering. The spirit of water chose me, and I decided to leisurely stroll on the dirt path that ran alongside a loud bubbling mountain stream.

Without warning, I felt an invisible force stop the movement of my feet. I looked down and saw a large velvet black butterfly on the front of my right shoe. For several minutes, I gazed in awe as it slowly let its wings down to the ground, lifted them up to a position of one wing, and back down. My normal response to beauty and God's grace is tears. So much water gushed from my eyes that I feared drowning this stunning creature. The black butterfly had come to symbolize the vulnerability, the fragility, and yet also the power of the feminine spirit I so desperately wanted to be. The one wing reminded me of my yearning to be whole, to be in communion with the Divine in a body. Meeting the butterfly was a reminder that the Mother had not forgotten me—she wanted me to set my burdens to rest.

As I approached the riverbank with a pocketful of stones that represented parts of my life story, I sensed a numinous power in the air that was staggering. To my right was a hollowed-out mound of dirt that formed a womb for hundreds of small yellow butterfly wings. There was absolutely no trace, no evidence of their bodies, just scintillating wings pulsing with heat and death, pulsing with the stillness of pure essence. As I did on the pyramid in Mexico, my knees folded ever so gently, bending reverently in astonishment. In the silence, I heard a whisper that resonated with the pulse of translucent wings: *I would only be free if I made the choice to believe that my body, although important, wasn't the primary determiner of my happiness. What was significant was the body of information I chose to attach to.* The multiplicity of my fractured-fairy-tale existence had to be rewritten through eyes of a tender Mother as opposed to the not-good-enough, burdensome judgments of Ma. Maybe my wings were more beautiful than I thought, and it was time to place my stories in the womb of the Earth and let the waters soothe my warrior nature. No need to deny the harshness of my path, no need to fire any more rounds of *you failed* ammunition. Maybe my wings weren't as broken as I thought, and all my analyzing was nothing but hot air.

Shifting into the compassionate energy of the Divine Mother was life-changing. During the week I was at the training, the volume of my daily jackhammer headaches began to subside. Every birdsong, every rustle of the leaves, every ripple of water dancing in the stream was a symphony never heard before. I believe I heard the song of the Universe that morning, like those times as a child when I could hear the plants singing as they awakened in the morning sun. It felt safe to be home in the world, in the arms of a loving maternal energy.

CHAPTER 16

Egypt: Giving Voice to the Divine

A bird does not sing because it has an answer.
It sings because it has a song.

—JOAN WALSH

In 1995, I was invited to do a workshop on near-death experiences as part of an organized pilgrimage to Egypt. The woman who invited me was a spiritual friend and colleague, and she thought I'd be a breath of fresh air, given my sense of humor and "irreverence" about spirituality. I had a reputation for being as respectful as the Pope, and yet, as I was in high school, if I saw something as BS, I'd start giggling. I didn't take myself too seriously, no matter the sanctity of what I was involved in. On this trip, I was intimidated to be on the roster with celebrities like Marianne Williamson and Elisabeth Kübler-Ross (who didn't attend due to illness). I was a country bumpkin: unknown, unpublished, and I didn't even have a business card. But, with Frank at my side, why not be the holy fool and say yes to the invitation?

My presentation was scheduled for the middle of the week. I began by recounting my near-death experience, and then led shamanic journeys to connect with Egyptian ancestors. My near-death story did not fit the norm as recounted by most survivors. It wasn't focused on being dazzled, converted, motivated to write a book, and set the world on fire with the "truth." As a result, some of the other presenters were dismayed to hear me admit to my disillusionment of having to return to the drudgery of everyday life. It seemed to them like a spiritual betrayal—that is, not uplifting or inspirational to the conference attendees.

Given my tendency to believe that external authority was superior to my inner guidance, my confidence turned into a bowl of unset Jell-O—until I realized the audience was receptive to my story. In fact, because I spoke of the underbelly of near-death—and not from the expected *all is light and love* perspective—several people were drawn to my authenticity. For once in my lifetime, I was validated for speaking what others dared not think about or reveal publicly—and with a sense of humor.

That evening I was scheduled to lead a sacred ritual in the Great Pyramid at midnight. Armed police patrolled the street in front of our hotel, not only because there had been a shooting that morning, but also due to mounting tensions surrounding the upcoming elections. I'd initially wanted to take a leisurely walk to the pyramid with Frank, but I opted for a five-minute cab ride with two other women, blissfully ignorant that the ride itself would turn into an initiation.

The driver gave me that creepy-crawly feeling, and when he deliberately turned off the headlights to the van, goosebumps popped up all over my skin. He drove past the pyramid slow and steady as an ancient tortoise, going deeper into the cold, silent desert, ignoring our anxious pleas to turn back. The light of the crescent moon penetrated the darkness, making our eyes shine like cat's-eyes marbles, magnifying our terror. We were petrified that we'd be stiffed for money or worse. Always the person to break the tension with humor, I started to boom out in my Kate Smith voice, "When the Moon comes over the Mountain." The driver was not impressed with the impersonation of my childhood idol. He parked the car, turned off the motor, slowly turned his gaze in our direction, and flashed a leering grin. Not to be intimidated, I prayed the rosary, out loud, just as the nuns taught me in grammar school. He laughed like a wicked witch, so I pulled out all the stops, claiming I was one of the important leaders of the conference and that the police would soon be searching the desert for all of us. In my sternest nun voice, I barked, "You are going to be in BIG trouble if anything happens to us." God knows why, but he started up the engine, and we were back to the pyramid half an hour later. Apparently, people were concerned by our disappearance and had alerted the police. When we stepped out of the cab, the driver was wrenched from his seat and beaten by several guards. I cringed to witness this kind of brutality, yet I was grateful we were unharmed.

Upon entering the Great Pyramid, the previous distraction disintegrated like tissue in hot water. Spirit directed me to go to the top of the Grand Gallery, a steep, narrow passageway that climbed to the King's Chamber. *Oh dear God,* I thought. *How in the world am I supposed to be spiritual when just looking up that dim passageway makes my head spin like a top?* I swore under my breath, hoping no one heard me. *Okay, Annette, get a grip.* I retreated to a secluded corner, praying, *Okay, Spirit: take over!* I gingerly began the long climb up, clutching my drum in one hand, sensing that many spirits of the pyramid were entering my body to support me. I was glad to have them as my guests. Once at the top of the climb, I lit a vigil candle at my feet, and, as I lifted my drum, a spirit began drumming me. All I could do was let my hand move with the rhythm pulsing through my body. The other participants in the ritual reverently and silently climbed in semi-darkness, called by the drumming and my chanting from the top of the passageway. Together we entered into the pharaoh's burial space.

For three hours, shadows of the Buddha, Jesus, and the pharaohs flickered larger than life on the stone walls of the chamber, and otherworldly sounds flowed effortlessly from a space within me that I didn't know existed. It was a visceral experience of being drenched in the power and wonder of Oneness, transforming me into a wordless melody of God's voice. With profound awe, I can say it was as if the Divine and I were united into a Sound, connecting all of us in that chamber into a strand of ancient pearls, awakening a universal memory of Love and Peace. Yes, God's life force experienced itself through my body.

At some point during the ceremony, while the rest of the group continued chanting, each of us lay down in the sarcophagus of the pharaoh. When I entered that sacred space, I felt the stone shiver vigorously, and I was blinded by a flash of white light. Within seconds, my whole body was exquisitely soothed, the cold tomb magically transformed into a rocking cradle. I then heard the scraping of a stone being rolled away—and Jesus was before me, glorified, dazzling as a stream of sunlight after a storm. He reached out his hand to me and we touched—a touch that connected every bone, every muscle, every drop of blood in my body. Finally, I knew God within my body, the energy that held me in existence. I was no longer *out there* but rather *in here*. In the cold sarcophagus, I knew I wanted to live, not die.

It was three a.m. when the ritual ended. As we left the pyramid, one of our Egyptian tour guides told Frank that my voice reverberated so loudly that he was sure the desert sands began to dance. One of the guards was superstitious and wondered if the ancient ones had returned through me to have them clean up their lives! The next day, those who attended the ceremony were aglow with the power of Spirit they'd experienced the previous evening. Many asked me, "How can I learn to do what you did? How do you do *that?*" I had no answer. It wasn't something I learned, nor could it be taught—it was a divine energy I remembered.

At the time I believed I was merely a vessel for the Spirit—a hollow bone. Lately, I've come to realize that, while this is true—we are a vessel, a host for the Divine—there is something more. I'm not an innocent bystander to Spirit—I am a partner with God, a co-creator with Life, so that the Great Mystery can have the experience of being human and evolve it through me, through each of us. The stunning consciousness of this communion is what I began to realize in Egypt. But, as elevating as this was to my spirit, it created a dilemma. I was torn between wanting to set the world on fire with this consciousness, this memory of Divine Union, and wanting to appear a normal person living an ordinary life. My need to belong and be accepted in this world blinded me to the realization that there is no separation in this consciousness, and all that is asked is to Be this essence. The complexity of this simple truth still boggles my mind.

Some of the people were angered that someone so insignificant as me had been given "prime time" for this event in the pyramid. They seemed to have sudden amnesia to the fact that no one had wanted the midnight shift, and it was given to me by default. There were several critical comments made about my "singing." It was dismissed as high drama and "showing off." It didn't take long for me to start slipping into the old rabbit hole of not being good enough. Whenever I was authentic, I'd hear the voices of Ma and my ex-husband, one sitting on each shoulder, saying, "Who the hell are you anyway? Who appointed you to be God's messenger? What right do you have to 'stand out' amidst people who are far more sophisticated, learned, and more experienced than you?" I thought, *Maybe I am a show-off, but nothing inside me says that is true.* In fact, I wasn't "owning" the cosmic energy that sang me that evening—I just let it be. Even so, I found myself pretending that being God's songbird wasn't significant. Behind closed doors, I wept, grateful for Frank's presence. He helped me see that the most effective response to people was silence and a smile.

Singing in the pyramid prepared the way for an event that occurred a few days later when we visited the Temple of Horus. He was the son of the goddess Isis and her husband Osiris. Horus was depicted as a vengeful god of great might, and our Egyptian guide confided his misgivings about visiting this site. "Something always happens," he said with trepidation. As our group approached the temple, one of the women had a severe asthma attack, triggered by the stifling heat and her allergy to horse dander and the dried manure on the streets. Various healers swarmed around her, using crystals, incantations, magnets, and whatnot to help her breathe. I could see her life force being squeezed out of her body. Her eyes were bulging like a swamp frog from the constriction in her lungs. I finally went over and, not too elegantly, insisted that they get her to a hospital. "If you don't, she may be joining Horus very soon." The tone of my voice commanded respect and she was immediately taken to medical care.

The tour continued on to the Temple of Horus. Half an hour later, as our group was praying in the innermost room of the temple, someone ran in and reported that the asthmatic woman was dying. Our Egyptian guide, who remembered his experience at the pyramid, demanded I sing. I wanted to tell him that what happened in the pyramid was not under my control, but after a brief prayer, a clear, wordless sound, half an octave higher than my normal voice, poured out of me, filling the temple. I "saw" invisible Egyptian kings walk around us in circles and could hear the clanking metal of their armor. We were being protected. When the singing ended, as in the pyramid, I experienced a temporary physical weakness as the energy of the Spirit diminished within my body. Later, we learned that the woman recovered and would rejoin our group within a few days.

Two days after this experience, we visited the Temple of Hathor, the goddess of fertility and motherhood. My body trembled and my head throbbed with unbelievable discomfort while we were in this space. The pillars and the carved stone murals of her face had been vandalized by Christians, who wanted to destroy her influence as part of a pagan, earth-based female cult. I walked away from the busy chattering of our group, wandering by instinct through several rooms, one of which I felt certain was a birthing room. I sat on one of the stone benches, remembering how, as a teenager, I'd go to cemeteries, stand in front of the tombstones, and step into the life of the person buried there. Part of me thought this was crazy, but I loved my time with the ghosts. Here in Hathor's Temple, I felt myself time travel back to a ceremony with ancient women, following the birth of a child. I heard a joyful chant sing in my head: *There is such joy in being born. Come celebrate our new life.* I was unaware how loud I was humming until our Egyptian tour guide came up, grabbed my arm, and said, "You are sitting in an ancient birthing room, and you will sing—you will sing for the Goddess. Come to the innermost sanctuary of Hathor."

I again protested that I could not "sound" on command, but he insisted and brought the whole group into the heart of the temple. The Spirit of Hathor knew exactly what the group needed in that moment, and I cooperated, surrendering to embody her voice for the greater good. As others joined the mantra I'd been given, an astounding descant sang through me, in harmony with the other voices but rising above them. Frank told me later that a woman, a professional rock singer, gaped at me with her mouth falling open. Several people with ailments were healed, and others broke into song and dance to praise Hathor. Perhaps some people will think I am being grandiose in writing about such experiences. But they were moments of bone-deep memory that I was one with Divinity. I am just an ordinary, bumbling mystic, and yet my essence is to be a melody of the Divine. Who I am is a sound that needs to soar like a mighty symphonic wind.

The lead Egyptologist on our tour later told my husband that he was on the roof of the temple when the singing began, and he'd had an out-of-body episode. Devout Muslim though he was, he told Frank in tears that, in my singing, the goddess had returned, that the temple had come alive again. He wanted me to stay in Egypt, to awaken the spirit within other ancient ruins. As seductive an offer as this was, a whisper reassured my soul: *You also have been disfigured from personal trauma, and your ruins need further restoration. Your voice will be heard when the time comes.*

The woman who had suffered the asthma attack was in Hathor's Temple during the impromptu ritual. On the last night of our Nile cruise, she told Frank that, during her brief stay in the hospital, she'd undergone a near-death experience. She was at the point of crossing the barrier between the worlds when she heard a "hauntingly beautiful" voice that surrounded her entire body. She told Frank that, when she heard me sing in Hathor's Temple, it was my voice that had sung her back to life

In the midst of such transforming energies, my irreverent sense of humor bubbled up to keep me grounded. Whether it was taking myself too seriously or encountering spiritual practices that just seemed too daffy to me, sometimes I just had to bust a gut with belly laughing. It's not that I disrespect other spiritualities or alternative modalities of healing—heaven knows, I've tried most of what is offered on the market and some that were down the alleyways! On the Egyptian trip, everything from dial-the-dead services to depossession from aliens was available. While I'd partaken in many of these kinds of healings in my lifetime, at one point of the trip, it all seemed rather unbalanced and almost surreal. I was reminded of clients I'd encountered over the years who sought to bypass the process of transformational psychological inner work by wearing expensive crystals and fetishes and performing prescriptive formulas for cures and "fix-me" outcomes. God knows, out of desperation and exhaustion, I'd done the same. So, when I decided to plan a spoof, I was laughing at myself as much as I was at the "woo-woo" spirituality. The spoof, which was free of charge, was for me to channel the spirit of an animal that tended to be dismissed because it was ordinary and rather dumb. What my mother would describe as "stupid." To heighten the anticipation, I didn't specify who the spirit was.

That evening, I skipped dinner, taking the time instead to dress fashionably and prepare the opening lines for my presentation. The first question came from a woman who wanted to know if she would find her soul mate and how long would she have to wait. I closed my eyes, bowed my head reverently, drummed a bit, sang a few prayers out loud, and then burst into loud chicken squawks, climaxing my answer with an after-your-head-has-been-cut-off chicken dance. My arms and legs moved spastically, but my face was expressionless—I was possessed by the spirit of the Great Chicken. When someone said they were having difficulty deciphering the language of the chicken spirit, I'd hesitate for a second and start my performance all over again. Not one single person caught on, or at least no one dared confront the Great Chicken! It was all I could do not to pee down the legs of my silk pants. In the process of my outrageous antics, I had this aha moment: I saw a mirror image of myself. I was no different than any of those searching for ways to eliminate their pain. The sad truth is that they, and I, would accept an external authority—in this case, innocent mischief—over their own wisdom. The Great Chicken had the last cluck on all of us!

The following morning, our group decided to ride Arabian horses in the desert. The only other time I'd been on a horse was in my early thirties, and I'd failed miserably in my attempt. The horse did nothing but circle a tree, refusing to move forward. The instructor commented that the horse was connecting to my fear of life and it was probably best for me to dismount—the horse wasn't going to go anywhere, and neither was I in my emotional condition. As the horses were brought to us, I started to feel faint. The beauty and nobility of these animals was unparalleled, and their life force was intimidating, to say the least. And while I carried the spirit of the Great Chicken with unflappable dignity, the power of a horse frightened the living daylights out of me. I watched Frank eagerly mount his horse, and decided I could get on as well if I remained centered and connected with Frank's confidence. I telepathically communicated with my horse to stay by Frank's side!

Halfway through our adventure, Frank and I decided to take a breather from the hubbub of the crowd and meditate on the Pyramids in the distance. At first, I thought it was a mirage, but there it was—a field of energy lifting the façade off the Pyramids, unveiling exquisitely carved images of Isis and Osiris kissing. I looked over at Frank who was visibly shaken by something as well. When I asked if he was feeling okay, he smiled and teared up. He took my hand and whispered, "There is nothing, nothing but Love. That is the essence of all—pure Love . . . nothing else matters." We'd both seen the exact same depiction of Isis and Osiris.

Since our marriage, I'd struggled with tremendous guilt about the grace-filled power of the love that Frank and I have for each other. Somehow, I bore a deep-seated religious wound that I was betraying God in loving Frank so intensely. Once the veil lifted off the Pyramids, a cloud of duality lifted from my consciousness. The truth was that it was impossible to separate human love from divine love. We both grasped the depth of how each of us had been freed from loneliness and craziness through Love. The tenderness of this revelation enfolded us in a peace beyond understanding. Tears of gratitude—gratitude for being alive—formed a roadmap through the sand and dust on my face.

That evening, two women from the conference invited me to join them on another horse ride into the desert, this one before sunrise. They expressed concern about the shabby treatment some of conference presenters had given me, and they thought a brisk ride at dawn would be the perfect boost to lift my sagging spirit. Their graciousness touched my heart, so I agreed, even though I don't function well at five in the morning.

As we walked to the stable, I was flabbergasted to see the Sphinx of Giza looming over the back fence. Quite the ominous presence at dawn! The owner of the stable appeared, dressed in a simple dark-brown linen robe, followed by his robust dimple-cheeked wife. She came over to me and wrapped my head and neck with a soft white scarf. A mother wrapping her child in swaddling clothes could not have been more tender. I stumbled over my words like a skittish colt, asking that I'd be given a demure, well-behaved horse. The husband smiled, semi-toothless, and motioned for me to look over his shoulder. Out stepped his twelve-year-old daughter, dressed in a blue serge gown and a white veil, pulling a gray-white donkey for herself, and a white horse for me. The father gave strict instructions to his daughter not to make the horse go *chi-chi*—her signal for *Let's go full speed ahead until we get swallowed up in the dust!* Her body slumped in obedience, but her eyes flashed, *We'll see . . . we'll have some fun.*

The other women galloped off on their supercharged black stallions, while I on my horse, the girl on her donkey, did the shifting-sand shuffle, barely disrupting the top layer of sand. At times, the girl would stop, twirl on the back of her donkey, and twitter "chi-chi?" I pretended not to notice.

An hour later, my reverie was broken when the father came riding up and said, "You special lady. I give you gift—stones from over there." The *over there* referred to the second largest Giza pyramid, which was inaccessible to the public. The night prior, I'd had a dream in which I saw how women found refuge in this space during times of persecution. Then Isis led me to a secret chamber of a pyramid in which an entire city was in darkness. She handed me a candle, whispering that I was to awaken the light within the women of the city.

The father sped away to the pyramid, returning with two unpolished pieces of white alabaster, one large and one small. My heart quivered. What was this about? Why was the stable owner choosing to give me the stones? *Okay, what will it cost me this time? No one says I'm special without there being a price to pay.* Unlike the threatening look of the cab driver in the desert, the father's eyes radiated kindness and unconditional love. Then a queasiness surged through my belly, almost toppling me off the horse. I knew this man! His aquamarine-colored eyes were those of the cab-driver Jesus in my dreams.

The father saw my obvious unsteadiness, so he took the reins of the horse in one hand and, with the other, held my hand and led me back to the stable in silence. Nothing could be heard but the faint whistle of the wind and the muffled thud of hooves in the timeless sand. Was I delusional, or was this the Spirit of God in ordinary human form, leading an ordinary woman, seized by the Divine, out into the dawning of day?

And two stones: one bigger than the other, a perfect reflection of how I experienced my life. My spirit was far greater than my human form, and the discrepancy and my inability to truly integrate body and soul was problematic. Maybe the stones were reaffirming that I and Frank were the same essence as these elemental gems. Was this a cryptic message from the Divine to help dispossessed women shift into a consciousness more attuned to the hidden world of mysticism? In that moment, my mind was swirling into a vortex of wonder and fear. I blinked my eyes and let them say the words I couldn't manage: "Thank you."

As I dismounted the horse, the daughter grabbed my face, locking her rich brown eyes with mine. She burst into sobs and heaving sighs. I tried to comfort her, but she only relaxed when I cried with her. Was she an old soul who recognized the lost innocence of my life, the blank years of lost passion that subdued my stallion nature? Did she sense the grief of my spirit from the Mother, the feminine? She pulled at the blue-crystal rosary bracelet I wore on my wrist, and without hesitation I placed it in her delicate hand. As we parted, her wailing continued to pierce the sunrise, leaving me shivering from more than the crisp air. I suspect a cynical person would interpret this encounter as her anger for not receiving money from an American tourist. Maybe. The chill in my bones told me differently.

In Egypt, the hard shell that imprisoned me cracked open to reveal that I was not the woman I thought I was. I showed up as a prim and proper spiritually elevated person—a façade that covered the layers of personal shame I lived with. Granted, I was comfortable, at home, in the divinity of my voice. It was as natural as warm bread and butter. I could have been in sacred ritual twenty-four hours a day if my body could have sustained such ecstasy! I still wonder about my sanity in channeling the spirit of the Great Chicken, and yet, that was another face of the Divine Feminine, and She wanted to be heard also. Chickens in high places are my best friends.

CHAPTER 17

Medicine Man

. . . Our life dance
Is only for a few magic
Seconds,
From the heart saying,
Shouting,
"I am so damn Alive."

—HAFIZ

Less than three months after my experiences in Egypt, I had a dream in which I heard that a "shepherd" would soon appear on my spiritual path. I met him un-expectedly when a book fell off a shelf in a local bookstore, making me wince with pain as it landed on my big toe. As I stared at the back cover, and realized the au-thor was the man in my dream, my body began to visibly shake. I was immediately intrigued when I read that he was both well known in the field of psychotherapy and was recognized as a shaman by indigenous tribes all over the world.

I picked up the book, randomly opening to an entry from the author's personal dream journal—and realized, I'd just had a similar dream myself a few nights ago. While such synchronicities were normal for me, I still had that "this is spooky" reaction. In the author's dream, he described seeing a plant with a white trumpet flower, a plant whose root was bound by white light. In my dream, I was diving into a white trumpet plant, seeking to unbind the root of the plant from a darkened filament—an image of my perpetual drive to release myself from the darkness of not being worthy. Was this person my next teacher? Why did I feel compelled to connect with him? My logical mind was skeptical, and yet the pounding of my heart confirmed what I was intuiting and what my dream had foretold.

I located the author easily as he was a professor at a well-known college. When I called, the tone of his voice was a bit standoffish, but, in retrospect,

I would have been the same had some unknown woman called me and rambled on like a runaway steam engine. I sensed his reservation about me: *Oh dear, another tumble-weed-flaky woman crashing at my feet in a desperate attempt to be saved.* He indicated he didn't meet individually with people, but if I wrote him a letter of intent, he would consider meeting me in person.

As I pushed the button to raise our garage door, anxious to get my eloquent letter to the post office before closing time, a gentle voice whispered in my ear: *This communication will forever alter your life.* I was so discombobulated that I didn't notice I'd inadvertently pushed the button again, this time making the garage door come down on my head!

Two days later, the author called, very excited about my spiritual journey, and said he'd received signs from the Spirit that he was to work with me. Apparently, on the day he read my letter, a treasured sacred object, a deer figure, had fallen off his wall and broken an ear. I hadn't told him yet that my spirit animal was a deer. Later in the day, an earring appeared on his front porch, and it didn't belong to his wife or anyone visiting his home. At the time, I made earrings similar to the one he found.

I, too, received a sign. In my office, an amulet bag hanging on the wall mysteriously turned over and dumped a small bear fetish onto the carpet. The fetish was something I had not seen before. I didn't see the significance of this until I walked into the shaman's home. There above the mantle was a painting of a large black bear, and the bear was holding the broken body of a deer and staring accusingly, angrily, at the skyline of the city in the background. My husband and I were both startled by this image, thinking he was like the bear carrying my wounded humanity, very concerned how depleted I was and how defeated I felt in the "real" world.

The instant I met the medicine man, I knew him as a spiritual brother. He exuded jubilance, and the vibrant flame of God burned deep within him. I'd never met another human whose obvious passion for the Divine equaled mine, but he was extremely grounded and in his body. I was a bit overwhelmed. After exchanging pleasantries with Frank and I, the shaman took a seat at his baby grand piano bench. When his hands touched the keys, he became one with the instrument, creating the most incredible seamless improvisation I'd ever heard. There was no distinction between him, the piano, and the melody. The spirit and he were making love with cosmic notes.

As he began playing, I went into a trance, stepping into vivid, extraordinary landscapes in nature, all of which felt familiar and like *home*. First, I was a deer in cool waters, then I froze as thunderous clouds appeared in the distance. I was aware of impending danger, even death. I darted blindly into the forest, stumbling against trees, searching for a safe haven. The rocks, the wind, the trees—all remained a silent presence as I trembled, fearing the scent of human flesh, terrified someone or something would block my path to union with God. In the music, I could hear a song in my heart, whispering that the waters of the ocean, the bark of the tree, the smoothness of a river stone, and the heart of a doe would heal the sickness within my body and mind if I took the risk to live an integrated life. I had to place my front hooves in the world of spirit and my back hooves in the earthly realm.

When the music ended, I struggled to return to my body, but out of the corner of my eye, I saw the toe of Frank's polished black shoe, and I came to. The shaman then led me into his healing room, which was located in his basement. We sat across from each other, gazing into each other's eyes. Within minutes, one of his eyes shape-shifted into that of an eagle, and it felt as if my human defenses broke down, leaving me spiritually naked. My body began to shake like the rattle in his hand, and I was aware that balls of light were flashing out of many ceremonial objects in the room, all showering rays of light into the right side of my body. My bones vibrated as if they had been unhinged, as if I'd been morphed into a skeleton for the Day of the Dead celebration.

This was high drama in spiritual theater, and on this stage I was a female body whose belly turned into a furnace of love. Five minutes prior, my energy level was lower than a dying ember, but, as we both shook like epileptic trees in a windstorm, I was tempted to just keel over with ecstatic wonder. At times, I felt as if I entered the Soul of the Universe, the space of utter silence and blackness. At other times, I became a universal woman, a vessel of evolution traveling through all of Creation. Looking back, I was awakened to spiritual memory, meaning that I began to drop the concept of my individuality as separate from the Cosmos. During the times I heard jumbled, cacophonous music swirling around my head, I responded by singing a single high-pitched note—a note that eventually calmed the energy into love and peace.

Some people would consider an experience like this as psychotic, or the product of an overactive, hysteria-prone imagination. How unfortunate. Certainly, diving into such an intense experience with a fractured mentality could have been disintegrating. But it wasn't for me. I wasn't a lunatic, as a lot of people, including me, had labeled me. In Egypt, I entered unearthly realms of mystical power, my voice breaking the barriers of whatever fears lived inside my heart. In the presence of this shaman, however, my earth-bound, mummified body began to unwrap, I experienced a fierceness and power in my essence that I had never imagined, and I knew why I'd been sent to study with this man. This life force of spirit was incarnation to the fullest, a communion of body and soul that arose from within my whole being, including my flesh and bones. I've known many people who have used psychedelics to achieve the kind of aliveness I felt when shaking with the spirits. I didn't need anything for mystical union except to allow myself to be ignited. The shaman recognized this passion for God within me, a divinity that never stopped trying to be the movement of my life.

Following our meeting, the medicine man served as a mentor to me, and we continued to correspond by mail. My nighttime dreaming became so intense, that sometimes I had troubling discerning what was the real world and what was the dream. It became clear to both of us that I entered a dream university at night, a time when the Universe itself designed the curriculum and chose which pages of life I was to study. That was a time I was directly infused with spiritual knowledge.

Within a year, the medicine man gathered a circle of twelve people who were interested in expanding their spirituality through the process of "shaking with the spirits." I was totally seduced by the power of the energy that surged through my body once he began primordial African drumming, usually in pitch darkness. The only words I can use to describe what it felt like during our sessions was experiencing the *nothingness of everything*. All memory of pain, generational in-sanity, and despair evaporated into ludicrous concepts. What a radical shredding of the personal identity I'd created: I went from perceiving myself as a demented, contemplative, sickly, nunnish woman, to a vivacious woman with African blood flowing through her veins and a fiery Spirit in her body. I understood for the first time in my life that we are all atoms and molecules of the Universe, of God, and that in dancing we blend into one harmonious, embodied whole.

I am grateful to this shaman for many things, but one in particular resonates with me. I'd lived all my years with a mentality that my goodness was intertwined with a need to suffer for Christ. After one of our sessions, I had a dream that shook loose the brambles of this distorted thinking. In the dream, Jesus took off his crown of thorns and places it in a gentle stream of water, blessed by his Mother. She emerges from the water, changing all the thorns into small balls of light through her healing touch. I woke from the dream, recalling the face of Hathor in the Egyptian temple, and the promise of new birth. The crown of dispossession and mental illness that the women of my family had worn for generations, the assaults that damaged their vulnerable womanhood, was touched by the power of the Divine Mother. I hugged myself, yearning for the mother I never had, beholden to the Mother who loved me.

Spiritually, I was comfortable with the rising of the feminine spirit, but in everyday reality, I was loath to explore the issue. To me, it implied that I'd have to be messy, unorganized, spacey, and motherly, and have to hang around with women, wear nice clothes, and wear nail polish on my toes and fingernails. I could handle being strong and untouchable but not vulnerable—no way. Living as a feminine spirit in a body meant I'd have to love all of me unconditionally, and that seemed more impossible than skydiving in the nude. In my isolation, and in my need to possess and be possessed by God, I had devalued the physical and relational aspects of life. The medicine man woke up the woman hidden under the burka of my disembodied spirituality.

Living as a feminine spirit in a body meant I'd have to love all of me unconditionally, and that seemed more impossible than skydiving in the nude.

It would take time for me to live into this new awareness, but I was peaceful in putting new pieces into the puzzle that was my life's path, embracing shoots of new life poking their heads up like spring crocuses. I was comforted by dreams of being an African priestess, a healer of children and women in ancient villages, a woman who healed with laughter and song. I even dreamed that maybe Africa would be my next destination, but it didn't matter—a spirit of lightness was breaking through the armadillo protection I wore in life.

As the meetings of the "shaking" group came to an end, the medicine man invited his mentor, a holy woman from Japan, to bless us for the next step of our journeys. This elderly woman was as gentle as a lamb and yet she had healing powers that surpassed anything we could dream of. I witnessed her spirit during an early-morning ritual when we gathered in a large field. Her arthritic legs and swollen feet carried her slowly to the center of the group of workshop attendees.

She stretched her weathered arms toward the heavens in prayer. Wisps of her thinning hair escaped like innocent children from the bun resting at the base of her neck. Prior to her gesture, the sky had been cloudless, a sea of robin's egg-blue. As her prayer ended, dark storm clouds suddenly rolled into the sky, almost bumping into each other. Thunder rumbled louder than freight trains crashing into each other. We began rattling with fear, anticipating the earth splitting open and swallowing us. The wind whipped the branches and leaves of the gigantic trees nearby into a frenzy until they swayed and seemed to bow in submission.

Just as quickly, a stillness hushed over us, merciful as a pure silk scarf, and a shaft of light broke through the gathering darkness, illuminating the ground at the tiny feet of this humble frail, plump woman. The power of God kissed the power of this woman. My knees buckled to the earth, speechless—as did the knees of the others. No one could utter a sound.

We were in circle that evening, awaiting her special blessing to us. She stood in front of each of us, bowed in simple elegance, smiled ever so sweetly, and lightly touched our foreheads. I expected to be greeted with the same gestures, but she raised my bent head, and her eyes reached deeply into my eyes. For a moment, I thought I'd die from the touch of her motherly gaze. Without warning, a loud sound and a gust of air blew from her dainty lips, and I felt impaled in my heart. Her energy knocked my breath to somewhere below my belly button. She then looked at me, looked at the shaman, and said, "Listen to him."

As we left the group that evening, she hugged me again, and a look of deep concern glided over her eyes. My first thought was *She thinks I'm dying*. My second thought puffed up my ego: *Wow, I am really special. She singled me out from the entire group*. Fortunately, I quickly remembered my encounter with other spiritual teachers and didn't succumb to my ego need to be affirmed for my spiritual gifts. I believe that her directive to listen to the shaman was about embodying my spirit. I could go on being "high on God," or I could begin focusing on the truth: that my out-of-body experiences were not the primary contract I had with life. I was as comfortable with spirit as anyone could be, and yet, something was moving me to places I really didn't want to go. I was in the midst of an evolutionary shift in my spirituality, and, true to form, I had to kick and scream before I'd surrender.

CHAPTER 18

When Is This Going to End?

And I tell you, ask and you will receive; seek and you will find; knock and the door will be opened to you.

—LUKE 11: 9–10 (NEW AMERICAN BIBLE)

Just months after I was with the medicine man, my physical pain flared up and I found myself sinking into a cesspool of despondency, a direct result of *never feeling well.* As Frank put it, "It's hard to feel good about yourself when you feel like a pile of shit, day in and day out." All my best efforts couldn't stop the inner tidal wave that slammed itself against me. My spirit glowed like an alien ship, but my health was a flickering will-o'-the-wisp.

The recurring dilemma for me was this: as a shamanic practitioner, I was skilled at working in unseen realities. In an altered state of consciousness, my head stopped pounding, my life force surged with incredible energy, and pain didn't exist. Afterwards, within an hour or so, as the cosmic energy evaporated, I felt stuffed back into the confinement of my bodily reality—and pain popped up, spreading like a weed. Shamans, doctors, alternative healers all had their version of "why" I was miserable, yet my spirit was dogged in saying, *something is missing—don't surrender now.* I was determined not to capitulate to the interpretations of other authorities. I had to face the internal demons that persisted with this negative chatter. I came into the world with a gift, and I was failing to deliver it. I was disgusted with myself for not being well; for not doing "it" right, though I had no idea what "it" might be. After all I'd been given, here I was blindly dragging my ass through the muck of my mind again. I was caught in the tangled roots of patriarchal, cultural, and religious lies of "do the right practices and you'll be cured; live selflessly and you'll flourish as God's chosen one; there is an answer to every problem we face." What I needed at that time was reassurance that much of the pain was the emerging feminine consciousness evolving within me.

I hadn't given up, however. I began making rosaries to sustain my sanity. I put my army boots back on, marching again to Eastern and Western doctors in search of an answer. I walked around gazing at the world through sunken eyes, held within darkish circles, giving me the appearance of a raccoon or some alien zombie. I had difficulty walking, crippling head pain, and diminished vision. The doctors were baffled. One doctor thought that my endocrine system was shutting down for no observable reason. Another medical doctor, trained in Eastern traditions, looked at me, dropped my chart, and simply said, "I'm sorry but you have multiple sclerosis. You have to go with Western medicine." A Chinese herbalist said, "You not very live. You go to China—see my father." I was referred to a medical intuitive who thought I had a brain tumor or that I was suffering from the residue of a prior exposure to polio, perhaps from my older brother's childhood illness. My dreams and shamanic journeys indicated something different, informing me that I had a virus, possibly multiple viruses, in the lining of my brain. There was also an MRI report that found that I had a ruptured disc in my neck, but since it was not "resting in the proper place," it couldn't possibly be the source of any pain. Final conclusion: Maybe I needed to have my head examined.

Reluctantly, I set up an appointment with a psychiatrist at a prestigious hospital. I barely said my name and social security number before he abruptly left the room and came back with records of my breakdown twenty years prior. For a moment, I was in a time warp, remembering the incident at the tribunal when the priest dismissed me as crazy based on medical reports. According to them, I was severely depressed, suicidal, and my health symptoms were psychosomatic. After reading these records, the psychiatrist said I was having a "relapse," meaning I was inside the cuckoo's nest again. I countered with my theory about having a virus, listing the history of attacks on my nervous system, including mumps, meningitis, rheumatic fever, encephalitis, scarlet fever, and exposure to polio.

"Where in the world did you come up with this idea?"

"From some dreams, and I believe in them."

"Well, *that's* stupid."

"And you, sir, are stupid and arrogant. Perhaps *you* are the one needing medication for depression. My body is smarter than you. Don't you get it—I ought to be crazier than a bat, but I'm not."

I stormed out of the room still wearing the examining gown, dragging my white turtleneck shirt, but leaving my shoes, black polyester pants and purse on the chair. I didn't realize I was half naked, until I saw the quizzical looks on people's faces as I pressed the elevator button. Thank goodness I chose the bathroom door and not the psychiatric unit to make myself presentable to the outside world.

Outside in the fresh air, I began hyperventilating, my mind a spinning gyroscope, and wondering if I ought to just cross the street without looking and leave my fate to oncoming traffic. *Oh God, I couldn't do that to Frank!* I adored him, so I got into my car. I took every wrong turn imaginable in the parking garage, pounding my fists against the wheel, wishing I could die and shut down this circus freak show. It is horrifying to sizzle with anxiety, to be bowed down from the pain of jackhammer headaches, and to constantly be told, "Well, you are a mystery. You must be doing something wrong." My response to them was "You are right—it's wrong for me to be alive." Inwardly, I stubbornly thought, *Damn it to hell, someone has to hear me, someone has to believe me. I am not a lunatic, there just isn't a rational explanation for this pain.*

Looking back on all that I coped with, I can see now that everyone, including myself, missed the core diagnosis: the grief of "holy longing." I didn't have the awareness that being returned to the earth in my near-death experience resulted in similar grief as if I'd lost a human spouse or close friend. Just as people long to be reunited with their loved ones, and they never "get over" their loss, so I longed for the return to Love beyond the bounds of this life. I remembered direct, unmediated union with the Divine, and this memory ached to be embraced by *Life* itself. The tension was killing me.

This unnamed grief, along with other frustrations, fueled an internal volcano that surfaced when I was attending a retreat in Death Valley. Walking up the steep incline to the retreat center, in the midst of the blistering heat, with no visible signs of human life, was both breathtaking and otherworldly. At one point, I dropped my suitcase as the heat and the fluid in my eyes produced what I perceived was a mirage but wasn't. There in front of me was a wind-whipped rusting wire gate. To pass through the narrow opening, I would have to detach the gate from a dented steel pole, which was blazing hot and was half-buried in the untouchable sand. I thought, *Oh God, what am I in for?*

The first exercise of the retreat was to walk out on a narrow finger of rock that jutted out from the mountainside. There were no safeguards, nothing to hold onto. You couldn't afford a loss of balance or a misplaced step. It was death-defying. When it was my turn, and I was the last person to step forward, I walked out to the end of the finger. Standing there, held by nothing but crisp air, thousands of feet above the canyon floor, something erupted from within my bowels. My right arm shot up, and I raised a white-knuckled fist to God. I hissed, *You'll never beat me down! You're not gonna get me!*

I gingerly walked backwards off the ledge. God only knows why I hadn't dive-bombed into the canyon. Back on the mountainside, I couldn't believe what I was feeling: defiance . . . of God! How was I going to come to grips with this revelation? What entitlement and audacity on my part to defy God! And yet, was this defiance an expression of my life force, its tenacity to stay alive? In hindsight, this was the moment that one of my core beliefs hit rock bottom. How dare God not reward me, the good Catholic girl, after everything I'd done!

Our next challenge on the retreat was to shimmy down a crack in a cliff to the ground below. To get to the bottom without plummeting to our death, we had to wedge ourselves between the two walls of the crack, our backs against one wall and our feet pushing against the opposite wall. There was no safety net beneath. We only had the encouragement of a helping buddy forty feet below who had already completed the exercise. Of course, I waited, watching others descend with great gusto. My turn. Didn't anyone realize I was an exercise dropout and that I could barely walk without tripping? I screamed like a banshee: "I don't care if the freaking buzzards pick the flesh off my bones. I am *not* going to do this." But my buddy kept encouraging me, and I relented. I placed my back against one wall, my feet on the other wall, and my butt wiggled itself down to safety. At one point in the descent, I realized, *This is working, I'm doing it!* and I lifted one foot from the wall in excitement. "Sweet Jesus, honey, don't take your foot off the wall! You'll kill yourself," shouted my guide from the bottom.

There was one more challenge that day. We had to wriggle like snakes through a tunnel created from a rockslide. Groveling on the earth was not my idea of spiritual transformation. Another "Sweet Jesus" and more rolled out of my mouth—the other participants thought I was being funny.

At the end of one of his presentations, our retreat leader instructed us to find a safe place outdoors and meditate on whatever was blocking the intimacy we desired with God and ourselves. I chose to sit down on a humongous hot boulder, unaware of a rattlesnake sunbathing there. Why my skin didn't fall off in the oppressive heat, I'll never know. Then I heard the sound of the coiled rattler and hissed back, *Buddy, it's not my day to die . . . so scram . . . maybe tomorrow.* I shut my eyes as if this was the most normal thing to do when facing death so early in the morning. Later, when my wits returned, I wondered if this had been a heat-induced figment of my imagination, but the tracks in the sand left by the departing snake spoke for themselves.

The coup de grace came a couple of days later in the sweat lodge. An inner voice commanded, *Get out before disaster strikes . . . your body cannot sustain this kind of heat.* I crawled out of the teepee, fully aware that I was violating the protocol of the ceremony. It had been hard enough on me to strip to the buff with all the other retreat participants. Now, lying on the ground outside the teepee, I was totally mortified to be a sweat-lodge dropout. Directly in my view, however, like a saving grace, was a huge tree perched on the hillside, split almost in two by a lightning strike, yet still held together by the very bottom of the massive trunk. Shit. I was looking at myself! Like a helpless baby, I curled up in a scratchy woolen blanket, bawling and wishing I could just disappear into thin air, or find a way to heal the division within myself. I'm not sure which is worse: to be in denial of one's issues, or to be incredibly aware of them and feel clueless about how to deal with them.

There was another retreat leader, an awesome woman, who was kindness personified. She offered to take me home with her for a week, to help with the physical and spiritual emergency that she saw I was experiencing. Her intention was to have me live as normally as possible while I integrated the transformation I was going through. Needless to say, her compassion caught me off guard, but I gratefully accepted her offer. The protective barriers around my heart were broken, and my vulnerability was frightening.

For a week, I followed her regimen: sleeping seven to eight hours a night, eating three well-balanced and carefully prepared meals, taking long walks in the nearby forest preserve, watching comedy shows on TV, buying new clothes that were colorful, not black and white, and taking time for regular but short meditation and prayer sessions. Being in touch with the rhythms of daily life, the rhythms of my own body and the wonder of life as it flowed through my veins, felt very weird. This earth angel taught me to live in the mystery of life instead of always trying to understand and figure it out. Although my headaches and body aches were not cured, I felt incredibly loved and nurtured. As the time came for me to leave this safe environment, this woman had a dream that predicted I would shortly be facing another breakthrough, and told me not to be afraid, that the Spirit would be there to guide me.

CHAPTER 19

Medicine Woman

*[A]ll the greatest and most important problems of life
are fundamentally insoluble . . .
They can never be solved, but only outgrown . . .
requiring a new level of consciousness.*

—CARL JUNG

And breakthrough it was, on the occasion of my fifty-fifth birthday. It was going to be a special celebration with my sons, their wives, and my two grandsons. They were all traveling long distances so we could be together. The evening before they were to arrive, I developed a life-encapsulating migraine. I burrowed under the covers, an ice bag over my head, while images flickered before my eyes in rapid, erratic rhythms. Around midnight, utter panic gripped my body as an explosion of fire ripped through the top of my head. I saw myself leaving my body, climbing a ladder, reaching for the Light. I heard a voice say, *Unless a cure is found for the pain in your head, you will die.* Frank intuitively woke up at this moment and called my name. I slumped back into my body.

It took true grit to hide my distress from everyone the next day. They could see I was not well, and they knew I often had migraines. However, I'd managed to conceal the scope of my health issues as well their connections with my spiritual journey. In their eyes, Ma was a "trooper" and Frank never failed her.

After everyone returned home, I dragged my exhausted bones to sit in my favorite chair. As I sorted the mail that was piled on the dining room table, I came across an article sent by my shaman friend and fellow workshop facilitator. The article was about a Native American woman living in the Northwest who had a gift for curing people who suffered from intractable viral conditions. I swore under my breath, wondering what the hell kind of masochist I was to even consider looking this woman up. *This spirit stuff hasn't cured you yet, so why the hell go back to it?* I threw the article into the recycling bin and quickly retrieved it wondering to myself, *This cannot be a coincidence—what do you have to lose?* I found the healer's phone number, and she returned my call in ten minutes. I described what I was going through, to which she replied, "You are on the brink of death. Be here by sundown." I mustered a weak laugh, thinking, *This could make a great beginning for a John Wayne movie!*

I called United Airlines, sobbing, barely coherent. The ticket agent gently walked me through every step of getting an emergency ticket at a reduced fare. She presumed someone had died. "No, I am dying . . . and I don't want to," I managed to blurt out. When asked what hospital I'd be staying in, I sputtered, "A teepee in the woods." Without missing a beat, she replied, "I didn't hear that. You will arrive at the nearest emergency room in Portland, Oregon. Is that clear?" I whispered, "Of course. God bless you."

Early the next morning, with only a toothbrush, a change of underwear, and a hairbrush I packed in a tattered black sports bag, I said to Frank, "I won't return until I am well." The anguish in his eyes stung my soul like icy balls of hail, and yet unconditional love welled up stronger than his fears, filling my spirit with the essence of pure mercy. "And you know I'll be here when you return. I love you forever." Frank often says that his only real suffering is not being able to take away my pain. If it is true that the Divine weeps with us in our brokenness, then Frank elegantly lives the call to be Love wrapped in skin. With him, I've never doubted that I walk and breathe in the presence of God.

An hour before reaching my destination, my alarm button was triggered when I saw the plane I had to change to. I'd never seen such a small vehicle. It could have been part of my son's erector set, and the ceilings were too low for anyone except dwarfs. I asked God to please squeeze my flabby thighs and drippy Kleenex into the narrow seat, but, even more, to make sure there was a can opener to extract me once I arrived in Oregon.

With great cheer, the medicine woman's assistant picked me up, and drove through mazes of mountain roads, going like a crazed coyote. At one of the stop signs, I opened the car door and threw up. I left the window partly open to trick my dry heaves into waves of anticipation instead of fear. I was embarrassed enough already, and I didn't want to be denied the medicine woman's magic—if she had any—for messing up her car with barf.

At the camp, I was immediately placed in a structure made of willow branches covered with olive-drab tarpaulins. How appropriate to be lying under faded

Army cloth, given that I was losing my battle for life. Inside the dome-shaped "hospital room" was a twin-sized mattress lying on the bare ground, a kerosene hurricane lamp, and several roses in full bloom, placed in a mason jar near the entrance. I took my glasses off and lay down, too weary to do anything else.

I sensed the presence of the medicine woman before I saw her. She was petite, wore tight denim jeans, and had wild, steel wool hair that looked as if it had been electrocuted in a hair dryer. But it was her voice that defined her. It combined the sound of boots crunching over gravel with that sound created when a wave recedes on a beach when hundreds of pebbles rub against other. She wasted no time beginning the healing ceremony, cleansing the space and my depleted body with hawk feathers. She chanted, "Grandfather sun ... grandmother moon ... I heal with the power of Jesus Christ ... believe and be healed." *Oh, my good God—you have got to be joking.* I wanted her to hear my silent screams, but nothing came out of my mouth. Internally, I was beyond fear, beyond sanity. *NO! NO! NO! How dare you pray to Jesus! How STUPID are you to think that he will do anything for me? He has abandoned me, left me here on the earth to suffer with no relief! NO- NO- NO!!!* Even worse was hearing my mother's voice in my head, *Stooopid stooopid—you're going to trust this ignoramus?* Within seconds, as if drugged with a spiritual anesthetic, I passed out.

The medicine woman reported later that I was unconscious for twelve hours—although I had lucid moments in which I felt spiritual beings pulling out my spine, cleaning it, and restoring it. I was not spared the excruciating pain of these experiences. I also recall having my brain placed within an orb of rainbow-colored lights that vibrated with sound. When I awoke, the pain in my head, the pain in my body was gone—apparently, I was cured of the viruses. With all my senses heightened and freedom from the emotional turmoil of my polarizing beliefs, I was certain I'd returned to God's sanctuary—not unlike what I felt in near-death. But, after a few deep breaths, there was no doubt that I was in my body—free of distress.

Normally, the medicine woman chose to isolate herself in her "sacred trailer home," deliberately separating herself from the "white folk" who sought her help. She broke this taboo with me, spending hours with me, exchanging stories about our journeys, our fears, our hopes, our craziness. From the moment we saw each other, we knew we were soul sisters who struggled with being disempowered women, burdened with the wound of insanity. She rolled on the floor when

I shared a quote with her from the comedienne Lily Tomlin: "Why is it that when you talk to God, it's called prayer; but when God talks to you, it's labeled schizophrenia?"

Both of us had undergone near-death experiences and a "brief reactive psychosis." We agreed this can be a sophisticated psychiatric label to describe the dualistic dilemma faced by "madwomen"—they are intuitive, mystical, can commune with spirits and dead people, have prophetic visions and dreams, and yet are afraid to live in the real world and are uncomfortable with normalcy. We agreed that madwomen are called witches, who turn into bitches because their voices are squelched.

After my recovery, the medicine woman and I chatted away, both grateful for the brief kiss of psychosis and the gift of courage to stay the path. She recognized that plunging into the tangled thicket of my family's mental illness was an absolute necessity. She knew that each thorn of personal pain was coated with the crazy quilt pattern of my mother, my grandmother, and my aunts. Every cell in my body grasped that I could have been another statistic on the family tree, a caged songbird executed by the torture of a darkened mind.

One of our conversations focused on how different we were in our approaches to the spirit world and in the ways we received information. The medicine woman's spiritual practice was rooted in firmly established earth-based traditions and wisdom. There was nothing weird to her about connecting to, talking, and working with the spirit world. She also did not "leave her body" to travel to the unseen realms as I did. She merely sat on her bed that was decorated with bark and hawk feathers and talked with "council" (supportive guides) and one invisible Native ancestor who, as she said, "tells me all, and I follow blindly." She was a hollow bone through which the wisdom of her ancestors and of spirit animals flowed, a power of enormous healing, and she didn't question what she was given.

I, on the other hand, had both mystical experience and cellular memory of indigenous ways that could not be explained. I also had a profound yearning for union with God, for a connection that went beyond being just being a messenger or a medium for the Divine. The medicine woman truly thought this was nuts! For her, being the hollow bone was the bridge between heaven and earth. My desire to *be* a cell of God living in my body was suspect to her—and dangerous to my health. From her viewpoint, I was disrespecting tradition and trying to escape how humanly miserable I felt about myself. From my perspective, I was questioning and attempting to break through traditions that didn't resonate with the memory I carried in my bones, in the core of my authentic self.

I shared with the medicine woman an experience I had while doing a presentation for a college anthropology class. I'd been asked to involve the students with drumming and journeying, and perhaps include a simple ritual. Prior to the class, I consulted with the spirit guides I worked with, who gave me a very clear ritual to offer. For the students, the experience was remarkable, and they were opened to realms they never dreamed of. As I was packing up to leave, the anthropology instructor approached me, with tears running down his face. He asked how I had knowledge of this "secret" ritual from an obscure tribe he had researched. I looked at him dumbfounded and told him that I had no knowledge of this tribe or their rituals. I elaborated that I was not a Native American, that I was a woman with a bachelor's degree in English, a master's degree in social work, and an initiate in shamanism who received ancient information by working directly with Spirit and spirit guides. He shook his head in disbelief but decided I was telling the truth and gave me a hug for gratitude.

After four days at the medicine camp, I returned home in a state of bliss. I recall walking through my neighborhood, thinking I was tripping on some kind of hallucinogen. I could see brilliant-colored auras around the chirping birds and see the blue print of the leaves dripping with sunshine. All of nature sang in stereophonic notes, reminding me of my childhood days when the daisies and the pansies sang duets for me! An ecstatic energy and radiance of God and of the Universe pulsated in me with a power I'd never felt before. It was as if the veils between the seen and the unseen dimensions had dissolved.

Resurrection was short-lived, however, and three days later I woke up vomiting, barely able to hold my head up because of the stabbing pain. I was angry and confused—this couldn't be happening again. *What the hell did I do wrong?* I dialed up the medicine woman. "Abominable" and "staggering" are feeble words to describe the tongue-lashing I received from her. "You are resisting the Spirit. You don't want to be healed. If you do it right, God will give you the reward. If you fail to be cured by the healing powers I have, then it's your fault. The spirits never lie."

As she delivered her knockout punches of shame, all propriety vanished from my mouth and I verbally kicked back. "Who the fuck do you think you are, spewing this craziness?" Swearing at a "chosen" and ordained shaman was certainly disrespectful, even arrogant. However, I'd come to know that my soul places my evolution over honor and sacred tradition. I knew I could not allow anyone, including myself, to dispossess me, to treat me as "less than." I'd come to understand that nothing kills spirituality like shame, and nothing cements a person's identity into victim consciousness like humiliation. Her assaultive words ripped open familiar wounds: *You are a friggin' failure—a heap of totally useless female flesh. Stupid idiot.* Ma was always a breath away.

But I wasn't the only woman dealing with agonizing thoughts. Her world-view also suffered a devastating blow. Everyone she treated, until that point in time, had been cured. If you believe miracles happen when you follow the pre-scribed ritual, then what if it fails? Are you "less than perfect" in the eyes of your community, in your own mind? Granted, many people might think this question is ridiculous; that, of course, a shaman would know it is not in their hands to bring about healing; that they are vessels for the Spirit. But who is so perfect, so integrated, that they aren't vulnerable to feeling inadequate? Maybe a trickster spirit delivered this lightning strike to remind us that, in spite of our good in-tentions in seeking a cure, something was still evading our consciousness—some mystery beyond our grasp at the time. It is not pretty when two fragile pieces of glass collide—and we did. We both felt we had come to nothing with the Spirit and were unworthy of our calling.

God knows why I called the medicine woman again a few days later. This time she was pleasant, although she asked for a half hour to consult with her guides before commenting on my symptoms. When she called back, the diagnosis from the guides was grim: "You have a brain tumor, and you must return to the camp immediately." I went into another tirade and told her that the guides need-ed to come up with something better than such outrageous information. What made me think she was dead wrong still baffles me. Nevertheless, I returned to her camp, trusting that another high-powered ceremony would be the winning ticket. Unbeknownst to me, the spark of the Divine Soul in me had a hidden agenda and was hell-bent on waking me up.

In preparation for a major healing ceremony, the medicine woman demand-ed that I undergo a saltwater purification ritual. Apparently, this was now an essential ingredient when asking for a cure from the spirits. It involved drinking several glasses of highly concentrated salt water (one quarter salt to three quarters water) as quickly as possible. I chuckled to myself thinking this is not what Jesus meant when he said we were to be salt of the earth. I wasn't keen on becoming a salt lick for the deer in the area.

Although I knew that that such a high concentration of salt would cause my brain to detonate with a migraine, I submitted to her orders. I was still caught in the belief that the ancient ways of an authentic medicine woman were superior to my inner wisdom and spirit guides. After guzzling the first of the three prescribed containers of salt-water concoction, I plopped my rear onto a toilet seat, anticipating a twenty-one-fart salute. I wasn't disappointed. My bowels exploded like a grenade, and my mouth spewed a fluid of different colors and consistencies. I sensed it wouldn't be long before I collapsed on the bathroom floor. The medicine woman became frantic, yelling that I couldn't die on her premises. I gasped, "You're killing me, you idiot! Do something!" I knew the extent of her terror when she offered me pain medication, something that, under normal circumstances, she regarded as an evil invention of demonic Western medicine. In my best military-command voice, I ordered the medicine woman to settle down. I still have to laugh as I recall that. I reminded her that I was the one dying, not her, and if she wanted to trade places, I'd be happy to share the remaining salt bomb cocktails.

The medicine woman decided to put me in the sacred teepee, even though I hadn't completed the traditional purification rite. Even though I smelled of salty crap, I was not going to die if she could help it. The interior of the teepee was meticulously prepared with cornmeal, herbs, prayers, flowers, and sealed with prayerful incantations. I stumbled onto the woolen blanket, wanting nothing more than a nap. But as Ma would have said, *No rest for the wicked.* A big brown and white barn owl appeared, flapping its outstretched wings above my head, a sign of imminent death according to the medicine woman's tradition. It was my turn to go berserk. I shrieked, "NO, NO, God damn it, you won't take me. I *will* not die. I'm going to live, so leave me the fuck alone!!" The medicine woman slapped her hawk-feather fan against her thigh, freaked out by the owl. I had a flashback to the time that my oldest son was dying as we watched the movie *I Heard the Owl Call My Name.* The medicine woman and I were both numb, in near-psychotic fear, trembling before this manifestation of the spirit world.

At the time, I thought I was out of control, but, in truth, some inexplicable voice, some encoding in my DNA and in my soul, remembered wholeness and would not surrender until the wonder of life became stronger than death. I heard something new in my voice in that teepee. The sounds were not the lyrical songs of the spirit as in Egypt. My song was messier, sloshing through the muck of a flesh-and-blood body, and my swearing and insulting words were its kick-ass power demanding its freedom.

I agreed to stay in the teepee overnight. I was guarded by a friend of the medicine woman, a Vietnam veteran who occasionally forgot he was not on the battlefield and play-acted scenes, making weird sounds. I wouldn't have minded his fantasies except for the fact that he carried a loaded gun and kept others in his car, in his tent, and everywhere he felt the need to protect himself. I passed the night squatting in a sacred position, offering prayers and sacred tobacco. I hoped no one would catch on that some whacky white woman had desecrated this sacred space by peeing there. I was too petrified to leave even to go use the bathroom in the medicine woman's trailer. I simply wasn't evolved enough to transform my terror into trust.

When I arrived home several days later, my eyeballs twirled in their sockets as I recounted this surreal adventure to Frank. I could barely believe it myself. I'd been faced with so many dysfunctional systems, and I realized that none of them served me any longer. I believed the medicine woman's spirituality would cure my wounds, and they did, but not as I expected. How ironic to think that Ma's legacy was intricately involved in all this drama. Ma never trusted anyone but herself, with the exception of my dad. I, on the other hand, didn't believe in myself, trusting everyone's wisdom but my own. And I trusted Frank.

Before I left the camp, I had noticed a peculiar pain in my skull, along with muscle spasms, headaches, nausea, and a mysterious "scratching blood" rash on my scalp. At the time, I dismissed all of this as post-intestinal trauma shock waves, and I never mentioned it to the medicine woman. I felt that my only way out was to pretend to be cured. So, I was on my best behavior in the days after the salt episode. I cleaned up all my swear words and did my daily prayers. All I wanted was to return home to Frank, my heaven on Earth, eat a pepperoni and onion pizza, and guzzle down a bottle of Diet Coke. My organic regimen could resume later.

Back home, my mobility became a struggle. I'd try to walk, but my legs stayed on the chair. As if I had a light-switch dimmer behind my eyes, my vision deteriorated. I found myself sleeping more than usual. I mentioned to my chiropractor that I was feeling a bit off and showed him my scalp. It was crimson red on one side, and I was drawing blood from scratching. He laughed when I told him that a Western doctor, whom I'd visited the day before, said I had a bad case of dandruff. My chiropractor was also a practitioner of homeopathy. When I told him what part of the country I'd been in, on a hunch, he gave me a remedy that miraculously took away the rash within fifteen minutes. The remedy was for a black widow spider bite. Then I remembered the medicine woman furiously dismantling my tent one day, mumbling "black widow." She didn't allow me to lie on the ground after that. Maybe the black widow spider was another spirit manifestation, like the owl in the teepee—to wake me up.

It is humbling to admit how much the black widow spider reflected the trap of dispossession I'd fallen into. I, too, was painfully shy—ashamed of everything about me except what I could do spiritually—turf I'd defend to my death. And just as the spider devours its mate, all my frustrations trying to mate with patriarchal systems and people left me raging, ready to attack anyone who dared to gag my voice or steal my freedom.

When I journeyed to the spirit of the black widow, she informed me that my toxicity was nothing more than my syndrome of *you're not good enough and never will be.* I also had the distorted view that pain was my abuser and my body was the victim, always being betrayed. The black widow's bite reminded me that, when I accepted the wisdom and perception of others over my soul's truth, I was both betrayed and betrayer, both victim and my own persecutor.

I have full respect for this medicine woman. I truly love her. For me, she was a voice of what she termed Coyote Medicine. To her, when the spirit of Coyote appeared in your life, it was a red flag alerting you to another fork in the road. Old beliefs and situations would appear at your doorstep, presenting you with the choice: to either intentionally release negative patterns or to continue a path of destruction and suffering. I am grateful that my soul and my voice broke through in her teepee, further shredding the remnants of a deeply held belief that external authority was superior to my inner knowing.

• • • • •

While the effects of the spider bite abated, I still stumbled a lot, and my head pain continued unabated. Disheartened, I decided to call a dear friend who lived on a farm with her husband in Wisconsin. Besides Frank, she was a rare soul who understood the gargantuan struggles I grappled with. Her nonjudgmental friendship and hospitality made her home a safe haven for Frank and I to retreat to on many occasions. We had studied alternative spiritual traditions together, and we were both fascinated with shamanism, rituals, and the healing aspects of Mother Nature.

When she invited me to visit, neither of us could have anticipated the drama of our drive to the farm that night. Sheets of blinding rain slapped against my friend's van as if we were enemies in a foreign territory marked for obliteration. I still recall with amazed horror how the rain and wind battered us with a maniac fierceness, forcing the windshield wipers into spastic contortions. The streets and farmlands were deluged with water, while lightning bolts ripped the endless sky, sending fiery, jerky blue bolts dancing around our vehicle.

All I could think was how this must have been what my mother experienced that day when she crossed the bridge during the flood when I was twelve years old. Holy crap and sweet Jesus! Was this karma blasting me for wanting her dead, or was this just a treacherous storm that we happened to fall into that night?

"But I don't believe in coincidence, and screw the karma theory," I hollered to my friend. Just then, a flash of lightning ricocheted off the van's silver trim. "Jeepers creepers." I yanked the scarf on my head tightly under my chin to keep my hair from standing straight up as Aunt Anna's did the night lighting struck our kitchen table. "OMG, girlfriend, we are going to fry in water, or I will land in the loony bin." There were nervous giggles, and rosary beads coming out of my friend's purse.

Although we were semi-blitzed with awe, there was nowhere to go but forward unless we voluntarily marooned ourselves in a cow field. Amazingly, we arrived safely though very bedraggled. The next day local news programs reported that many of the county bridges we'd crossed had been washed away by the flooding. We chuckled over the contrast between me being stranded in the desert at night in Egypt just a year ago and now almost drowning in cornfields.

After sleeping for a day, I was awakened by the voice of a spirit guide: *Go outside and start digging up the bull thistles.* Bull thistles were taking over the pastures of their farm, choking off other plant life. The worst infestation was in the horse paddock by the barn.

Really, I thought. These five- to six-feet-tall thistles had thorny stalks and spiny leaves that made my skin look like bleeding freckles when I brushed against them. I snoozed for another half hour until the insistent spirit sent me the same message. *I am serious. Go start digging.* Ever the obedient, albeit grumpy, woman, I went outside to find a shovel and begin my task.

Out in the horse paddock, the temperature was over ninety degrees, with no breeze and no shade. Protected by gloves and a long-sleeved shirt, I begrudgingly started to dig, chop, and pull. I'd work on one thistle, and get speared by its neighbors. After an hour of sweating and swearing, I collapsed into my favorite friend, a pool of hot stinging tears. *Okay, God: you really think this is funny? Do you enjoy seeing me turn into a self-pitying blob, once again begging to feel like a healthy human being? If this is a joke, your sense of humor is cruel and uncalled for. And if you think this will heal me, then you're the one who needs a shrink.* I was so annoyed! The goats were frisky and liked nothing better than to nip at anything they could reach on my body. I wanted to repay them by butting them with the shovel, but I knew I wouldn't win. They were having too much fun. Then there was the high-pitched yappy dog that chased a nearby cat, who leapt over the wooden fence, hit the electric wire on top, letting out a yowl that stopped even the goats for a second.

I was on a mission from God, and so, amidst the horse poop, I came upon a thistle that would either kill me or cure me. It was over five feet tall and its roots were ensnarled around a very large stone. I attacked it furiously, wrenching my shoulders and wrists. "Damn it to hell," I muttered, "this is crazy." But then a *wind* came—an otherworldly, baby's breath messenger that stopped every movement in my body. Even the animals hushed.

Annette. Be still. Look up. The prophet Moses heard a talking bush, and I had a talking thistle. As I lifted my eyes and wiped the sting of my sweat from them, I saw my friend's horse, Precious. Her reddish-brown coat glistened in the sunlight with beads of sweat, making a striking contrast to the white markings on her forehead and nose. As she stood at the brow of the dropoff overlooking the paddock, her ears perked, her tail swishing sassily, her presence was breathtaking and regal. As I leaned on my shovel, enraptured with the image of this animal, the words "Precious, you are magnificent" soared up to the horse, and an eerie sense of oneness formed between us. Almost magically, we each took a step closer to meet the other. Without warning, her foot slipped over the ledge she was standing on, and she slid down the steep hill of rocks and earth, landing on her back. She slammed into the fence, one leg hooked in an open space between the wires.

The sound that escaped from my throat could have shattered atoms. Believe me, this was not an Egyptian song channeling God's peace. My eardrums were vibrating from the alarm in my voice as I walked toward Precious as in slow motion, whispering, "Do not be afraid. All will be well. We will free you." Inwardly I was screaming, *Sweet Mother of God, Marsha will never forgive me for killing her horse.* To this day I can still see the alluring power of this horse's eye. It resembled a black hole in the galaxy, with tiny specks of light floating in and out of liquid terror. *Oh my,* I thought, *I am looking into my own eye.* I was startled to see an image of a diaphanous white silky scarf float in my vision. I knew what this meant, as I'd had seen it before. When my grandson Nick was born, as he lay naked and shivering on a steel hospital table, I saw his filmy white soul begin to leave his body. Without any apprehension, I simply called on the angels to bring him back to earth. Now, in holy dread, I did the same for Precious. Once I observed that she was reunited with her body, I commanded, "Holy Spirit, free her!" Like a noodle slathered in hot butter, Precious's leg slid out of the contorted trap it was stuck in. She rose to her majestic height and climbed back up the hill, a small rivulet of blood trickling down her leg.

When the veterinarian came that night to check on Precious, she remarked, "I never would have believed the story unless I saw the indentation of the horse's body in the fence . . . this is miraculous." I wasn't surprised by this outcome, as I trusted that the spirit guides understood how important Precious was to my friend. Equally stunning was the way that the long thistle root I'd been wrestling with effortlessly popped from under the rock as my shovel barely grazed the ground. Like the horse, I walked over to the fence, a bit unnerved that I was walking normally, and hurled thistle and root over the fence. I trembled. I'd been told that thistles protect traumatized land, and here I was looking at myself, not unlike my reflection in the horse's eye. With the life force of a thistle, I was fiercely determined to uproot the ancestral lie that I, and other women, were not good enough. That was the soil we grew in. I'd developed spiky thorns of distrust not only to physically survive but also to protect the sweet, lovely lavender flowers that crowned each prickly branch. I, like other women, am determined to guard that part of me that no one can touch, that nothing can destroy: that is the mystic, the Divine, planted on the earth. My feistiness refused to accept the diminishment of being crazy and weird.

Over the next few days, I thought of the irony that "Precious" was my dad's favorite name for me. Though as a teenager, my physical appearance more resembled the swaying, flabby cows grazing in my friend's pasture rather than the sleek beauty of the horse, Pa always said, "You look great." I knew he was lying, but I didn't care since I was not prone to seeking flattery for my appearance. My Achilles heel was wanting respect for my spirituality. Like Precious, prior to her fall, my ears perked up whenever my spiritual teachers and shamans honored my identity as a spiritual woman. My flesh-and-blood imperfections paled against what I could manifest with the spirit world. And yet, I crashed and burned, like Precious, whenever I succumbed to the words "Annette, you are so gifted." What a conundrum: invariably I would either dismiss the comments so as not to be egotistical or get sucked into other people's power and surrender my authenticity. Precious was the catalyst to cleansing these distortions from my past, and she got back up on her feet through her life force as it connected with the power of Spirit in my voice. In Egypt, in communion with God, my voice awakened the spiritual memory of the ancestors. On the farm, in connection with a horse and thistle, the poison from my ancestors was uprooted—I was able to walk again.

In spite of my chaotic relationship with the medicine woman, I returned after five months to her reservation to complete my initiation. Healing with indigenous wisdom was second nature to me, and yet, so many of her traditions were intriguing to me. Also, she and I had a soul bonding which was unexplainable. As our relationship deepened, she invited me to join her in the desert for a three-year period. Our task would be to break open the wisdom of certain ancient stones, with which she had been entrusted. Her guides were certain that the stories from the stones would be for the healing of the planet. She felt I had the right connection with Spirit to bring forth the wisdom of the stones and to decipher the messages. As with the invitation from the Egyptologist, I was very tempted by this recognition of my gifts. But cutting off all ties with Frank and my family for three years went against the calling of my heart. When I left the reservation, I was humbled and honored when the medicine woman gave me part of a deer's leg as a protection and a reminder of the longing I carried for God and the spirit world.

A few months later, on my birthday, our next-door neighbor came to our back fence and asked Frank, "Who are you, really?" Frank was puzzled and asked what he meant. The neighbor hesitantly recounted that he'd seen a deer with antlers standing at my office door earlier that afternoon. That our neighbor appeared slightly befuddled was natural. Our backyard is fenced in, we live in a densely populated suburb, and the nearest forest preserve is two miles away. The neighbor went on to say that the deer had been pawing at the door, then proceeded to chomp the plants surrounding the maple tree, slipped past the back gate, and began walking down the alley. "That deer suddenly disappeared right before my eyes . . . Scooby Doo spooky . . . and I wasn't drinking."

Because I relished such paranormal events, I giggled. However, that evening, when I looked for the deer leg on my special altar, it was gone. A shiver went up and down my spine. *Had I misplaced it?* No. I searched. It had disappeared. I knew the medicine woman could teleport herself, and I had no doubt she had reclaimed the gift she had given me. On that day, she broke all ties with her white-woman friend, for reasons I'll never truly know. But maybe she understood the ravenous hunger I had to grasp my human identity as a blessed woman. Maybe she knew it was time to set me free of her ancient traditions in order to claim the memory of the Divine I came to the earth with. On that particular birthday, I cried a lot, grateful for the imprint she left in my spirit, aware we needed to honor each other's path with the Great Spirit as good-enough women.

CHAPTER 20

The Call of the Mother

Love is
The funeral pyre
Where I have laid my living body . . .
Love is the funeral pyre
Where the heart must lay
Its body.

—HAFIZ

After nearly a decade of shamanic work, I became interested in facilitating a communal grief ritual based on the traditions of the African Dagara peoples. *That* raised eyebrows. "You are a white woman from Chicago—who says you are qualified to do that?" As usual, I went to Source, and in a shamanic journey, I was given clear direction on how and where to conduct the ritual. It was to take place on the sacred land of dear friends of ours, who lived about five hours from our home. One of the owners had been initiated by the Lakota Sioux and followed their traditions, so I agreed to modify the Dagara ritual and combine both traditions for our communal grieving. I invited about a dozen people to gather on our friend's property to publicly share their losses, not through a psychological process, but in silence, and through drumming, singing, and weeping.

The people who gathered for this were Caucasian yet African in spirit. For the most part, they were disciplined spiritual seekers attuned to their inner wisdom. They were open to allowing the power of the Divine to move them without analyzing the gifts they received from the Spirit. This was my clan and the sacred land was my home away from home.

The weekend began with an evening sweat lodge to prepare us for the long ritual the next day. Afterwards, I needed to talk, and asked Frank to walk the land with me. Our nicknames for each other are Bunny and Bear, and we often giggle that nothing is friendlier than to nestle my nervous bunny paw in the center of his secure bear paw. As we walked, a shawl of sorrow began falling over my shoulders, and teardrops flowed serenely as the moonlight waltzed across the lake before us. Something was troubling me about my spiritual calling, and I was restless without knowing why. I didn't have a problem with the practice of shamanism itself. Traveling between the worlds was effortless, and being One with Spirit was second nature to me. It wove together my mystical and earth-based traditions. I was never fearful of the journeys or of the information and healing energies given to me to relieve the distress of people so desperately seeking wholeness. For the most part, I could dream of no better mission on the earth.

But, as I reflected on several stories of people who had sought my assistance, I shared with Frank some of my growing discouragement with people who were skeptical about the Great Mystery and the unseen dimensions in general. "Tell me what this means." "How do you know what you are seeing is not just your imagination?" "How do you know it's true?" "How could you possibly know about that?" "Someone must have told you!" The latter occurred often when I would describe, for example, a specific article of clothing the spirit of the dead person was wearing in the journey or when a nickname was revealed.

Even the more open-minded spiritual individuals could be resistant to the gifts from the spirit world. They wanted a literal, easily understood explanation of Spirit's gifts/messages, instead of being open to an unknown spiritual power that could potentially transform their life. I had underestimated the power of the "fix-me" mentality in our culture and the need to be in control. While I understood the neediness of people who wanted shamanism to be the magic bullet that would end their problems, I was fatigued. While I sympathized, and while I was more than willing to explore the possible meaning of the messages and images I received from Spirit, facing a barrage of questions immediately upon returning from a trance state felt like an assault on my energy field. It was something like being on a silent retreat and coming home to sugar-high children. Not to mention I felt guilty for not being able to detach from people's reactions. For goodness sake, where was my evolved spirit that could rise above it all?

Frank and I ended our walk, back where it began, at the lake. There, comforted by the gentle lapping of the water against the old wooden pier, and by the rhythmic croaking of the bull frogs, I burrowed snugly against Frank's chest. "Why am I so unsettled, Bear?" I reminisced to Frank about the young woman who came to see me for a shamanic consultation on the recommendation of her therapist. The day she came in, her first remark was that she felt a little "off," that her head was not "right." I wasn't surprised by what she said, as I had developed a pounding headache, accompanied by fuzzy thinking, about ten minutes before she arrived. I knew from past experience that this was a warning for me to be alert to some kind of organic medical condition underlying the spiritual symptoms. As we chatted, I became certain she needed medical attention, and I didn't need to do a journey to confirm my suspicions. However, I knew she'd accept the information through a journey more readily than from my intuition. The guides were crystal clear: *she needs to see an MD today—she is on the road to a massive stroke.* I could "see" a cloudy mass moving over her brain, and a darkness beginning to flow down her left arm. Staying calm, I gently relayed Spirit's concern for her health, and I made sure she realized how imperative it was that she keep her doctor's appointment scheduled for that day. She was grateful for the information but was adamant that the shadow was purely symbolic of her negative attitude toward herself. I didn't argue about the symbolic nature but was clear about the danger in reality. That evening, a social worker from a local hospital called me to say this woman was in the ICU following a massive stroke. They'd found my name and phone number in her pants pocket. She had managed to communicate to the staff that they were to call me and say, "Sorry—you right." I wept. And while I accepted from a detached spiritual perspective that this was her contract with her life's path, I could not escape the notion that if only she had been open to an awareness of both/and, there could have been a different outcome for her. *Yes*, Spirit speaks in symbols *and yes*, it manifests in the body.

But there were also times when people believed the messages from the spirit world. I thought of the time a woman came to me about a breast cancer diagnosis. In the journey, Spirit not only gave information about the kind of treatment she was to pursue, but also said the cancerous cells were not in the area where the doctor was focusing. There was a hidden cluster right behind a rib. Not having a medical background, I could only advise her to ask her doctor to check for another mass or tumor beside the one being operated on. The woman's doctor was rather offended by her request, but the client insisted, not revealing why. It turned out that the targeted tumor was benign, but they found a hidden one that was malignant. It was in the area Spirit had shown me. With the early detection and the tumor's removal, she was restored to full health.

As if I were a quaking aspen, I tightened my grip on Frank's hand and prayed

I'd feel at peace before the ritual began. Both of us realized that shamanic work had become my priesthood, a call I'd had all my life but one not allowed within my Catholic tradition. Was I losing my spirit? Was I simply burned out? Or was something else happening?

The following morning, over community breakfast, one of the participants shared that he and his wife were fostering a fifteen-year-old teen, an orphan from Cambodia, who recently had immigrated to the States. His entire family had been massacred, and he had witnessed this slaughter as he hid beneath some nearby bushes. Moved by his tragedy, several of us invited him to participate in the ritual, if only by carrying the tree stumps to the ritual space or stripping the bark from the limbs of the trees. He responded by tipping the brim of his sweaty gray baseball cap, which was oversized for his melon-shaped head. It slid right over his eyelids, so only his nose and closed lips were visible.

After breakfast, everyone helped build an altar for the ritual by gathering tree limbs, branches, leaves, stones, and feathers found on the land. Communication was done through gesture and smiles, arms reaching over others' arms, with seldom a spoken word. The project unfolded magically, as if choreographed by unseen ancestors. Everyone added a personal talisman to adorn the altar, an offering to the Spirit.

In the afternoon, we gathered in circle to begin our ceremony. My directives were simple. Each person, when they felt ready, would step forward into the center of the circle, and release their personal or collective grief in whatever manner they were led to express it. Some might choose to wail, some might be silent. Some might choose to drum, and others might dance and sing. What I emphasized was the need to ask Spirit specifically what grief, what losses the Divine *Soul* wanted them to release—as opposed to any of their preconceived ideas. I explained that all of us have ways to make sense of the miserable emotional swamps we dive into, but the spirit uncovers the beliefs and lies that blind us to the underlying root of our pain. The issue wasn't liking or disliking what the spirit reveals. The loving intention of Spirit is to help us first remember and then evolve the Soul dimension of our authenticity. In other words, it's not to fix anything—it's a matter of exposing the roots so they can be brought into the light for healing.

I shared some examples with them. One was a woman who wanted an immediate cure for her migraines, which she said were "killing" her. She was disappointed when her journey revealed she was to work on releasing herself from brutal self-judgment. Another was a man who wanted to divorce his wife, but the Spirit guided him to first divorce himself from being a workaholic and being obsessed with material possessions. I also shared that, for years, I was convinced that, if I'd had a different, saner mother, all my troubles would have only been pretty bubbles floating in the air. The real issue was my belief that "I'm crazy, unworthy, and I hate being alive in a body." Admitting that really made me squirm.

As the ritual began, the earthiness and raw energy of our African drumming effectively emptied our minds, creating a spiritual high, allowing Spirit to crack open the layers of unresolved sorrow we were entrenched in. I quivered in anticipation, waiting for the moment when, with my face to the sun and my eyelids softly closed, I called forth the power of the Great Mother with one swift twist of my wrist. I held a rattle that produced a sound like thousands of pebbles on the seashore being swept by an ocean wave. It was an invitation to the Spirit and the ancestors to lift the sleepiness off people's spirits, and to come dance with us and transform us.

I was very attached to my rattle. It was a simple gourd, wrapped in tiny pieces of deer bone strung on faded twine. When I shook it, the sound propelled me into galaxies beyond my mind, and ignited tones and vibrations from the inner chambers of my heart. The harshness of the deer bone pieces of the rattle was softened by the mystical tones that streamed from my mouth, sounds of love that originated from the stars above my head, from the wind wrapping around me like bird wings. I was free, a harp singing in the high winds. Visions flashed across my inner universe like comets, bringing information for different people on how to proceed with the ritual. I didn't have to plan anything. All I ever had to do was show up and shake the rattle.

As I looked around the circle of people gathered for the ritual that day, I watched a tiny white butterfly fluttering in the wind. It reminded me of a young girl, ten years old, whom I held in my arms, just after she died. She often came to me in the form of a white butterfly, to warn me that change was about to happen. This day, there was lightness in the butterfly that was unsettling for some reason. It was fluttering against a burden I couldn't quite grasp—or maybe cope with.

It was a sweltering day with no shade from leafy trees. We were in an open space, and the heat singed our innermost being. As the intensity of the mourning increased within the circle, I felt the wind shift, as if an invisible giant hand were behind a curtain of air, creating a path for Shanyu, the Cambodian boy, to join us. There he stood, head bobbing, shoulders slouched, his blue jeans riding high on his bone-thin body. The shirt we'd given him, with an image of a wolf howling into a lightning-laden sky, was inside out and backwards. One could almost hear the cries of his parents and family members dropping into heaps before our very feet.

Without any warning, his frail body fell forward with dignity, Mother Earth gently catching her fallen son. Not even a whimper came from him as our drums stopped, and the spirit of the Mother hovered over him, breathing new life into him. The invisible blood of memory silently poured out from his body and soul into the belly of the Great Mother. When he was ready, he stood up and turned his cap around, lifting the brim so that his eyes appeared. He bowed to us, came over to me, and a smile of love rippled over his face into my heart.

As this young boy walked away to the nearby lake, I shuffled my feet toward the center of the circle, grateful that his warm body had prepared the ground that was calling to me. The drumming resumed. The thumping pulse in my head was louder than the drumming of the circle. *Dear God, what is happening to me?*

Standing within the vibration of everyone's grief, the vapors of loss rolled through me like an unexpected sea squall. I gripped the damp handle of my womb-shaped rattle as my knees buckled to the dirt. Like being in a movie scene with no director, I was a desperado, clawing for life, ready to die but not knowing what for. Maybe I was delirious or dehydrated, but I felt transfixed by the echoes of deeply embedded fears. The participants in the circle were oblivious to my death throes. They had no idea that I was being stripped naked within the landscape of the Soul. They could not see that the Divine Mother had surreptitiously come to claim me as her own. *Annette, it's time. Weep. I will lead you. It's time to remember who you are, Annette.*

Whose voice was I hearing? What was I to cry for?

No, no, you can't be asking me to surrender my identity as a shamanic healer. This is my worthiness. Enough already! I finally found my home. Don't ask me to be a tumbleweed wandering in the desert once again. No, no!

What would people think of me if I weren't a revered shamanic leader, if I lost the gift of sounding with my rattle? What if the godliness that just poured out of me like liquid gold turned into plain water? All I could think was *What have I done wrong? Had I failed the Spirit? Was my life meaningless?*

Annette, it's time. Weep. I am here with you.

I laid down my beloved rattle.

Looking back on it, the call to put down the rattle was the work of the Divine Mother, setting me free. I feel ashamed to admit that shamanism had, among other things, been a way to cope with ordinary human life. Unless I was offering spiritual work, I had to deal with my insecurities, limitations, and face crippling anxiety whenever I had to interact with other people. With the exception of Frank, no one guessed that I was scared shitless by the messiness of relationships.

Also, hidden from most people was a strange dichotomy I wrestled with. Though I readily accepted that I was a spiritual woman led and moved by the Spirit, I would get nauseous if someone told me what a wonderful person I was. *Oh, that's not me—that is the work of the Spirit.* On the other hand, when confronted by critical comments, I absorbed the negativity as truth. *Yup, you must be right. I do everything wrong.* Furthermore, I'd been taught by my religion that, when insulted, turn the other cheek—offensive people need love, not retaliation. While this is true, I developed a mistaken belief that setting boundaries and speaking out against cruelty was pure egotism and, therefore, sinful. I was convinced that "evolved spiritual people" rose above criticism and the earthy crap of trashy emotions.

All of this fit right into my nearly unconscious attitude that being a flesh-and-blood individual was a lowly vocation, insignificant. I was convinced that matter didn't matter. What a light-bulb moment to admit that I was a slave to a certain image of spirituality, and I'd ripped my human dignity into shreds yearning to be only a divine spirit. It shocked me to realize that, by living from this lopsided perspective, I'd unconsciously recreated Ma's behavior. She bought new bonnets and white gloves for Easter to cover up the shame of our poverty. I chose to wear my Sunday-best spirit to hide my shame as an inadequate human.

As I dismantled the ritual altar that evening, the Earth Mother—my Mother—put her hand into the hollow space near my heart, a space that had once been the nesting place for my rattle. I hung Ma's grief and mine alongside my ceremonial garb on one of the gracious pine trees. Swaying with sorrow, I sang a hushed lullaby to my beloved rattle.

I dragged my tuckered body to the sleeping quarters and slowly rolled onto the small cot nestled against the window of my room. I was grateful to have windows with no shades that evening, desiring to be bathed in the light of the stars and moon, aching for relief from the black hole of emptiness in my body. A Native American ancestor arrived that evening and slept outside the window. I'd seen him in prior visits to this land. His elegant headdress folded up as a pillow, while moonlight cast dim blue shadows on his heart. I was comforted by this invisible ancestor who understood my suffering, and by the spirit of my brave-hearted partner, Frank. He came over and hugged me tightly, saddened that there wasn't room on the cot for us to snuggle. Without words, he knew that once again I'd been seized and uprooted for one purpose: greater intimacy and communion with the Divine Mother.

From top to bottom
Pa and Ma, circa 1938
Grandma Helen
Pa with Pepe and Meme
Annette at two years old, 1944

From top to bottom
Annette at five years old, 1947
Annette and Frank on their
wedding day, 1981
Laying down the rattle, 1998
Annette and Frank, 2018

Windsong: An Embodied Mystic

CHAPTER 21

Lead Me, Guide Me

Grief is not the enemy
Grief is the life-giving, heart-expanding teacher

—TOM ZUBA

In hindsight, I see that the Mother wasted no time in guiding me in new directions. Following breakfast, we gathered in a closing circle, offering prayers of gratitude to the Great Spirit and to the spirits of the land for taking our grief into their soil. Although others shared, I kept silent about my own grief process. As I was about to leave, out of the blue, one of the participants stopped me. "You know, Annette, I feel sure the Spirit wants you to attend this alternative Doctorate in Ministry program I'm enrolled in. It's one place you can be acknowledged for your weirdness. You know, something like Ellis Island for mystics. And, honey, you certainly carry the torch for Spirit!"

I have to say my eyeballs crossed for several seconds. Here was this tall embodied goddess of a woman, wearing enormous pink-rimmed glasses, her hair piled on top of her head, held back with a sweat-soaked bandana, and she's telling me to apply for a DMin program that begins in a month? We stared into each other's eyes for several moments before I sputtered, "And you, dear one, are nuts." We doubled over with outrageous laughter.

"Okay," she said, "I may look more odd than you. But, honey, God is your best buddy, you hang out with the dead, you see things that the rest of us don't, and you think that's normal!"

"Of course, it is," I said through loud chuckles.

"Okay, then, apply for this program. You need a tribe of mystical lunatics, and we need you. We need you."

I wondered, *What the hell is she talking about?* But as she explained the purpose of the program, my heart skipped with excitement. I'd never heard of a doctoral program that studied the mystics, the wisdom of ancient traditions, and integrated them with contemporary spiritual movements. She made it clear to me that the purpose of the degree was to enable you to be a God-like force in the world. In other words, it prepared mystics to be social activists. "Why not," I thought. "I've done crazier things."

In my application to graduate school, I startled myself by writing that the primary reason for entering the program was to bring forth the Divine Feminine. I eloquently expressed how my personal story paralleled the tradition of Mary Magdalene: a woman labeled as a whore, possessed by evil spirits, and unworthy of her Beloved Jesus. I'd been condemned as the siren who defrocked Fr. Frank from his sacred calling, had been labeled mentally ill, and certainly I felt unworthy. Following the retreat, I was willing—albeit fearfully—to follow the Mother's call to integrate my mystical self with being a woman of power. It was time to step forward as flesh and spirit without excuses. Within a month of being accepted into the DMin program, I bought all the necessary books and went shopping for a California wardrobe. As I had in prior spiritual adventures, I placed my feet on the ground and let the great unknown guide me.

Before my studies began, the Divine Mother had additional plans for me. The first came through in a dream in which a holy woman from India appeared. She told me telepathically that I was to visit her, that she had a gift for me. The woman was petite, exquisitely beautiful, and had a red spot in the middle of her forehead. When I related the dream to one of my friends, she immediately said, "That is the Mother Avatar I am devoted to—my guru! I'd give anything to go see her in person."

"Okay, girlfriend, let's get a plane ticket." Losing a week's pay from our jobs seemed insignificant in light of this awesome opportunity. We flew to Germany and stayed in a delightful chalet. Each evening, along with two hundred other devotees, we waited in line until we were allowed entry into the Mother's small devotional room. When the Mother entered, it felt as if the walls expanded. Flashes of heat flooded my body, and I always felt a bit faint. We came forward individually and knelt at the feet of the Avatar. She placed her delicate, soft brown hands on our heads, unknotting whatever emotional or spiritual blockages we had within our energy-bodies. She never uttered a word. Once she lifted her hands, we looked up into her eyes for a moment and then returned to our seats.

While I was impressed and sometimes giddy after these encounters, it wasn't until the fourth day that I was knocked off my feet. One of the Mother's aides came up to me and whispered, "The Mother desires to have you come forth. Leave your glasses on the chair."

What? Have I done something wrong? My legs felt like Silly Putty and, without my glasses, I stumbled over people's feet, even landing in a few laps along the way. Tears were pouring from my eyes like a fountain, and my blouse was wet by the time I reached her. I dropped to my knees with a thud, and a rush of alarm coursed through me: her feet were ice cold, and my sense was that she wasn't really a body. She was an energy dressed in exquisite clothes, and her thin golden bracelets were sliding on air. Even gazing into her eyes was overwhelming. Despite my 20/900 eyesight, even without glasses I had perfect vision in that moment. It was an experience of floating in the space of the galaxies, and I even wondered if the Star of Bethlehem was in the center of her right eye. In a flash of sacred stupor, I heard my mind asking, *Am I dead? Is the Mother of all Creation looking at me? Is this Love? Is this God? Is this Wonder?* Within minutes, I was ushered back to my seat, and my friend reached over, grinning and crying at the same time. It was true—I'd been touched—we had been touched—by the Divine Mother.

Not long after this encounter, the Mother's second plan appeared in the form of a man whose entire life had been devastated by heart-wrenching loss. He was collapsing into ragged pieces of lifeless flesh. He'd been referred to me by several people hoping that the spiritual work I did might lift the crushing weight of his grief. He decided to make an appointment when he saw the date for one of my last scheduled shamanic workshops. It was on the birthday of his deceased wife. What still strikes me about this man who barely crawled into my office was the intensity of his bone-gnawing sorrow. As we sat on the floor facing each other, him sobbing like his insides were going to explode through his skin, he related how his wife, forty-three years old, was ripped from his life, fifty-two hours after the onset of chest pain.

Nine years prior to this most recent trauma, he and his wife had desperately clung to each other as their first child, their eighteen-month-old daughter, was erased from their lives by a rare blood disease. Now, he was left alone to father two sons, ages seven and three. With every swaying movement of his body, and his heavy sighs, the wood of my office walls swelled, absorbing his agony.

This man was open to me journeying on his behalf to retrieve the pieces of his spirit that had spun out during the traumas. I explained that the purpose of the journey was to restore him to wholeness, freeing him to move forward with the mourning process versus always feeling like he was being sucked into quicksand. While I could not assure him of any results, I hoped for his sake that Spirit might connect me directly with the spirits of his daughter and wife. After the journey, when I lifted my blindfold, I saw terror in this man's eyes. For a moment, I considered saying nothing. However, he reached for my hand and asked to hear everything.

I told him I saw a young girl at a stream, bent over, looking in the water. She said, "Tom is my daddy." Up to that moment, he felt he had lost his daughter—that death had severed their connection. Now he felt transformed and came to peace knowing he and his daughter were forever Daddy and daughter. The part of his spirit that split off had left the earth in search of her. His response, and mine, was profound silence, interrupted only by occasional sniffling and heaving sighs.

This man left my office less burdened, his consciousness shifted by his daughter's words. That was evident several years later, when his thirteen-year-old son was diagnosed with a brain tumor. He invited Frank and I to the hospital, and I quietly scanned his son's body. It was clear to me that his son would not recover, no matter how many people prayed for him, no matter what healing techniques were used. However, I agreed to do a journey on his behalf later that evening. In the journey, I saw a young teen standing on a dimly lit road, gray clouds foaming in the background. The boy looked forward and saw his deceased mom in the distance as an illumined figure. When he turned around to see his dad, the air became stagnant, taking on that greenish color before a tornado strikes, before death snatches a life. For several seconds, the teen hesitated between both parents, and then he burst into a brilliant flame, his smile penetrating the fire. He leapt into his mother's arms. A few days later, the dad called to say his son was home with his mom.

My time with this man was life-altering for me also, helping me to understand the possibility of both feeling and holding pain with people as well as stepping back and being a witness. I was able to hold the divinity of death for him and, in compassion, send droplets of serenity into the rubble of his annihilating grief. However, it was this man's vulnerability in expressing and embracing raw emotion that cracked me open. No one knew my terror of feeling the angst of this kind of horrific human pain. I'd spent a lifetime distancing myself from overwhelming, bewildering, and unspeakable emotions connected to loss. It was far more rewarding—and safe—to play with God. Believing that pain was the enemy left me half alive, a half shell of a woman. I thought back to the moment with the Mother Avatar in Germany when I knew her body was formless, waves of undulating energy. That was an ecstasy I could willingly enter into and enjoy. The woman Avatar's transparent formlessness restored me to a universal connection and interdependence with the Universe. With this man, the power of human grief formed and moved his very existence. In merging with this intensity, I could barely breathe, but I chose to dive into this man's ocean-deep eyes that spoke what he couldn't utter. Oh my. Like with the Avatar woman, I knew he was the presence of God, in human form, weeping the Divine's experience of human loss and love. I struggled to stay breathing.

Being with this man brought home something that Elisabeth Kübler-Ross told me at a conference I attended years before, when I was working at my local parish. I usually didn't ask questions at public forums, but I was enthralled by Kübler-Ross. Her wisdom resonated like finely tuned flutes playing in my soul. So, during the question and answer period, I naively commented that it confused me to see how fearful people were of dying, and to see how the loss of a loved one crippled people. I recounted the time my best friend's sister died after being gored by the bull on their family farm. I saw her father at the funeral home, vomiting over the porch rail, and I wondered, *Why is he upset? She's with God. There is nothing to be unhappy about.* I was a teenager at the time, and I would visit with my friend's mom and tell her when I "saw" her daughter walking into the room, and what she was saying. Her mom would cry and hug me. I told Kübler-Ross that this was natural for me. She stepped forward from the podium, staring me down as if she were a raptor bird. "You have a phenomenal gift from God, but—and I say BUT with capital letters—you are in love with death, Annette, and you need to fall in love with life." I was quite mortified, to say the least, but I accepted her warning.

Prior to the birth of my first grandson, a dream surfaced to confirm this awakening. In the dream, a voice spoke these words to me: *If you want to know who I am, look into his face. If you want to know how I feel, touch his hand. If you want to feel the warmth of my love, hug him in your arms. I am he, and he is I am.* In the presence of the broken-hearted man, a man I now call friend, I'd had a direct experience of this message. When I first held my grandson, I had no doubt that God was sleeping in my arms, and I melted into the love of a living God.

CHAPTER 22

Dark Mama, Earth Mother

I desire to live as the glowing mystery of Darkness
Manifesting always the Lightness of Being

—ANNETTE HULEFELD

In July of 1999, prior to being admitted to the DMin program, I had a dream in which Jesus appeared, clothed in tattered robes and bleeding from his wounds. I watched as he began to dance, morphing into the form of the Virgin Mother, who was clothed in a swirling robe of iridescent crystal beads. As I looked to the ground, Jesus's feet, clad in gray sandals, shifted into the beaded feet of a woman. I asked, "Who are you?" He replied, "I am the risen woman." As he uttered these words, the figure of an African man rose behind him, accompanied by rippling sounds from the cowry shells on his garment.

This dream puzzled me until I shared it with a shaman friend, who immediately laughed aloud. He said he personally knew the African man I described. "He is a Dagara medicine man. I urge you to contact him. You will find yourself in his village soon." I wrote a letter to him, and, surprisingly, he phoned me. We talked for quite a while, and, at the end, he offered to share his teachings with me in weekly private phone conversations. He was a guru in demand with a busy schedule, and I was astonished by his generosity. But, as it happened with some other teachers, I knew that we were somehow connected in this lifetime for a far greater purpose than I could foresee.

Several months later, I was invited, along with a dozen other spiritual seekers, to visit his village in Burkina Faso, in West Africa. The purpose of our trip was to spend time with the people of his village, to receive divination readings by the local shamans, and to visit the sacred cave of the Kontomble (little people from the unseen world of Spirit). I'd had many dreams of dancing in an African village, so I didn't hesitate a moment in saying yes to his invitation. I couldn't explain why, but I felt that, in going to Africa, I was going *home*.

The preparation for the journey was almost as challenging as the trip itself. For three months, I was plagued with an infection that refused to leave my lungs and sinuses. I was crazed wondering how I could board the plane feeling so ill. I tried every non-traditional remedy without success. Finally, I succumbed to a course of antibiotics and, voila, my symptoms abated for the most part and I packed my suitcases. I would have asked for a wheelchair and a morphine drip to get there, believe me! Every cell in my body was Africa-bound.

My fellow travelers and I were a varied group, but one hilariously funny gay man became my best buddy. He could out-fart and out-burp me at every turn. Together, we decided to be the laugh patrol for all the ponderous folks on the trip.

The journey to the village was comical, with eighteen people crammed into a minibus intended to seat ten at the most. We were so cramped together that our noses were literally in each other's backs or armpits. Live chickens ran loose on the back seat, and when we'd bump against protruding rocks, they'd send forth a flurry of feathers. All thirty-six suitcases, loaded with our belongings and gifts for the villagers, bulged and croaked like pot-bellied toads under a rope that miraculously tied them onto the roof. The bottom of the van often scraped the red earth, making a *rattle-rattle* noise that competed with the nervous chitchat escaping from our clenched jaws. The dim light of the moon hauntingly illumined this rag-tag pilgrimage of eager spiritual initiates.

Halfway through the trip, the motor of the van stopped, and we clunked to the ground. The driver yelled, "Look! Look!" To our right were tongues of flames, dancing through the air on a flying branch, which crashed to the ground by the side of our van. All chattering ceased. One chicken clucked. One of the guides stepped out and reported a fire within the baobab tree near us, blessing our arrival. "Wow," I sputtered. "Moses had the burning bush, and we get this."

We stayed on the outskirts of the village to sleep in the evenings. The only discordant sounds came from the pigs snorting and the roosters crowing at four a.m. When we arrived at the village compound the next morning, I was stunned by the appearance of several strong-bodied women—women whose faces radiated hardship, polished by the wind and the earth. The fierce heat of love from within the women's eyes stretched the pores of my being to receive all they had to offer. The shiny brown babies, snuggled on the backs of their mothers, were hushed, except for an occasional gurgle when a tiny finger popped from a hungry mouth. Vultures swirled elegantly over the terrain, landing with an audible thud of dominion on the rooftops. They probably sailed in a mystical state of near-drunkenness on the days when the animals were slaughtered, which our money and hospitality made possible. The vultures' presence created a heavy-breathing, brooding-storm kind of stillness. The tension eased seeing the naked children giggle and skip around the fire they'd made from the branches of the baobab trees close by. They'd throw a chicken directly into the fire, then squeal with delight when it was time to pluck all the feathers out and to rip off the meat with their fingers.

One afternoon, I saw a young woman climbing down a very steep wooden ladder, a baby strapped to her back, and with six-foot long poles precariously balanced on top of an enormous stainless-steel bowl on her head. She was dressed in a traditional wrap-around skirt and a silver lamé camisole top, an American symbol of femininity that escaped the Goodwill bin.

Two other women were in a nearby field, using long carved wooden pestles to pound millet in worn wooden buckets. In the midst of empty millet sheaves, a smattering of dried bushes, here and there a baobab tree, the drumbeat from the young women pounding millet turned into layered heat waves of the Mother's rhythmic heartbeat. I stood in rapt attention as the sound of the Mama pounded me and the Universe tap danced inside my body. I felt new life rising within me. Even the red dust of the earth seemed alive as it clung like static electricity along the edge of my tacky polyester black pants.

The ritual performed on my behalf was focused on one sacred intention: to lift the generational lies I was rooted in. My palms were clammy with sweat, my mind a swamp of conflicting emotions, and I gagged as the first animal chosen for me was a red baby goat. It wrapped itself around my legs, unwilling to be taken by the shaman for slaughter. Images flashed before my eyes—the faces of powerless, submissive women I'd known, including myself—images imprinted on the scratchy face of the goat. My God, I thought, how many of us succumbed to the knife of cultural and family abuse, when all we wanted was the softness of the Mother for comfort. I threw my arms around the sweet, warm creature, weeping, and asked forgiveness for the cruelty he was to take on my behalf.

But when I was shoved aside, and the shaman kicked my reluctant goat into submission, something inside me snapped. *Sweet Jesus, I am the dumb goat here. I have given over my dignity to external authority all my life—to my mother, to the*

Church—*in order to be worthy of love, to be acceptable, to belong.* The shaman glared at me for my display of sensitivity—or maybe the sun was in his eyes. I faked my willingness to participate in the ritual, yet inwardly I prayed to the ancestors: *Forgive me, but I am not able to accept this way of making me worthy.* There had to be another approach, and I trusted I'd be led to it.

Each person in our group was to receive a personal reading from the village shaman, and he would determine what other animals would be sacrificed for us. I was a bit apprehensive entering the hobbit-sized hovel of his room, but then I had to restrain myself from guffawing upon seeing a grungy, tattered poster of Eddie Murphy posted on the earthen wall. There was also a fifth of vodka by the shaman's side. At first, the shaman's translator shook his head, muttering, "He cannot read you. There is a white light around you that he cannot get through." I froze in place, thinking that nothing could be done on my behalf, and I was doomed to feeling shitty forever. Then I recalled I'd asked Jesus for protection that morning, so maybe the light was his shield. There was a pregnant pause, and then the shaman said I was dying from a generational curse handed down through my mother. He would ask his mother to kill a pig on my behalf. There would be other rituals, but this one was specific: it had to be his mother, and it had to be a pig. Between the heat of the day and the anticipated ritual for release from my mother's energy, I experienced waves of terror and profound weakness—dubious and yet hopeful at the same time.

Later in the week, we were gathered together for the sacrificing of the chickens. Chickens of all types were selected and represented different issues that needed healing. I was given a black-and-white guinea hen, an exquisite symbol of my dualistic mind, the split within that was killing me. I was suspended between living here on earth and being in other dimensions; living from lies of diminishment versus living from the truth of the Soul. The story I was told was that the guinea hen was chosen for me because, once killed, its feathers would scatter to such a distance they could never be retrieved again. Believe me, I was more than willing to be free of the burdens I carried.

When it was my turn, I sat hunched over, my butt barely touching the dusty earth, sure I was going to faint from the trauma of being a killer. A very kind elderly shaman gently nudged my hand for me to slit the hen's throat. He flashed his semi-toothless grin deep into my bewildered eyes. I commanded my arm to slice a V formation into my chicken's throat, but my arm remained motionless by my side. With the swiftness of light, the shaman swiped his blade through the neck of the quivering hen and threw her a short distance, where she landed at the edge of a narrow ditch. All eyes were on the chicken. My curse would be lifted only if the dying hen leapt up to the heavens, raw nerves twitching for the ancestors. My hen, however, just lay there, lifeless. Inwardly I shouted, *Jump, chicken, jump! Jump, chicken, jump! For Christ's sake, jump, you stupid chicken!* Just then, I became aware that the shaman was reading my mind. He was following the tickertape of thoughts and feelings rushing through me. He grinned, and I was mortified.

Meanwhile, the hen showed no sign of its anticipated death throes. *Oh, Great Chicken in the sky, tickle your hen, do whatever you have to do. Oh God,* I thought, *if that hen doesn't spring into action soon, I am going to remain here in Africa, trapped in my family's wretched belief systems, forever a fried chick.* With a shiver, the hen rose up, releasing a cloud of downy black and white feathers. As I watched them disappear from sight, the fluttering of my soul came to rest. Finally, both of us were in peace.

After the ceremony, the rest of our group went to the building compound, small-talking their nervousness away. Collectively, they sounded like columns of dictionary words falling off the page. I was tuckered out to say the least, both from the ordeal and from the sweltering heat. Several times during the trip, I attempted to share some of the profound experiences I was having, but my talky-talky companions were focused more on devising plans to create a water project for the village, bringing medical supplies to the struggling clinics. My journey to become more human and shift into the Divine Feminine energy didn't fit with their list of priorities, so I remained silent for the most part. They also became very animated when looking for places to fill their bellies. Without fail, the menu was: hot orange Fanta soda (ice cubes being forbidden due to the poor quality of the water) along with chicken and *pomme frites* (french fries). Waves of dry heaves overwhelmed me just hearing the word "chicken." All I could think of was slit-open chicken throats and spurting blood. So, my diet was reduced to double servings of fried potatoes and hot soda.

The next morning, we were invited to the home of another village shaman, which was basically an open cement space supported by pillars. Already feeling like a roasted acorn about to split open, I meandered from the group. I was drawn to stand near a pile of ordinary-looking rocks that had an odd magnetism about them. There, looking out on the vast horizon, either the energy of the compound or the ancestors of the village blessed me with a vision. Like a screen slowly rising up from an orchestra pit, *the* Mother of all creation came onto the stage. Even now, recalling her image gives me goose bumps. She was a stupendous ebony figure, with plump mounds of fleshy breasts. She radiated unconditional love—an abundant, divinely human woman. I wanted to sprint into Mama's body, but a wind arose from nothingness, becoming my skin, becoming my breath. I knew there was no thing between me and the Divine. I had dissolved into Oneness. For one brief moment, the seen and the unseen worlds were the same, and all questions, all fears, became irrelevant, non-existent. What mattered was that nothing mattered but being Love. My search for meaning was ended. I could stop whoring for God with all my traditions. My African Mama reunited my soul with my body. I was Home, I was in Love, I was undone, I was whole. I was in Truth.

In this reverie, I didn't hear the shaman calling my name to receive a personal talisman made from the bladder of my sacrificed four-legged goat. I was instructed to keep it happy with alcohol and blood. We were also gifted with a hand-carved knife to continue offering sacrifices once we returned home. I actually buried mine, along with my "goat girl" mentality, under a maple tree in our backyard. I made a vow to disengage from any religious or spiritual traditions that fostered violence against the feminine, and I promised to lay my negativity against myself to rest.

I didn't have much time to integrate the power of meeting the Mama that morning as our spiritual adventure involved traveling to another remote village in a mini yellow school bus. Once again, our challenge was to maneuver our derrieres expertly to avoid major black-and-blue bruises from riding over the jarring terrain. Pee breaks were complicated. If the bus lurched forward unexpectedly after the brakes hiccupped to a stop, you'd check to see if you'd already peed on the person in front of you. If you were lucky enough to hold out until you could exit the bus, then you ran behind a random bush, squatted, and prayed some huge bug wasn't waiting for your sweet flesh. Afterwards, you scooted back quickly, remembering you had to air-dry since there was no toilet paper. I am glad I brought an extra pair of socks to change into from my own dribbling.

When we arrived at our destination, we scurried like homeless mice into a dark, cramped cave that smelled of ram slaughter and bird entrails. For the African villagers, caves were gateways between the spirit and human worlds. Bats swirled around our heads, and I wasn't sure if I was going to laugh irreverently or pee a river. Serendipitously, I was seated in front of the sacrificial pit, alongside my best buddy, the gay man. Butt-to-butt and knee-to-knee, we shivered in anticipation of our next shock. A very thin, pruned-faced, seemingly deranged woman strolled into the cave, flailing her arms erratically. Her fingers stretched in all four directions, giving them the appearance of Silly Putty gone wild. Her mouth hung open, revealing toothless gums, and her eyes rolled loosely in their sockets, occasionally darting like pinballs in opposite directions. There was a translucent aura to this woman, almost as if her blue flowered dress covered a body that didn't really exist. She walked the length of the cave and returned walking backwards. She stopped in front of me, grabbed my arm, squealing with laughter that unsettled my heart. It reminded me of the Japanese healer's breath that cracked my spirit into pieces. Not wanting to be disrespectful, I responded by laughing quite loudly, which triggered her to move my arm up and down like a like a water pump. As she stepped backward, she stretched my arm as if it were a worn-out rubber band and released it with a snap. My arm recoiled and, unfortunately, the only place for it to land was across my best buddy's face—which he took in good humor. I sensed this woman was a cosmic jester, not a daffy loon—and she was setting me up. I appeared to be sane and well-mannered, but she sensed the depth of my sorrow, and she was poking holes at my ridiculousness. My outer veneer cracked in her gaze, so I could be a fool for God, living from a spirit of joy and sacred irreverence—not be the stuffy old fart my dad feared I'd become.

I whispered to God, Keep me sane.

After the woman left, the ritual began, with dead chickens flying out of corners I didn't even see, landing at my feet. Their still-warm blood splattered over me, creating indelible designs on my white t-shirt. I numbed out. The coup de grace was the slaughtering of a black ram, its blood mingling with that of the chickens. The sound of the gurgling blood in the ram's throat conjured up images of the slaughtering of women and children throughout the ages. It was as if my bones turned into a living battleground, merging my spirit with the blood of the sacrificed victims. I whispered to God, *Keep me sane.*

After the ritual ended, my buddy motioned to me that it was time to get out of this cave. Poor man, he was terrified. We crawled out on hands and knees, shaking and shivering. He then pulled me up to a standing position, and we ran over to a gigantic fallen tree trunk where he inelegantly plopped me down. He stared at me, I stared at him, and suddenly we could no longer contain the ripples of intense anxiety trapped in our bodies. We doubled over in boisterous laughter, and a thunderous fart burst out of me. My buddy fell off the log! *Are you for real? After this indescribable event and you do that?* A small group of children came running, screaming with delight! Suddenly I was a celebrity—*Thunderclap Hulefeld.* They quickly went to gather other village children and returned, dressed in Western finery, chanting for the silly old white lady to repeat the stupendous wind bomb! As we left the village, the children followed the bus, jumping up and down, giggling beyond control. The shaman told the bus driver to "gun it—get us out of here, and get out fast!" He teased me that I'd made an impression never to be duplicated. Tongue in cheek, I related that the breath of Spirit had blown through me, making fear evaporate into nothing but hot air.

· · · · ·

We were taken to our most important destination the following day. This was a sacred cave in the mountains, where, hopefully, we would encounter the Kontomble—the pitch-black "little people," visitors from the unseen realms. We were instructed to drop all intellectual and spiritual expectations before entering the cave: there was no assurance that these beings would appear to us. Unlike my comrades, who were anxious about their appearing, I felt unusually calm. I wasn't worried whether I would see them. I just knew this was where I was meant to be. I waited to hear the "boom-boom" sound from the top of the cave that marked their arrival.

The protocol for the meeting with the Kontomble was that we would each prepare three questions that the shaman would relay to them. The Kontomble would answer the questions with individualized prescribed rituals. The ritual could involve animal sacrifice or an offering of money, cowry shells, or perhaps some ash.

It was several hours before my turn arrived, so I spent time in the open air, content to commune with the spirits of the mountain and the stones. I noticed an old woman peacefully crouched in front of the cave. Her delicate frame swayed in the wind. Her features and patterned blue dress were the same as the wild-eyed woman's at the other cave. I wondered, *Is she here, or had she drifted in from the other world?*

When it was my turn and I entered the cave, I sucked in my breath, overcome by the pungent odor of great antiquity, decay, and musty dust. The darkness was unforgettable and yet familiar. My heart raced like a thoroughbred horse, champing at the bit to finish the race and be victorious. I had memorized my questions, fearing I'd become stupid in the presence of this being. "How do I serve the planet at my age? What ancestors could assist me in fulfilling my destiny? How was I to protect my health?" After I waited over an hour in this space, the shaman came to inform me that the Kontomble "were rushed"—meaning that I'd have to wait for another day for my meeting. One of my core issues was feeling dismissed by people in authority; another was feeling too invisible to be noticed. Looking back on it, I find it hard to believe my boldness. I smiled at the shaman and, like a nervous bride, surrendered to surging waves of energy that pushed me past him, onwards toward the space between the worlds where one of the Kontomble was waiting for me.

I was as blind as a bat in the darkness, and I felt woozy from the excitement. God almighty, what if I was going to die? I fell to my knees, or so I thought; I actually fell into the Kontomble's lap! I pushed myself up, perched myself on one bent leg, and handed over my monetary offering, hoping I'd be forgiven for being such a bumbling klutz.

Immediately, I felt the dryness of his skin scrape past my shuddering fingers, and he grasped my hand and arm with the sinewy strength of a mountain lion. Infinity opened in that moment, and pure generative energy went through my nervous system, my muscles, and my whole body. The lightning bolt that seared the kitchen table when I was twelve years old came back and kissed me, jolting me to life. The power of the universal life force gushed through the Kontomble's handshake. The physicality, the intensity of his raw power, so stunned me that I literally gasped, YES! YES! YES! He and I were one and the same, from the same Source. It felt as if all the skin of my body dissolved, and he recalibrated my cells into light particles dancing in the black space of the universe. My eyesight developed a clarity beyond explanation. I watched, entranced, and witnessed the Kontomble's piercing eyes transform into glittering circles of light, which exited through the back of his head and burst into a brilliant halo.

Streams of "Oh My, Oh My" rippled from my mouth as I saw Christ and the Buddha appear in this black man. I was immersed in pure love and compassion. I believe the Kontomble sensed the tension within me: a wild pulling toward the light streaming in the distance. Oh God, I knew this portal to other dimensions, and every cell of my body knew I could disintegrate and become a speck in the cosmos. I had been there, but this time I had to make a different choice. He was affirming me as a human, mystical woman and connecting me to the feminine consciousness. I was on fire with the Mystery, connected with the heart and soul of all of humanity. I sensed my personal existence sinking into and becoming united with the planetary consciousness of the Divine. That was the gift I was to deliver in this lifetime.

Although I actually spent five or ten minutes with this being, it seemed like eternity. I didn't hear the shaman calling me to leave with the group, as my sense of hearing had diminished. That was understandable, given that half of me was here and the other half was somewhere else. The shaman may have come to lead me out, I don't know. The Kontomble released his grip, slowly sliding his leathery fingers across the palm of my hand until we felt the coldness between our fingers.

When I stood up leave, I was in such a stupor that I lunged forward, accidentally landing a punch in the Kontomble's private parts or where I thought they might be. I then staggered out of the cave, my heart pounding in my ears, my legs wobbling like a rubber chicken's. I was inebriated with love. My buddy friend told me later that he knew how the apostles felt seeing Jesus transfigured on the mountaintop. As I clung to the rocks next to the mouth of the cave, he saw a translucent aura of light around me. It was as if my soul was clinging to my body like Saran wrap. My buddy started to bawl with me, offering his trembling arm as we looked for a place to sit down. I promised him I wouldn't repeat my thunderous rear-end applause as I had after the other cave. I could feel my body popping back into form as we chuckled.

Two men from the village, perhaps shaman initiates, walked over and offered me a raw piece of chicken neck. *Oh my! Oh my!* God knows why I was the only person to be chosen for this delicacy. Unfortunately, I didn't have my childhood collie dog to slip this awful thing to, as I did with the watery custard my mother forced me to eat when I was ill with rheumatic fever. I didn't want to be disrespectful, so I pretended to swallow the "gift" piece in one gulp. However, the two semi-clad young men had x-ray eyes, and they poked each other, tittering at my distress. I was going to have to taste the bones, along with the slimy stuff wrapped around the little neck. I gagged with such disgust, knowing I simply could not swallow the icky thing. They smiled and shook hands with me. At an opportune moment, I slipped the chicken neck under a rock, ready to vomit at any moment.

It was then that I again noticed the old woman dressed in blue, realizing she was standing in mid-air. There was no ledge for her to step on, and, in the blink of an eye, she evaporated into the ether. Had she come for me? Had Grandma Helen shape-shifted into her in order to comfort me? Or maybe there was no difference between the two of them. I trembled, wondering about the strangeness of this seemingly crazy woman, like Grandma, who had come to help set me free.

For several hours, my only words were *Oh my! Oh My!* oh my. I was so ecstatic that the group's nonsensical babbling on the way back to the village, and the sloshing of beer in their glasses during lunch, didn't faze me. The intimate union I'd experienced could not be shared with anyone. I was a woman resting contentedly in my Mother's arms, and my God had ignited the fire of my soul once again. I did manage to chug-a-lug a warm Fanta soda—no chicken, thank you—before retiring for the evening to the cement cell I was staying in.

The batteries to my flashlight were running low, but I still couldn't miss seeing the ginormous black bug hanging out on one of the barren walls in my room. Criminy—I'd just seen God, I was in Love, I was Loved, I was Love . . . so what's the big deal about a yucky creepy-crawly? If I had the gift to channel a sacred chicken in Egypt, then I could channel the African Mama to deal with this bug. I took in a deep breath and tenderly sang this creature across the wall, down the edges, and into the drain of the shower, a drain that was also the toilet. I made the sign of the cross for security and checked to make sure the mosquito netting was fastened snug-tight. I lay in bed, stiff as a corpse, hypnotizing my kidneys to not make urine.

On the final day of our pilgrimage, there was a large celebration for us in the center of the village compound. The temperature was around 120 degrees, or at least it felt that hot to me. I'm overly sensitive to heat, so I used bottled water to soak towels and wrapped them around my head. My legs and body felt so heavy I wondered if the eggs I'd been eating were actually time-released cement. I was resting in the shade when a young boy came to stand in front of me. My eyes traveled up his thin legs, and I found myself looking directly into the dreamy eyes of a cow's head, seemingly unaware that its body was several yards away! Each part of the cow was presented to me before it was skinned and cooked—to honor me because I was an elder. Oh my! I bowed reverently to legs, and even entrails, praying that my staccato burping would prevent me from throwing up.

Just then, to add to my discombobulation, my beaded necklace broke. I was heartbroken as I watched beads scattering into the red earth. The necklace had been hand-crafted by friends and family members who promised to pray for the safety and health of our group while we were in Africa. Even my seven-year old-grandson promised to light candles and call on Mother Earth and on the Wind every night so that his "Granbunny" would be safe. He told me afterwards that he stopped the prayers when his brother broke the energy of the circle by needing to pee at the wrong time! The undoing of the necklace was a not-so-subtle message from the spirit world that my life, as I had defined it, was over. I'd have to restring my life and create a new story.

As I salvaged all the beads I could find, a spunky older woman pulled at my arm, placing me into the center of a group of dancers. Her energy was quite different from that of the seemingly crazy woman who sat me in front of the pit where I watched the black ram get killed. This woman was a revered elder of the village, and she was inviting me to join the women. Although she taught me the dance steps, I was a spectacle of awkwardness, clumsily stepping to the left when everyone was jumping to the right. The women laughed uproariously, not *at* me but *with* me. I felt humbled by the warmth of their touch and their smiles.

The shaman told me later that the women recognized the gentleness and the power of my indigenous heart. Their invitation to dance was their acknowledgement that I was one of them in spirit. In the village, the women enfolded me as one of them, dancing, laughing, and gazing deeply into my essence, awakening the fullness and splendor of life. In the presence of Love, in the energy of their sacred space, both visible and invisible, there were no barriers, nothing to separate us from the unspeakable power of the Divine. I suspect these women would not have understood how wretched I had always felt about my body, and how deeply I hated waking up every morning to physical and emotional pain. They obviously loved their bodies and carried their flesh with dignity. Their intimacy with the ancestral spirits was our bonding as spirit sisters. They grinned at me as if I were amazing, and even my jiggly, flabby rear-end was a plus in their eyes. Who cares—being alive is the joy! Not your poverty or body shape or hardship. Get on with it, girl! I have no doubt they suffered physical pain—it is part of life, and cosmic memory—but they still danced, they still laughed, they embraced life. I prayed for the courage to carry this Mother heart back into my world.

When I returned home, I was unable to make sense of practically anything, including my psychotherapy practice. I decided to take a leave of absence for several months. It was as if I couldn't understand people's life dramas anymore. All I wanted to do was to simply sit with people and let love restore them to wholeness. But instead I coped with my disintegration by stripping wallpaper, delighting in the hot, sudsy scrubbing to remove the old glue. And I craved silence more than food or water.

If I smelled chicken, I found the nearest toilet bowl to engage with. Even visiting my friend's farm was now an emotional roller-coaster. I'd bought Frank an endearing brown goat that was cared for by my friends. I can just imagine what went through that goat's mind when I'd drape myself over his bony shoulders, sobbing, happy that he could romp around and have a life of eating hay and hanging out with the horses. And Frank—dear Frank—he understood I'd gone "home," that re-entry was more difficult than childbirth. He was a good shepherd to me, anticipating my every need, and was deeply attentive to the spiritual transformation unfolding before his eyes. No one could have been better protected as the butterfly me made its way out of the cocoon of old trauma.

When I landed in Africa, I knelt and kissed the ground—I knew this was my home, and I hoped that maybe, just maybe, I would encounter the Great Mother. I never dreamed I'd meet the Divine Feminine within me. And there, in a cave, I was grasped by a Being—a physical, mysterious Being whose touch was a Big Bang event. The cave was the womb of God for me, the space where the worlds were one, the space of Godness from which life is to be born and lived. I entered it as a mummified human, trapped by crushing beliefs and memories, but with one electrifying touch, the embodied creature, a Kontomble, broke through the falsehoods I had regarding what it meant to be alive in the world, and scattered them into infinity. Simultaneously, the schism between my humanity and divinity began to close—I prayed to embrace my existence as both a full human and fully mystical woman. I smile to think that maybe the child in me, who desired nothing more than to paint rainbows to wake people up to the love of God, was in essence a little Kontomble. The big difference is that riding a cloud was her delight and not living in a smelly, dark cave! After Africa, I had no doubt that clouds and chaos were a combo I had to embrace.

One final African adventure awaited me. No one warned me that the Kontomble manifest themselves, in bodily form, when they decide that a person is "one of them." I was surprised to have experienced a physical being in the cave, but when they transported themselves into our home in Chicago in the following months, I was convinced I'd crossed over into loony tune land. Imagine me telling my good Christian friends they were not invited to my home because a "little dark creature" could potentially jump into their laps. At first, the Kontomble appeared to me at night when Frank was away at our friend's farm. Suddenly, the doors started to rattle, the cabinet doors slammed. Furniture moved, and the toilets would repeatedly flush. Not to mention their insistence on wanting to sleep in my bed. It scared the liver out of me to wake up at three a.m. and feel someone breathing down my neck and sitting on my spine so I couldn't move. And their laugh was like the men who roared when I tried not to eat the slimy chicken bones. During the day, they'd walk past so quickly I only saw their shadow. The reality of their presence was confirmed during a drumming circle one evening, when one of the women screamed there were two little black people jumping all around me. I smiled. I didn't doubt their existence; I was annoyed I wasn't in control of their antics. I called the wife of the shaman we had gone to Africa with, and she assured me they were appearing when I was alone so as not to startle people who were not familiar with them. She advised that I leave them food and honey, and to firmly tell them to calm down when they were being mischievous. I complied for a few weeks but decided to ask them to leave after my wedding ring disappeared. It showed up several months later in the wax of a candle Frank had gifted me with on our anniversary. My ritual for removal was outrageous, to say the least, but frustration led me to weirdness. In my flannel nightgown and rubber boots, my shaman belt around my waist, I paraded throughout the house banging a drum and singing at the top of my lungs.

In my personal evolution, dismissing the Kontomble proved to be a defining fork in the road of my spiritual life. On the one hand, I loved being "chosen" by the "little people." This was a painful hubris for me—I was special and more acceptable to the spirit world and, thus, worthy. On the other hand, saying yes to being "possessed" by them, surrendering to their traditions, would have aborted the purpose of my soul's unfolding: reclaiming my voice and breaking the mantle of dispossession worn by generations of women in the family. Turning away from this kind of spiritual power was necessary for me to step away from an old pattern of being a submissive, voiceless woman. Wherever I was being led, I'd have to be aware of how the spirit world informed my consciousness, and honor the integrity that emerged from this process of co-creation within me.

CHAPTER 23

Midwife for the Mother

*The rippling tide of Love flows secretly out from God into
the soul, and draws it mightily back to its Source.*

—MECHTHILD OF MAGDEBURG

After Africa, I spent a lot of time vegging out, gazing at the birds in the backyard, and watching the flowers dance in the wind. I continued to be involved in my local faith community where I volunteered as a pastoral and bereavement minister. For the most part, I withheld sharing my personal spirituality, as I had no intention of scandalizing people with my adventures or calling into question other people's beliefs. The challenge was how best to serve the people I loved and retain my spiritual integrity. I found myself praying to the Divine Mother, asking to know what her next intention was. Some months later, I received a phone call from someone who was a friend, a professional colleague, and a member of my faith community. She was a charming, beautiful woman whose expansive smile adorned her face like elegant diamond jewelry. Those who knew her well, including me, teased her unmercifully about her Shirley Temple demeanor and about hanging around with a bawdy weirdo like me. However, my friend was facing a slow agonizing battle with the beast of cancer, and she asked me to be her spiritual companion.

Several people asked me to offer her a "bells and whistles" healing ceremony. Even though I was teased about being a "way out there woman" who banged a drum, they remembered the healing received by another friend, and they hoped for the same outcome. I hesitated, as I had an intuitive sense that the outcome this time would not be the miracle people were hoping for. In addition, I knew that my friend was a very private woman and would be uncomfortable with a ceremony that drew attention to herself. More importantly, she was a traditional Catholic: rosaries and medals were one thing, but adding drums and rattles to the mix was something else.

When it became clear that death was inevitable—her cancer traveling at a velocity that defied prayers and advanced treatments—I realized whatever I could offer her spiritually would do no harm, and it might bring her peace. Chuckling, I promised her that I'd be normal and leave my "woo-woo" rattles and drums at home. I substituted my tools by making her an amber-colored crystal rosary and loaning her my three-foot-high statue of Our Lady, Queen of Peace. Given my sense of humor, however, I first introduced the statue to her in an unusual manner. During one of my visits to her in the hospital, I wrapped the statue in a Winnie-the-Pooh blanket and strutted down the hospital corridor like a peacock in full feather. It didn't dawn on me that the shape of the statue looked suspiciously like a pile of concealed weapons! I was stopped by a nurse who asked, "And what are you carrying?" Without batting an eyelash, I said, "Woman, this is your mother, it's best if you fall on your knees." Mary's wrappings came undone, as did my friend, the staff, and visitors. Sometimes, it's best to face death with a smile and your mother in hand.

During months of weekly visits, all I could be, all I could bring, was the presence of friendship, rooted in love and peace. She was comforted by each visit as I began with prayers to Mary, Jesus, St. Michael the Archangel, and the Holy Spirit. Sometimes she asked me to softly hum some of her favorite songs from the Catholic hymnal. And then, sitting by her side, with her CD softly playing music in the background—always the same one—I began to deepen into the silence of God, the stillness of a human person drenched in divinity. I had the spiritual eyes to witness the encounters between God and her spirit, and no words were necessary for these moments on holy ground. We communicated through hand-to-hand squeezes and synchronized breathing. There were precious moments when our eyes reached out in wonder, and radiant peace glistened from the depth of her sunken eyes.

My friend never shared about our meetings, which was quite distressing for some members of her large extroverted and close-knit family. On the one hand, they were so gracious and grateful for these healing sessions. On the other hand, they were sad and bewildered that a mere friend could walk in and share such intimate moments with their mom, with their wife. Not only was I bound by professional ethics to protect privacy, but even trying to explain that I had spiritual sight would not have diminished the intense human grief they had in separating from her. How was I to explain that I could see where she was resting in the invisible realms, a space in which the gems of her life were being polished into glorious Light, and where she was expanding her awareness of the world she would soon enter?

Almost everyone who knew my friend interpreted her silence as a refusal to face the truth—that death was soon coming for her. Not so. She didn't fear death. She loved life more, and she wanted to protect her family from worry. She chose to keep this time private, just between herself and God, a loving relationship that had sustained her during some rocky times in her life, a relationship she trusted to carry her safely to the end. Her need during her illness was simple: "I don't need you to fix me. I need you to stay with me, watch with me, be with me." That was the nature of our connection together.

One evening during our prayer time, as my friend slipped deeper into a coma, I entered into another dimension with her as I sat at her feet. I saw Jesus place a veil of light over her, while Mother Mary and Mary Magdalene washed her feet, preparing her body for burial. A ripple of golden light formed an infinity symbol between us, linking my heart to hers. It was as if she'd been placed by God into the center of her own eternal flame, her soul slowly pulling away from all human attachments and rising out of the clutches of her ravenous disease. From that moment on, her essence was illuminated. This exquisite, mind-blowing touch of God left me incapable, in that moment, of feeling loss. It was as if my personal grief had gone through a car wash, and all I remembered was a consciousness of no separation between the visible world and the invisible, unknown dimensions— the past, the present, the future were all one seamless garment. As a therapist, I could have labeled this denial. As a mystic, I called it communion with Mystery.

A week later, death greeted me at the door like a hungry panther, checking the pulse of life in the environment and ready to pounce at exactly the right moment. I knew that my friend had been given "there's no hope" news that week. Even as her health was failing, as the good mom, she was determined to attend her son's wedding, which was just a few weeks away. She had purchased a chic champagne-colored beaded lace dress and hung it on the closet door, directly facing her bed. When her doctor told her that she was physically too weak to travel, her will to live collapsed. Death could now accomplish its mission.

On that evening, my spirit guides were clear that my role with her was only to be a witness and that I was not to allow the suffocating breath of death to seep into my pores. Anyone observing me would have thought I was a poster child for the serenity prayer. They couldn't see the apprehension that scurried through my veins like mice looking for a way out. My reliable friend, the Wind of the Spirit, graciously stepped in, making it possible for me to surrender: "Thy will be done, not mine."

Jesus stepped forth from the shadows of the room, dazzling in prismatic robes shifting into Death, moving forward, imposing in elegant, sumptuous black velvet. The union of Jesus and death approached her, not at all bothered by the sweaty sheets and smell of decay. I wept to observe how my friend had withered away, barely a whisper of flesh and bone, not unlike the emaciated women I wept over in Mexico. He placed his hand in hers, and, just as the dew drenches the grass, my friend began to glisten in Love. Days later she would be lying under a dense carpet of exquisite red, white, and pink roses, sprinkled with lilies and baby's breath. She danced out of life at dawn, lifted to the light by the song of chirping sparrows. With the morning breeze, she was carried swiftly to her home, free from life's limitations, into the endless bounty of God.

At the conclusion of her funeral service, I walked down the church aisle in stocking feet, singing, at her husband's request, *I'll be loving you always . . . not for just an hour, not for just a day, not for just a year, but always.* Always.

Needless to say, being a companion to my friend awakened a calling to be a midwife, or an angel with death, on behalf of the Divine Mother. I was comfortable in both the world of earthly form and Spirit, and what greater blessing than to be the hand that helped return the Soul back to its Source. For me, it's a time when the notes of our song play its unique melody of gratitude in having had the experience of life. In retrospect, I'd had an almost addictive attachment to the ecstatic high of shamanic ritual—something I don't regret. However, during those precious hours with my friend—in mystical stillness—I came to know the weaving of the Divine in and throughout ordinary life. In the process of my friend living and dying, somehow her humanity and her spirit co-created each other into new life, and Mystery sustained it all. And as if I'd been hit over the head with a two-by-four, I also realized that the method of prayer is not the issue—what matters is union with God.

I mourned the loss of my friend and wept copious tears for all the years I'd been dead to life. In the end, we were both unbound, each returning to the home we needed to be in. Thank you, my friend. I know that you are shimmering in the night sky—and I love you to the stars and back.

CHAPTER 24

Journey to Crete

When water and stone meet,
you hear the song of the Mother.
When earth and stone rest in each other,
you hear the story of the universe.

—ANNETTE HULEFELD

Not long after the death of my friend, I began having unusual dreams of pythons dangling from ancient trees and undulating cobras. In one of the dreams, I am sitting on the edge of a pool filled with brilliant turquoise water. A voice in the dream tells me that the pool is a sacred place of ancient memory, a place of evolutionary consciousness that is free of distortions and lies. A hooded cobra arises from the water and gazes into my eyes with such intensity that I sense my eyeballs are being punctured. Suddenly, the cobra lunges toward my left eye, creating a tight seal around my eye with its mouth. Apparently, the way I was perceiving life was due for another layer of initiation.

Very soon after the dream, a woman I consulted with about integrating psychology with spirituality and ancient traditions invited me to join a retreat in Crete, land of the snake goddess. Although I was intellectually intrigued by cultures that honored the power of the feminine and celebrated women as healers, diviners, dancers, and dreamers, I wasn't particularly drawn to snake goddess work, nor was I overly enthused about traveling with five women I didn't know, who were devoted to these traditions—just a bit too sensuous and earthy for me. However, the leader was both solid as a rock and softer than a cream puff; a woman who drew out my intuitive, goddess essence with tender compassion. Had I known how my body issues were about to be exposed during the trip, I may have prayed to let the damn cobra eat me, and skipped the retreat altogether!

Traveling to Crete was not pleasant. Our overnight accommodations in Heathrow, England, were in an obnoxious-smelling motel. I wondered if the greenish mold clinging to the walls and floorboards was going to produce murals in my lungs and suffocate me during the night. However, the mold was easier to deal with than the jealous feelings I had toward the other women in the group. It's embarrassing to admit that I wanted nothing to do with them because they were all young, thin, and beautiful, and they talked incessantly about flowing clothes, practicing yoga, and the rapture of eating organic vegetables.

I held back tears as I recalled the years when I took pride in being fashionable and looking younger than my years. Back then I was pencil-thin, bedazzled with brightly colored dresses and wore long dangling earrings I created myself. Now I used Clairol to color my fading roots, and I never bothered with makeup. The bags under my eyes were far smaller than my saddlebag thighs, floppy belly, and sagging derriere. Amidst these elegant women in Crete, shame numbed me to the core, as it was right in my face that my glamour days were gone with the wind. This was conspicuously apparent in my low couture wardrobe: baggy checkered cotton pants, coral-colored tops from J. C. Penney, socks with images of cows, frogs, and bunnies, and a white eyelet half-hat that had a bow in the back for the Kewpie doll effect.

During the course of the trip, the women were engrossed with shopping, drinking wine, and—far beyond my comfort level—commenting on how they maintained their Vogue figures. Thank goodness my inner dialogue wasn't posted on Twitter—it was nasty. *How unspiritual, how materialistic to be so self-centered, when we ought to be sharing about the nothingness of God or the rapture of mystical bliss.*

I can laugh now at my arrogance, but at the time I felt isolated and humiliated to be a woman in a fat body. On the other hand, I was equally ashamed of my snobbery and disdain for the beauty of the Divine in their female forms. It was one of those times when I felt like a puckered plum plopped alongside sweet juicy peaches.

I had little frame of reference to include myself in their conversations about the trials of watching their weight and eating only organic food. I certainly could empathize with their struggles for equality as ordained women within their religious traditions. I refrained from sharing the depth of my wound in not being allowed to be a priest within the Catholic Church. As for sharing my personal reflections on what it meant to follow the way of the shaman, I choked. In the midst of their intellectual conversations, how was I going to share about retrieving people's spirits, or tell them about seeing and talking with the dead? I felt so ill-suited for this group and yet trusted my inner urge to be with them.

It also didn't help that my attitude toward food was less than enthusiastic. Unlike these svelte young women, I was not into recipes for vegetables in exquisite olive oil or sweet strawberries covered in chocolate. The kind of food I really enjoyed wasn't the healthiest; it was fattening. And while I made deliberate attempts to eat vegetables and salads without complaining, I never lost weight. I became convinced that my metabolism was that of an ancient sea turtle, and I surrendered to being roly-poly. All my adult life, I dreamed of being able to take a pill that contained all the nutrients I needed to survive, so I'd never have to shop, cook, or eat.

I mentioned this idea to one of my therapists who, with raised eyebrows, emphatically stated that I had an eating disorder that had to be addressed immediately. While I understood why someone would come to that conclusion, I knew the real disorder was that I was not able to absorb the goodness of life, the holiness of the feminine and of Mother Earth according to other's expectations. I could immerse myself in writing stories and poems, run with the wind, fly with the angels, or cover a canvas with lush paints and brilliant colors. This certainly helped me deal with the consequences of having an overly sensitive, allergic body. Living mystically was far more satisfying for me than lathering up my body with scented lotions and body creams. In reality, neither one is better than the other. Unfortunately, I came to the conclusion that I was a dysfunctional misfit because my experiences with life and Spirit were a bit unusual.

Our sleeping quarters in Crete were sparsely decorated, yet spacious and comfortable, run by a charming, good-looking man who was a gourmet cook. We lounged on a veranda that overlooked lush green mountainous valleys and ate our organic food. It was certainly a shift from the vast barren red earth of Africa, and dinners of fried potatoes with sickeningly sweet soda pop.

A few days into the trip, the Divine Mother found a way to bring the real me out of hiding. Over breakfast, several of the women mentioned they were hearing weird sounds at night, including rattling doorknobs, as if someone were attempting to enter their room. Though I had previously kept it a secret, I told the group about the disembodied spirit who was visiting me nightly. The owner then confessed that a mentally disturbed man had recently committed suicide nearby. I offered to do a simple ritual to release the soul of this distressed man, and the ritual immediately put a halt to the ghostly antics. Although the group teased me about my "ghost-busting" gifts, I gained credibility in their eyes.

A favorite outing for our group was sunbathing on the beaches that ran for miles along the pristine turquoise water, the same color as in my cobra dream. I have to admit, my enthusiasm was tepid when I heard that nudity was the proper etiquette. Not being a graduate of charm school, I chose to be the rare body on the beach wearing a bathing suit. Had my mother been on this beach, she would have raised a ruckus over this indecency, spewing about "immoral floozies" all "destined to burn in hell." It made me smile to imagine the chaos she would have started. What I loved about the beach was the wildness of the wind that picked up the sand and hit us like a sandblasting machine. The other women in the group tried to protect themselves by wrapping their naked bodies in towels and continuing to valiantly write in their goddess-decorated journals or read trendy novels. I sat on the edge of the water, drenched in sand pebbles, finding the whole scene hilarious. In fact, a lifeguard came up to me and said I was disturbing the peace with my laughter.

The highlight of our retreat was to visit the Cave of the 99 Holy Fathers, located just about a mile from the villa where we were staying. We walked to the cave, unbothered by the steep, slick pavement, dumbfounded by glorious panoramic mountain vistas. Along the way, goats pranced and roosters crowed like princes, entertaining the chickens and bunnies cooped up in the neighboring yards. The heat of the day made my legs operate in low gear, so I was content to lag behind the group most of the way, engrossed in the splendor of the environment.

When our leader found the opening to the cave, she warned us that the half-mile descent into the cave could trigger some personal fears. It was easy to understand her warning as we climbed down narrow decrepit iron stairs and held onto a railing encrusted with pigeon poop. At the bottom of the stairs, we began a further descent on a treacherous stone path that was covered with unexpected slime and oozy wetness. Although we had cavers' lights on our foreheads, it was hard to see the sudden dips between the stones. No one thought it was funny when I began to hum "Just a closer walk with thee." We fumbled when the humidity turned our glasses into white fog, or when the person in front of us suddenly disappeared around a corner. Due to my age, I was the designated caboose for the snake line of "goddesses." Having the backpack of the person in front of me to fall on was a bit comforting, although I don't think the feeling was mutual.

Our destination was a small open space that resembled the womb of a mother. I quivered when one of the women informed us that she heard there'd been an earthquake in the area just prior to our arrival. Criminy. Death is one thing, but the idea of possibly suffocating under tons of earth and rock was not on my bucket list. We entered the chilly space timidly, our nostrils filling up with that moist fragrance of rainwater that is in the air after a storm. We lit tea candles, and then we noticed a crumbling icon of Mother and Child on a stone shelf, along with burned out candles from previous travelers and several small pieces of crystal. As we sang to the Ancient Mother and called to our ancestors, I felt the downy wing of a bird vibrate against my cheek and sensed the gentlest of fingers wiping my sweaty brow. This was not the powerful, full-bodied Mother in Africa.

Once the candles were extinguished, we plunged into a darkness of noth-ingness that defies description. Maybe this is what it is like to go blind. I even wondered if this was another form of death or if was even *actual* death—a pure dissolution of the body into immortality—like a sugar cube in boiling water. I had absolutely no trepidation as I surrendered to swimming in this blissful sea of infinite Love. There was no separation between my skin and the stone I was leaning against, leaving me to marvel if the mountain's stones were also liquefying into waves of energy. My body, the earth, and the Divine were all one essence. I was stardust, I was rock, I was earth, I was me.

I could hear the sound of "Silent Night, Holy Night" ringing in my ears, as if the Divine Mother were rocking me with her voice. Within God's hug, the clammy coldness of the earth on my bottom couldn't diminish the peace I snuggled into in that moment. I might have ecstatically spun my existence out to the Great Beyond had it not been for the nervous laughter of some of the women who were uncomfortable sitting in the darkness. I asked the group if we could remain for just a few more minutes. And then, I became aware of Grandma Helen's presence. She was an image of splendor, dressed in blue stars and wearing her hallmark tiara. Her smile was as innocent as I remembered it and her message to me was simple: *Thank you for lifting the curse of mental illness that plagued seven generations of women in our family.* I desperately tried to restrain my tears, but, like the time I met the Kontomble in the cave in Africa, I was overcome with Love, and a river of gratitude flowed down my cheeks. It was a rare moment: I sensed the importance of my life's journey and felt that I had not failed in my mission. This was confirmed when I saw, in my mind's eye, the spirit of an opalescent bird enter my body, radiating sparkles of energy throughout. Her name was Windsong and she stunned me into a silent stupor.

The Divine Feminine was alive in me, was me—and was also the Universe that held me in her essence. I was given one wing for the unseen worlds and one wing for the earth, all connected in my body.

I've often been told that there is no real time in an altered state. How long I was with Grandma or in a state of bliss is anyone's guess. I was startled to hear the leader's voice announce we were going to leave. We turned on our headlamps, the brightness of which was a shock to my system. I had a flashback of stumbling out of the cave in Africa, delirious with awe. Climbing out the cave in Crete was rather effortless, except for one time—when someone had to push my derriere up through a narrow passage. When we emerged into the light of day, I still looked like a frumpy old lady, but my spirit was young and renewed, pulsing with the energy of a liberated exotic bird.

While I had powerful visionary experiences at the ancient ruins of several sites in Crete, it was a small roadside chapel that completed the final missing piece of my quest: to remember myself as a woman of grace. While the rest of the group went sunbathing au naturel again, I walked around the small village and was drawn to the entrance of a tiny whitewashed chapel. A perfectly formed egg-shaped white stone rested on a cement slab to the right of the door. I picked up the stone, entranced by its smooth-as-polished-alabaster exterior. Tears bubbled over my sunglasses as I held the stone, cradling it as if it were an abandoned baby. Although it weighed well over ten pounds, it was lighter than a chicken wing as it rested in my arms. I chuckled, imagining what my companions would think if I told them I'd found a lost stone that whispered to me, *Take me home.*

I am not a person who removes objects from sacred sites, as it feels like an irreverent and selfish thing to do. And yet, like a mother reunited to a child she had given up for adoption, I could not let go of this rock. I swaddled it in my newly purchased sweatshirt and placed it in my backpack. Later, returning on the tour bus, I felt ridiculous sitting bent over my heavy package. The next morning, the rock made it clear to me that its home was near the Cave of the 99 Holy Fathers. I was very relieved. How in the world could I have explained this stone to a customs inspector at the airport? I told the owner of the villa of my intention to go back to the cave, and he assured me that, if I weren't back within a few hours, he'd come searching for me.

As I huffed and puffed up the steep incline of the road, I panicked that I'd lose my way or keel over. The noonday sun was hot enough to fry an egg on the pavement or to transform my rock into a baked potato. I looked up suddenly to see the Blessed Mother dancing in front of me. Oh my! I'd met the Mother before, so I had no doubt about the reality of her appearance. She seemed to be levitating, supported by shimmering snake patterns that were moving, showing me the direction that I needed to go. After checking to see that I was alone, I joined in her dance. It still tickles me to picture myself, an aging cookie-dough shaped woman, dancing on hot gravel, with something in my backpack bobbing against my butt. This was a far cry from the ethereal encounter with the delicate white butterflies that flitted around my head at the Temple of the Sun in Mexico!

Upon reaching the top of the mountain, I could not find the entrance to the cave. I followed some frisky goats, thinking they'd help me, but after a while I just felt like a child, running around in circles. I'd forgotten that the spirit of Wind always comes to me when I sit in stillness, and this time she sent a yellow butterfly fluttering near the brim of my straw hat. I followed the gentle creature as it fluttered in circles over a small bridge that stood between the path to the cave and an-

I imagined being a woodland fairy, flitting over the glittery drops of water bouncing against the leaves, listening to the whispers and rustlings of Mother Earth.

other trail that led to the village. There, in the middle of the stone bridge, was a perfect womb-shaped natural space, a micro replica of the space where we had prayed in the cave. As my heart trembled, I carefully restored the stone, this wonder of nature, to its rightful mother. It belonged neither outside of a church nor deep within the darkness of the Cave. It belonged in the open air, nestled in the memory of the mountain. Oh my gosh: I was the stone! The Divine in me found me and was now restoring me to my true nature and authentic mission in life. The bridge was the Mother, my body, like Windsong, reuniting me as the messenger for the consciousness of how we are both divine and human—in this life. Like the stone, I carried that memory, and it was not to be part of the traditional Church—it was to be embodied in the universal Mystery. Speechless, my wobbly knees bent in adoration.

I started back to the villa, taking my time to enjoy the pastoral landscape. One particular area caught my attention. It probably was someone's private sanctuary, partially hidden, near the side of the road. As I peeked through the overgrown bushes, I saw a secret garden, lush with bright-pink blossoming trees that encircled a tiny sparkling waterfall. The tranquil pond below it was brimful with magical stones of all shapes that made my imagination go wild. I created fascinating stories—it was more fun than reading the clouds.

As I entered this fairy-like island, a dilapidated, dusty blue pickup truck slowly rumbled by, leaving an ever-so-faint covering of dust over my face and clothing. In the back of the truck was an ordinary gray donkey, with large perky ears. God only knows how or why our eyes intertwined, just for a second. We recognized each other as fellow beasts of burden. I felt giddy: like this gray work ass—unburdened, getting a ride—my ass body could no longer bear the weight of the oppressive stories and memories I'd been carrying. I wanted to jump onto that pickup truck and slobber the donkey with kisses of gratitude, and tell her to run away—to retire from carrying everyone else's crap. Stop the ponderousness and kick up your heels!

Just then, the truck driver gunned the engine. Startled, I tripped over a boulder and slid on my rear down a slope that dipped me in and out of patches of wet mud. My ass landed in an enchanted mini-forest. As I slowly got back up and secured my feet on the grass, I drank in the wonder of this magical clearing—the sun-kissed flower petals, the twittering of itsy-bitsy birds. I imagined being a woodland fairy, flitting over the glittery drops of water bouncing against the leaves, listening to the whispers and rustlings of Mother Earth. I was fascinated as I "listened" to the story flowing from the crevices of a boulder that had the appearance of an ancient woman's face. This rock had fallen from the mountain, perhaps shaken free by storms or by rumblings deep below the surface. She said, *I hear the vibrations of essence, the rhythms of Life. What emanates from me is from the beginning of time. When water and stone meet, you hear the song of the Mother. When earth and stone rest in each other, you hear the story of the Universe.*

I walked a few steps forward to stand up to my ankles in the chilly stream. I poured my life's story out into the ripples circling around me, surrendering my pain, watching it sink and dissolve into the water. I heard the song of the Earth Mother, and I lifted my voice, joining hers, dedicating myself to riding the wind of her love. I accepted that She and I live from the same cosmic memory, that I am an element of her Soul, that we live her story within our bodies. Now, like the shy child who was consumed with God, who talked to the trees and worms and dirt, my body could rest in the beauty, in the perfect Soul of the Divine Mother, and be restored to my rightful place within the Cosmos. Had there been buckets of paint nearby, I would have painted fabulous rainbows in the sky as the sun bathed my rosy cheeks and chubby arms with happiness.

CHAPTER 25

Laughter as Healer

What is laughter?
It is God waking up!...
It is the sun poking its sweet head out
From behind a cloud
You have been carrying too long
Veiling your eyes and heart.
It is Light breaking ground for a great Structure
That is your Real body—called Truth.

—HAFIZ

Not all my encounters with the Spirit were intensely serious. Some were funny, and some were far-fetched—the kind that "proper" folk don't talk about or admit to. I've always known that Spirit played along with me. I'd find myself saying yes to situations that then took a surprising turn. Often enough, they woke me up to the shadow side of my quest for wholeness. The incredible situations usually succeeded in uprooting beliefs that were hiding deep within me and not quite ready for exposure. I wanted enlightenment to be a cascade of sparkling water, but it usually turned out to be an avalanche of falling rocks.

Once I went along with a group of women I had mentored in shamanic practices to attend a conference presented by a group of visiting Peruvian shamans. I loved these women, as all of us were spiritually disciplined and irreverent—we had no trouble laughing at our own idiosyncrasies when it came to spirituality. The conference appealed to us because we were devoted to earth-based spirituality and devoted to *Pachamama*, the Peruvian name for the Great Mother. We piled into a friend's white SUV packed with food, soft drinks, drums, sage, and crystals.

Upon arriving at the conference, we first walked through a dried-up field checking out the different workshop offerings. We decided to participate in a healing circle for the release of ancestral burdens. We gathered in an open tent, where a group of male shamans were lively engaging in their native tongue. Before we knew it, a translator whisked us aside and told us that the shamans were telling us to disrobe. Everything, including earrings and rings, was to come off. *You've got to be kidding me. Stand stark naked in front of everyone?* I almost blurted out an obscenity but chose to pray to Holy Mother Mary. Then I thought, what if stripping to the buff was *the* answer to ending my migraine headaches and undiagnosed pains? And a crazy idea calmed me: *So what if strangers gawked at my pudgy dimpled butt? If I take off my glasses, no one will be able to see me!*

I agreed to this humiliation and set my mind to not passing out. An elderly, weathered shaman appeared at my side, screaming incantations and rubbing uncooked eggs up and down my body. Some of the eggs broke, spurting gooey blobs even down to my toes. I knew this meant trouble. The band of healers gathered behind a table to confer with one another. One of them was holding his head and screeching, looking back at me and rolling his eyes. "Well," I thought, "he must be in touch with my migraines, or my mother is after him."

The shamans returned to the circle. One of them doused me, head to foot, with ice-cold vodka. Another lit a torch and held it inches from my body. *Sweet Jesus, my day to become Joan of Arc was here!* My spontaneous reaction didn't measure up to the protocols in spiritual handbooks—I started peeing like a racehorse, then a booming fart escaped, and I broke out in gut-crushing laughter, squealing like a piglet caught in a fence. My dear friends, standing behind me, added to the drama with their hysterical snorts and giggles.

Heaven only knows how I managed to put my clothes on after that. I was drunk with the sillies, and I couldn't cork it back up and behave like an adult. None of us could. To top it off, I was told I had to wear a woolen cap—the kind that has earflaps—for five days, even though it was ninety-five degrees in the shade. I was also given strict orders not to tell anyone, including my clients, why I was wearing it. I told Frank, taking the risk that the healing would still be effective if I revealed it to an evolved being.

My laughter at the Peruvian healing ceremony was not mockery. I recall what the medicine woman told me many years before: humor shifts negative and distorted thinking by breaking the ego's stranglehold on our emotions. When this disruption occurs, the Spirit slips in and takes charge. I recall how outraged I was when she told me I'd been gifted with the kind of humor that erupts at the most inappropriate time. "I already feel like a lunatic, and my self-esteem is in the toilet. And you're telling me this is a spiritually ordained gift?"

After the Peruvian ceremony, I understood the gift. It was time for me to laugh at myself. I finally saw the extremes to which I was willing to go in order to get relief from the layers of pain I lived with. Somehow being torched that day released me from my addictive, at times groveling, relationship with God, yearning to feel good and be good enough. The obsessive seeking for answers evaporated like the vodka fumes. Very honestly, I thought of Ma and her possessiveness: she probably had found a way to ward off the pig sacrifice in Africa; but if the naked body and vodka fire ritual hadn't sent her flying into the ethers forever, nothing would. I'm grateful that in that ritual, my insanity lost its battle in a sea of the sillies.

After this unusual encounter with Spirit and myself, I returned to my doctoral studies, which were an extraordinary experience. The immersion into world religions and mystical traditions was the perfect antidote to help me transition out of my involvement in shamanic practices and to pursue my love of learning. An unforeseen surprise was meeting a fellow student in the doctoral program, who introduced me to an exquisite, evolutionary, and Divine Feminine approach to mysticism and dreams for our modern times. The angels entrusted her with a body of information about universal sacred principles—energies we are contracted with—that serve as a divine blueprint for our human mission. I was enthralled with the spiritual teachings of this colleague, soaking up the new concepts as if my life depended on it—and it did! I am grateful for a significant shift in my attitude in terms of understanding mysticism that resulted from the information about these sacred principles.

Prior to my studies, I was one of Rumi's followers—one of those "woo-woo" mystics who became intoxicated with his words, a spirit who'd surrender all of her life to have that one drop of Oneness with the Lover. One day during class, however, I became so nauseated reading my favorite poem about the chickpea and the cook that I wanted to vomit. This poem was, for me, a classical approach to the disembodied asceticism required to lead an exemplary mystical life. The story relates how a simple chickpea tries to escape the boiling water it has been immersed in. It reaches the rim of the pot, clinging for its life, waiting for its moment to jump to freedom. But the cook comes along, whacks it, plunging it back into the water for further cooking. It wasn't perfect enough. For years I had embraced all the religious and spiritual teachings that focused on the purification of our lowly, sinful, imperfect human condition in order to be in divine union. I believed that holiness and salvation were based on suffering—and the more the better. My journey has been an intentional whittling away of these falsehoods. That day, as we read the poem in class, I began to cry, shaking with anger. But then, I felt the presence of a spirit, gently tapping me on my forehead, saying, *Enough Annette. You are Beloved. There is no need to be cooked to perfection for anyone, including God.* I sobbed louder, trying to explain to the other students why I was having a spiritual meltdown, but some were a bit scandalized by my words. They stared in disbelief: *How dare you disagree with the guru, with the mystical, poetical genius.*

The issue for me wasn't about the rightness or wrongness of the poet's words. I was faced with an old dilemma: What was it going to take to believe that I am already worthy, that the Divine is my essence? Could I trust the blueprint I was contracted with, a sacred imprint that didn't have any contingencies in fine print? "You'll be cooked when we tell you, honey. Do this correctly or, under penalty of law, you'll never see Home again." I was way overdue in setting aside the expectations of perfectionism in order to be a true mystic. Through the depth of my colleague's teachings, I could settle into a new framework and move forward.

Finally, I had a perspective whereby I could accept that the highs and lows of my life experiences weren't necessarily due to personal/psychological failure or resistance to wanting to be alive. No, every encounter, every experience, every illness not only awakened another *good enough* seed of consciousness within me, but also unfolded another layer of universal principles and mysteries that the Divine and I agreed to co-create with in this lifetime. In essence, the experiences themselves were not the focus—they were merely the Divine yeast in the dough of my existence. Each experience lifted another layer of grief of perceived separation from God in being human; each encounter brought me closer to realizing the Divine Feminine was not only the mystical Mother but also a reality within me.

In ancient times, becoming a mystic was based on stringent practices that were not necessarily embodied or integrated into everyday life. The body was viewed as the enemy and something to be cleansed through mortification practices. In our time, living a mystical life involves a total immersion into the wildness and the softness of life. I often think of it as being thrown into a giant evolutionary blender where our foibles, our failures, our negative thoughts are detoxified. This may be similar to being a chickpea in boiling water, but for me there is a radical difference: it's about embodiment and messiness. As embodied divinity, we are not cooked to be perfect or to be made worthy. This is not about boiling ourselves into blobs of godly mush—it's about cooking away the debris that prevents us from *being* the human messenger to deliver the divine soup into the world.

In my own process, the cooking pot is my body, and the boiling water is life and community. It is the feminine consciousness, the divine life force that has been cooking me for years! The only whack on the head is to be reminded that it's impossible to live outside of this Divine energy and each day is an intentional choice to be engaged in and with life.

CHAPTER 26

Farewell, Ma — Rest in Peace

In the Eye of the Mother, all darkness clears
In the eye of the Mother, all light draws near

—ANNETTE HULEFELD

People often asked what happened to my ex-husband and what happened between Ma and me after my marriage to Frank. I was always hesitant to share how uneasy I was around my ex when we had gatherings for the grandchildren's events. For the sake of family, I was cordial, and I stayed close to Frank's side. My ex had a good relationship with our sons, and I'd protected them from the darkness I'd experienced. Unfortunately, his life was cut short, the year of his retirement at age 62. No one knows for sure the cause of his death, and he was not found in his apartment until five days later.

While I don't often feel creeped out by things, the fact that my ex died on Frank's birthday rattled my cage, to say the least. I decided to assist my sons in preparing a religious service for their dad in the church we had worshipped at for many years. The evening before the service was Halloween, and our grandchildren were sleeping with us that evening. Around midnight, the oldest grandson, who is quite intuitive, leaned over and said to me, "Gwanbunny—Gwampa is standing by the bed, and he wants to tell you something." I looked up to see his spirit staring at me and, in that instant, felt a ball of hot energy blast through my stomach. I had no doubt my ex was still in the physical realm, and his message was one of anger for my decision to divorce. I told my grandson "thank you" and spent the next hour praying to release the negative energy I'd been hit with. I'd always sensed how devastated he was by my rejection, although he never comprehended the power of his dismissive and domineering behavior.

My connections with Ma during the years of my spiritual pilgrimages were sparse. At first, when people asked me about her, my response was a blank stare, chagrined to admit that I had very little contact with Ma. I only returned to my hometown to celebrate major events or to help during serious health challenges. I tried to please her by sending meaningful gifts for Mother's Day and Christmas. She always—and I mean always—responded that it wasn't the right color or the right size, or it "was cheap." I recalled the time I'd purchased a 24-carat gold charm for her necklace, engraved with the word Mom on it, and a small diamond in the center. When I saw her wearing it, I remarked that I was glad she liked her present. "Well, I keep my best jewelry in a safe and only wear the cheap stuff. If someone steals it, it won't be such a loss." I decided that I'd made a wise decision in not sharing my spiritual jewels with her—that way, the preciousness would remain intact. Somehow this particular rejection confirmed that, for all practical purposes, Ma and I both shared a similar destiny: motherless children with empty nests.

Ma's later years were a mixture of enduring the intense pain of arthritis and the erosion of her mind, which deteriorated into Alzheimer's. It was as if she had stored her destructive childhood memories in a sheltered area of her mind, and then one day the stagnation couldn't willfully be sustained any longer. I'd witnessed many occasions when Ma's behavior could have been interpreted as cruel and insensitive, and yet, her remarks and corrosive actions masked the underbelly of her wounded childhood. I recall, with compassion, the time my younger brother and I returned to our hometown for an early Christmas celebration. We figured that Ma needed help with her Christmas decorations—and it was her favorite holiday. Ma's bone-on-bone arthritic knees and her excess weight made it impossible for her to navigate the dangerously narrow attic stairs of her home to bring down dozens of boxes of decorations and the thirty-five-year-old artificial tree. Our offers to help were met with "You both are too stupid and clumsy to do anything." At the time, I was sixty-one years old, working on a doctorate, and my brother was forty-nine and owned his own technology company. Ever the comedian, he broke into song, using the refrain from Handel's Messiah: "Stupid, stupid, Hallelujah, Hallelujah!" He conducted the invisible orchestra, howling with laughter. Ma was really upset and accused us of making fun of her, to which my brother replied, "You are so right, and we are your offspring. Hallelujah!" My brother's laughter was infectious, and it was the only weapon that ever diffused Ma's critical disposition. In spite of herself, she cracked a smile: "Okay, smart-ass. Quit being so dumb and get going—and don't break anything or I'll have your hide."

My younger brother and I were irreverent for sure, and, during times like this, we wondered why in hell we reverted to such infantile behavior, even as we approached our senior years. He and I would sneak up to the attic together, doubling over as we remembered Ma's reaction to our unseemly behavior at the dining room table following midnight Mass: chuckling, belching, and "breaking wind" (Ma's circumlocution for farting). When we were kids, it was considered the most heinous of crimes, and, as often as we could, we'd muster enough wind to be sent to jail—sitting on the toilet until we learned to control our rear-ends better. As adults, Ma would simply excuse us from the table, muttering her disdain at having brought up such uncouth human beings. Dad would chuckle with glee at Ma's upset, not even attempting to hide his delight.

On the occasion of this particular Christmas holiday, after my brother arrived safely at the bottom of the attic stairs with the ornaments, Ma gave her permission for us to enter into the *holy of holies*. This was the name we gave to the front room, the parlor. The door to this room was kept locked, its key residing in the mounds of Ma's bosom. Being invited into the parlor was an honor granted only to *worthy* people: the local seminarians, the pastor of the church, doctors from the local hospital and their wives, the saintly nuns—and now us.

Neither as children nor as adults was our family allowed to sit on the furniture unless we were dressed in our Sunday best. When Ma wasn't within earshot, we'd say a prayer of thanksgiving that we were unworthy wretches, because the antique furniture was agonizingly uncomfortable. The cushions looked like velvet but felt like prickly horsehair with burrs. The back of the couch was adorned with lion heads and pointed wooden paws. If you forgot and leaned back, your body shouted "attention!" and you'd immediately shoot straight up. Furthermore, we were not allowed to chew gum or eat M&M's while sitting in the parlor. Ma feared that some drool might slip past our lips and drip onto the rug or upholstery. She was an immaculate housekeeper, and she prided herself on keeping her special museum spotless—minus dust, minus any evidence of human contamination.

In spite of these restrictions, that day my brother and I proceeded to slowly walk in front of Ma into her sanctuary, bringing one of the kitchen chairs for her to sit on. She sat perfectly poised, barking orders, as we placed all 350 of her handmade fake-jeweled ornaments on the shabby artificial tree. Any suggested placements contrary to hers were met with "over my dead body," with my brother and I winking in agreement. Strange as it may seem, I still get melancholic about this decrepit tree. My brother and I referred to it as "Saggy Boobs." Its branches were so overburdened with the glitz and gaudiness—all to impress the neighbors or, more likely, to keep the spark of magic alive in Ma's soul.

As I placed the ornaments to her specifications, my attention soon shifted from the decorations and her critical comments to her appearance. Ma took great pride in how she looked, even if she were just picking up the newspaper from the back porch or getting the mail from the box on the front lawn. She never missed her weekly hair appointment, and with hairnet and spray, she managed to control any straying locks of hair. Ma's skin was flawless, like her mother's, so the only makeup she needed and wore was bright-red lipstick—which matched the red painted trim of her kitchen cabinets. Ma usually dressed in matching skirts and sweaters during the day—unless it was cleaning day, meaning that she would wear clothes suited for the ragbag. But not so on this day. Ma's classy sweater was replaced with a paint-stained threadbare housecoat, with buttons missing down the front. Her hair, unlike her mother's silvery-white curls, was uncombed, exposing various shades of red and blonde hair dye above her gray roots. Until that day, I didn't know Ma suffered from Bell's palsy. Depending on the angle from which you were looking at her, one side of her face seemed to go up while the other side remained at half-mast. She managed not to smile, which helped mask her condition.

I felt a twinge of pity as I watched Ma hobble to the front porch, which was only a few feet away from the tree. She wanted to sort through her collection of Santa Claus figurines and music boxes, all of which she was proud that she'd bought at half price. It was obvious Ma was in agony from the pain in her knees, so I offered to get the Santas from the wooden chest and place them in her lap where she could unwrap each piece at her leisure. Her pointed red-polished fingernail shot out straightaway, settling on the edge of my wrist, arresting my well-intentioned offer: "I know you will break every goddamn thing I own. I'll do this myself. Get out of here." I did, trembling from the fierceness of the terror I'd seen in her eyes.

Ma gingerly unwrapped each Santa from their tissue paper, held each one to her heart as if it were a baby, and turned on its music box. When all of them were playing at the same time, nearly seventy of them, she became entranced by the dissonance, smiling as if taken up into a rapturous vision. *You better not shout, you better not cry, you better not pout, I'm telling you why: Santa Claus is coming to town.* I gasped for air, my stomach turning, trying to hide the whimpering sounds that arose in my throat. I was staring at the shell of a hopeful child for whom magic was still believing in a jolly old man who would make her dreams come true, who'd make sure no more lumps of coal were placed in her stocking.

Wrapped in the entrancement of Santa, Ma didn't realize I'd left the porch. I found my brother in the kitchen and begged him to take me for a drive through the winding back roads near our town. I hoped the change of scenery would ease the jitters rattling every nerve in my body. Leaning back on the seat of the car, I shared with my brother that I thought I'd become immune to Ma's fierceness; I even took for granted her seemingly impenetrable resistance to showing any vulnerability. Yet, in that moment of Santa and the wounded child, I recognized how safe, how sacred her possessions were to her: they were trustworthy; they wouldn't hurt her or disagree with her; and they wouldn't abandon her. Preventing her "dumb kids" from breaking her favorite things was just another way of keeping bad things from happening—of perma-sealing the grief of an endless black hole of loneliness and buried insanity.

Once upon a time, *I* was her wind-up Santa toy, someone to whom she wanted to sing the song of her lost dreams, a child to heal her robbed childhood. When I left home, Ma couldn't believe she'd raised a daughter who was so disloyal and ungrateful. Good-enough daughters stay close by and do what their mothers desire. The shock on the porch was admitting that it was one thing to laugh about Ma's outrageous behavior, but a totally different arrow to the heart to witness the rawness of her torment—the exposed grief of an abandoned motherless child. All I could pray was *O my God, Santa, whoever you are, wherever you are, I believe in you, come to her, love her, and, for God's sake, keep our hands steady so nothing gets dropped.* I wept again, knowing that Ma wasn't fundamentally insensitive or cruel; she was a lost little girl, trying to create a life in the midst of the ruins of broken dreams and promises.

A watershed event occurred eight years prior to Ma's death. On a bitterly cold snowy morning, my older brother and I were to take her to the hospital for knee replacement surgery. Promptly at five a.m., my grumpy brother turned into a gentle butler, patiently walking in front of Ma, placing rubber mats under her feet so she wouldn't fall on the sheer ice. Ever so slowly, she inched toward her white Cadillac, idling in the driveway. She repeatedly complained of a "bad feeling" she had about this surgery: "Something awful is going to happen today. I just know it." My older brother brushed aside Ma's fears, convinced this was just one of her many "Chicken little, the sky is falling" pessimistic moments. As they wheeled her into surgery, she angrily said to me that something was "not right," and the waves of swirling panic in her eyes convinced me she was having a premonition. And she let me know how old and ugly I looked with white hair. The surgeon grinned and said, "Well, have a nice day." I winked back at the doctor, faintly amused.

In terms of Ma's physical health, the surgery was 100 percent successful, but her foreboding about "something going wrong" quickly became reality. The cocktail of the anesthesia combined with the pain medications were enough to unleash the beast that had been growing like English ivy in the nooks and crannies of her mind for years—Alzheimer's. The terror that Ma managed to keep at bay through art, music, volunteer work, and service to her family ripped through her mind, free to roam and eat her alive. The progression of the disease reminded me of the invasive root system of the fir trees on Ma's front lawn. Unbeknownst to us, they eventually cracked the basement wall and destroyed part of the foundation of her home. No one realized that Ma's increasing rage and erratic behavior was one of the languages of this deadly disease.

After a short stay in a rehabilitation center, Ma was transferred to a nursing home that Pa had arranged to get her into. It won several awards for being one of the best facilities in the state. Ma didn't care; she demanded to be taken home. It soon became clear the staff also didn't want her there. During one of my visits, her doctor requested a conference to discuss Ma's treatment plan. He was at a loss for words and obviously dismayed about how to handle Ma. He stated that she was the most troublesome patient they'd had in thirty-five years. Nurses and hired help had turned in their resignations, unable to handle her steamroller criticism, incessant arguing, and fighting. I still get a chuckle when I remember the doctor telling me, "You don't understand how awful your mother is. She insults people all the time and calls them a horse's ass. And she flings her food tray against the wall."

I intervened with the staff, asking them to replace the carrots, mashed potatoes, and lobster—which she hated—with her comfort foods: thick-sliced bologna, grilled cheese sandwiches, and chocolate milk. Their response was they were regulated by law to provide her with a balanced diet. "Oh, for God's sake," I replied, "she hasn't had a balanced diet since she was born. I'll sign whatever papers you need to make her happy." I also agreed to do an in-service training for the staff, free of charge, on how to use humor when sparring with Ma. It worked, and several aides came back to work.

Whether it was the medication, God's grace, or Pa's death, Ma's demeanor softened a bit as her loss of memory increased. For the most part, she spent her days sitting on the edge of the bed, clutching a plush stuffed bird I gave her, and sometimes saying the rosary. At night she slept with two hairbrushes under her pillow and her purse wrapped around her wrist, protecting the sapphire bracelet Pa had given her. Sometimes she'd strip naked and play peek-a-boo using the bed sheets. Other times, Ma would take her long, wispy white hair and pull it over her face; then she would giggle or suddenly pose like a statue, pulling her hair over her eyes, as if closing the curtains on her life—and then weep. The most distressing times were when she screamed, "I have to go home. Take me home. I have to go home! Why won't you take me home?"

As obnoxious as Ma was, it was unsettling to observe how rapidly her life had been annihilated. The only comfort came in realizing that she'd remember, then forget, then remember, then forget. When this pattern happened with insignificant matters, it was amusing. For example, she loved chocolate-covered nuts, and, without pausing, she'd eat one nut after the other until all were gone. A moment later, she'd reach in the empty bag for another nut and shout indignantly, "What goddamn fool just ate my chocolates?"

During the last year of her life, Ma no longer recognized me. She would whisper hoarsely, "You are really nice, but don't tell my daughter. She would be *really* mad." The nurses were baffled that such comments didn't upset me. Actually, I was relieved to observe how the Alzheimer's set Ma free from the sludge of traumatic memories that imprisoned her for most of her life. So much diminishment proved to be a divine mercy in the end.

On one visit, I had stopped first at the nurses' station to thank them for their patience and for taking good care of Ma. They needed encouragement, and my reminders—to let go of trying to make her behave and to lighten things up with laughter—lifted their spirits. As we chatted about Ma, a piercing scream bounced off the dull ivory walls of the hallway. Even the drugged-up residents, drooling and slumped over in their wheelchairs, were startled out of their stupor, spontaneously joining in with a chorus of babbling words. I recognized Ma's voice and ran down the hall toward her room, holding my breath to avoid inhaling the vapors of industrial cleaners, fresh diarrhea, and rotting old people along the way.

When I entered her room, I found the nurses' aides doing everything possible to convince Ma she was not being poisoned or attacked. "Marie, calm down . . . you're being crazy again . . . you are scaring everyone on the unit." It was clear to me from Ma's outburst that she stepped into her time-travel machine and landed at the orphanage. She was once again a terrified abandoned five-year-old, fighting the nuns, refusing food, and demanding to go home. As panic seized her body, she began to shake, her eyes bugged out, then darted back and forth, giving her the appearance of a trapped animal. I wanted to reach out and touch her arm, but I hesitated. If Ma didn't remember me, then a touch from a "stranger" could intensify the vortex of agitation spinning inside her mind.

As I had done with Grandma, I hummed her favorite song, the "Ave Maria." Slowly, as she followed my voice, her heavily veined hands reached for my hand. "Ma, it's me, Annette." A transparency of Divine Love descended between us in that moment, slowly breathing us together. We locked eyes and, like watching scenes from a movie, I witnessed a review of the traumas of her life, culminating in a crystal-clear insight into the core of the distrust we had of each other: *I am not good enough, you are not good enough, we are not good enough for each other.*

I leaned toward Ma, ever so close, an action that, prior to this moment, always made my stomach churn due to past memories. All I could say was "Ma . . . Ma, I love you . . . Ma, I always have and always will." Her entire body trembled, my words rippling through every fold of flab on her frame. Peace washed over her milky, cataract-covered eyes, and a spark of light, similar to the Christmas star on her tree, peeped through. Like a child gulping for air after a long cry, and then collapsing from exhaustion, Ma slowly settled into her soft pillow, her flawless skin glowing softly. For a second, I thought she was dead, but not so. I heard the faintest whisper of her voice: "Thank you. I love you, too."

I could not remember the last time I'd heard *I love you* from Ma. I looked over my shoulder and saw some of the staff standing at the doorway of Ma's room, crying, holding each other arm-in-arm. They'd known my mother for years, even prior to her stay in the nursing facility. Both here and in other settings they'd been tongue-lashed by her many times, so what they witnessed must have seemed surreal. There were no words for any of us—we hugged and sobbed, grateful that Ma's light had turned on and been seen.

I returned later and sat at the foot of Ma's bed as she peacefully snored away. My mind drifted back to the astrological reading I'd found after Pa's death—how stunned I was, and how unglued I'd become after reading it. But reflecting in the silence, by Ma's side, a compassion washed over me—as if the breath of God were tenderly bathing me. Prior to this moment, I'd come to peace with Ma except for one thing: how to embrace the crippling torment of a young mother who interpreted an astrological reading as a death sentence for her daughter at the time of her birth. How tragic that my mother had accepted someone else's authority as truth and then let this be her roadmap in bringing me up. I thought of all the times I had succumbed to the same pattern—not knowing my own voice, and blind to its truth because of unconscious and unresolved wounds of the past. Given Ma's heritage, particularly her ruptured relationship with her mother, she made the sanest choice possible: to keep me under lock and key so I wouldn't end my life. That was the role of a good mother.

Soft, gentle tears warmed my face, and, as I took one last look at Ma before leaving that evening, an unusual memory surfaced as I stepped away from her bed. I recalled the time when Ma purchased an exotic bird as an anniversary gift to herself, right before her knee surgery. Her devotion to this bird equaled her devotion to saying a daily rosary. The first thing Ma did was to clip the bird's wings. "Now, now, it's time to get back in your cage where it's safe and no one will hurt you. Mummee is here." Twice a day, Ma unlocked the door of the elegant bamboo cage, wrapped her gnarled arthritic heavily ringed fingers around the bird's brightly feathered body, and nestled it against the irregular heartbeat of her bosom. She'd croon French lullabies to the bird and make up little ditties in sing-song style: *I love you, little baby. Come to Mummee and never go away. Never leave your Mummee. I won't ever let you go.* I had one of those OMG moments—that was Ma's image of my relationship with her. It all made sense. Ma's smothering possession was so repulsive to me, and yet, for her, she was determined to be different from all the "crazy women" in her family, determined to be the good-enough mother that kept her daughter—her sweet exotic bird—safe.

On April 14, 2010, Ma's worst fear became her reality—she died alone. I was told that a nurse came by after supper and found her tray of untouched food, Ma's little mouth open like a baby sparrow's, waiting to be fed. We were told that sometimes people with Alzheimer's forget how to breathe, and I assume that is what happened. She crossed the great divide and couldn't find her way back in. I decided to do a shamanic journey on her behalf shortly after her death, as my spirit could feel her restlessness in another realm. I saw her sitting on a park bench, dressed in my father's old woolen overcoat, her pink flannel nightgown showing below the hem. She looked so forlorn, a wailing abandoned child, with her thins arms tucked in between her legs. My spirit approached her, and I told her she was dead and offered to take her home to Pa. But she shouted I had no right to be alive if she was dead. I knew it was time to ask Mother Mary for assistance, and she didn't let me down. Mary appeared as an oval-shaped blue sphere, singing like an ancient crystal bowl. Her voice scooped Ma up into its vibration, and Ma became one with her. I sighed with relief, happy to be Ma's midwife into a dimension where finally she'd know her Mother loved her.

Just as I'd prepared my dad's funeral, so was it my task to create a loving farewell for Ma. While it was true that we lived in a small ghost town and that many of Ma's friends had passed on, the emptiness of the church at her funeral reflected how forsaken Ma's life had become. The social worker from the nursing home remarked how unfortunate it was that Ma had burned all her bridges, and people just gave up on her. I agreed how easy it was to see Ma only as a self-centered person who bullied others to get her way. There was no denying that Ma's fierce nature and cutting remarks left deep wounds on people, including her family. Very few people were aware of how her rudeness and her need to be right and for others to be wrong—*all the time*—was her way of asserting she was smart, decent, and good enough. Her crusty exterior protected her vulnerability and hid her wounds, and yet, on many levels, she was no different than most women: she wanted to be heard, she wanted to be loved, she wanted to be affirmed for her gifts and, most important, to be admired as the best mother ever.

. . . she wanted to be affirmed for her gifts and, most important, to be admired as the best mother ever.

I delivered a heartfelt eulogy that brought tears to my younger brother's eyes. I sang the "Ave Maria" in Ma's honor, relieved that, for once in my life, she wasn't there to criticize. My brothers teased me that they expected to see her rise up out of the coffin, yelling, "You're off key, stupid. Do that again." I couldn't help chuckling, thinking of the fifty-five years Ma had sung at every funeral and wedding in the church where we had her funeral. She was confident of her voice, demanding to be the only soloist in the church choir, blatantly scoffing that everyone else either sang off key or had the voice of a toad.

As I watched the cemetery attendants lower her casket in the plot right next to Dad's, and as we shoveled clumps of earth into the open grave, I felt my inner giggle demon rise up. I remembered Ma's last request of me—something I could not deliver. She asked that I find a stonecutter who would design a statue of the Blessed Mother for her grave. This statue was to contain a music box that played a recording of Ma singing the "Ave Maria." She wanted the music programmed to play every hour, even at night, so that everyone—the townspeople, visitors, even the deceased—would hear her voice. This sounds bizarre, but it was an ingenious idea, albeit eccentric, to have others remember that she was a woman with a voice. And, by God, she never believed she'd get the respect she deserved, so she'd mark her placement on the earth. As we left the cemetery, I smiled and apologized for failing her once again, knowing her divine consciousness would finally understand.

CHAPTER 27

Stroke

Grief and pain are the doors we enter to find truth.
To create the miracle.
To shift our perception.
Our path to peace and love.

—TOM ZUBA

By the ripe age of seventy-two, I'd reached a certain level of acceptance about the way my life had unfolded, and writing my story helped me put things in perspective. A new chapter, however, began in December of 2014 as I tried to hang a sparkly white nativity star in the window of our home, at the top of the stairs. The step stool was two floors down in the basement, so I decided to use a plastic child's chair to stand on. I double-checked the rollers to make sure it wouldn't move when I stood on it. What I hadn't counted on was having the spring-loaded curtain rod pop out of its socket as I accidentally leaned forward. Like a domino effect, the wheels of the chair unlocked, rolling out from under my feet. *Crap*, I thought as my teetering body was heading straight for the staircase. Double crap as the eerie ghost of Grandma Helen's face appeared—she died by falling down her front stairs. I lunged to my right to avoid the stairs, causing me to crash headfirst onto the hardwood floor. Thank goodness my eyeglasses spread eagled across my cheekbones instead of shattering. My arm wasn't so lucky—it snapped like a brittle twig.

I sustained a concussion, and my broken arm required surgery. Having shattered my other wrist a few years previously, I was prepared for the searing pain and the annoyances in getting my clothes on and other bathroom duties. For several weeks, black, green, and bluish blotches appeared on my face, arms, and hips, giving me the appearance of an abused woman. Medical personnel looked at Frank suspiciously as they asked about my safety. The purple goose egg on my forehead didn't help matters. What distressed me the most was that

I was completing the first draft of this book, and now the project would have to go on hold. I've prided myself on being a disciplined spiritual practitioner and a person who faces her emotional dragons every day. I didn't expect the barrage of emotional skeletons that seemed to dance around me after the fall, spewing the familiar, haunting taunts: *Consider this a sign to throw in the towel—the book is not important anyway. What makes you think you have anything to offer?*

In reply to these voices, my heart gently reminded me of my mission: *to share the story that the Divine lived in me, to evolve the family heritage, and to honor all women who believe they are crazy and do not belong because they have not embraced being mystics in everyday life.* The diametrical opposition of these mindsets gathered in intensity like the surf that indicates the coming of a colossal storm. I felt polarized in my ministerial and psychological work, constantly wondering, *I accept that my perspective is out of the ordinary, so where do I belong? Am I mentally ill and refuse to admit it?* I had no doubts about my place with Frank, but on every other level, I had to force myself to dampen, to bury my instinct: *Let me out of here—it's too damn hard to be human.* And, trust me, this was not something I shared with anyone. To the outside world, I was a perfect specimen of the normal creative good-enough woman.

Forty days after my fall, the perfect storm hit. I was at a clinic, doing physical therapy on my wrist. At 9:37 a.m., like a killer whale suddenly emerging from the ocean depths, a tsunami of nausea rocked my body. I've never had the words to describe what it felt like to be slammed into a sinkhole of devouring terror and to have my body dumped overboard, slumped against the wooden armchair I was seated in. My spirit slipped out from under my skin and swirled over my head, staring down at me in shock. My right arm lashed out like a bent windshield wiper, while I tried to scream out, *Don't let me die, don't let me die.* What spilled out of my mouth was unintelligible gibberish—as if I'd turned into a knocked-over can of mushy alphabet soup. My physical therapist's eyes suddenly riveted on me like a poised alligator, as she dialed 911. The whole left side of my body was dead weight, so it was a struggle for the medics to plop me onto the gurney. They asked me to repeat some ridiculous sentence, and I could not parrot it back correctly, sending my anxiety level higher than my blood pressure. Even though my vision was blurry and doubled, I sensed that many people in the clinic were gawking at me. I tried to stare back at them in a frantic attempt to attract their support, hoping they'd keep me alive—or at least, that they'd pray.

In the ambulance, a kind, good-looking medic kept reassuring me I'd get the help I needed. But I knew this wasn't going to be like a near death—an experience in which my body would be wrapped in bright Light, eager to step into euphoria. As the sirens blared, every cell in my body shuddered with panic. *Jesus, why can't anyone hear me swearing my brains out to you? No, no, no. Please God, I'm not done with this life yet. I have a book to write. Holy Mother of God, I cannot become a burden to Frank.* I had flashes of myself strapped in a wheelchair, with Frank weeping, while tenderly wiping the drool from my lopsided mouth. The worst terror was that my words never found a way out of my brain—they were pathetic guttural sounds thrashing against my skull.

It seemed longer, but it was probably only twenty minutes or so after my stroke, when I realized I was talking to the medic. Slowly, yes, and in simple phrases, but actually talking! Though I couldn't move my left leg, at least my whole left side felt as if bags of sand had been lifted off. The medic leaned over and with tears in his eyes said, "Honey, you're going to be all right—you are going to be all right. Keep praying and hold my hand. You're coming out of this." The smile on his face made my heart sing, and I promised I'd pray for him all the rest of my days for taking care of me.

The next morning, after completing a battery of tests, the cardiologist—accompanied by several curious medical school residents—came to my hospital room. He was visibly befuddled and just said, "You are a 'miracle lady.' People who suffer a stroke of this magnitude don't end up walking and talking, much less begging to go on a trip to Jerusalem in two weeks. You ought to be at the end of the corridor with the paralyzed folks." Although his bedside manner wouldn't win him any congeniality award for tact, I got the message and kept my tears at bay until everyone left the room. Apparently, I'd dodged one hell of a bullet and "thank you" seemed hopelessly inadequate.

I had no doubt that I was one those "lucky" ones, but I was naive about the physical and emotional impairments I'd struggle with—some of them for many months, and some for several more years. My ability to process information quickly and my reading comprehension were impaired—something I kept to myself. Furthermore, my memory was wrecked, and I couldn't remember the names of people closest to me and where I kept basic things in the house. What was especially debilitating was that now I had double vision, which caused me to develop mild anxiety attacks whenever I sang for church services. It was as if whole notes were strangling half notes on the music score, and I'd sing melodies that weren't on the page. In the past, I would have laughed about making up words, but now shame dripped over my head like a wet dishrag. I was now clumsy as hell, tripping over chairs, jabbing my fork into the table instead of into the salad bowl, and bumping into people. I was tempted to put a placard on my back: *No, I am not drunk. I see two of everything, and I can't tell if you are here or there.* I felt like a silent lunatic. Thank goodness for the eye specialist who assured me that my symptoms were the result of having a stroke and not caused by a brain tumor.

What also broadsided me was the insidiousness of a strange type of depression that oozed into my consciousness like dark molasses, almost snuffing out my ability to connect with people and life events. It didn't help when everyone said, "Wow, you look great! So glad you are doing so well." I wanted to be nasty and hiss out that I felt I was repelling down my old, crazy family mountainside—one minute, swinging with confidence that my godly spirit was guiding me, and the next moment, petrified I was being sucked into Ma's mental cesspool of *not good enough, insane woman.* I'd come to a point in my life that *maybe, maybe*—I could have some authorship over my life, some modicum of control. But this physical trauma returned me to a primal state of childhood, when I had no control of what happened to me with my mom.

There was a miracle, however, in the emerging awareness that all the mind muck was nothing more than the residue of polarizing conflicts that had built up into a bloody clot in my brain. Like a boil that bursts, all the infection got released, and this time my body once again said "enough" to me. Enough with the constant search for answers, enough with the wrestling of where I belonged on the earth, in community, in family, in my body. The stroke, like the lightning strike on the kitchen table when I was twelve, disengaged me from the final remnants of Ma's influence. I came to a profound understanding of the meaning of peace, not a peace without conflict but more of an attitude, a space from within me that allows for a "both/and" living. I could release the concepts of something being good or bad, something being either this way or that way—all of which are divisive and potentially destructive.

How this translated into daily life for me was an awareness of the flow of life versus the tension of life. I'd always recognized I was a "tough cookie," meaning I'd followed the hero's journey faithfully, determined to find the cause of my pain and never accept defeat. While this focus kept me alive, it also suppressed the consciousness of the Divine Feminine—a paradigm I was born to bring to birth. I have no doubt that whatever separates us from wholeness will destroy us in time. I, for one, am grateful my body and soul were a united front during this time, preparing me for my next spiritual adventure.

Six months prior to my stroke, I'd signed up for a trip to Jerusalem with a local church group, and my cardiologist cleared me to travel. I hoped that my occasional unsteadiness on my feet wouldn't be a burden to the group. I had visions of falling down on someone as we climbed down uneven steps in dark places, sending them reeling.

Every site we visited was memorable, but one in particular had a great impact on me. Our group debarked from the tour bus, and I found myself walking gingerly down a smooth but slanted stretch of the sidewalk. Without warning, a riptide of anguish washed over me like a freak cloudburst of rain. As I stumbled for a place to rest, I heard our tour guide say, "and this is where Jesus came to weep over Jerusalem." I stared out onto the city, frightened by the rapid pounding of my heart and a growing headache. Was I on the verge of another stroke, was I dehydrated, or was something more happening here?

A vision of Jesus appeared in the distance, and I heard him say he'd come to the earth to bring peace, not to establish a religion or dogma. He was broken-hearted over the divisiveness of religion and the ruptured relationship between humanity and God. And then, as if a shroud fell from my eyes, a realization of God's massive love in choosing to become human flooded my consciousness. *Dear Jesus*—it took my breath away.

Droplets of regret began to drip from my heart as I recalled how often I'd shouted to Jesus, *You must have been out of your mind to become one of us. What kind of a cuckoo bird willingly chooses to take on suffering, tragedies, illness, death, ridicule, and poverty?* Jesus didn't care about my neurotic machinations. Within seconds, I sensed him standing close to me, reminding me that—like him—I too was a particle, a flame of God, and that I'd said yes to being wrapped in skin and bones in this lifetime. I still didn't like it! I despised the pain of it. And yet, I had the same woozy *oh my, oh my* feeling as I had when the Kontomble touched my hand in the African cave.

Afterwards, I wondered what the group would think of me if they knew what I'd just encountered. Thankfully, when we returned to the tour bus, I had a seat to myself and no one questioned my need for a nap. When we arrived at the hotel later that evening, I excused myself from the group, saying I needed an evening to myself. As I settled into the perfectly ironed bed sheets and comfy plump pillows, I ached to have Frank with me. He was the only person I knew who could resonate with the depth of my experiences. He could listen to my bubbling emotions and just be present to the power of Spirit pulsing through my veins.

As I reflect on those hours alone, I see that I was in a spiritual intensive care unit. All my life, I'd wrestled with God, my spirit, with my mind obsessively protesting, Why did life have to be so difficult—so damn complicated? Why isn't God's love enough? What was I missing? I'd believed for many years what the gurus had told me, that misery is the result of thinking you are separated from God, not in union with God. Granted, so much of my pain was a yearning to be Home, but, as a mystic, I've never felt separated from the pure intelligence and the heart of the Divine. It's only when I've had to squeeze all of me into this less-than-perfect body, plugging into the rational-mind socket of our culture or the minefield of family craziness, that I felt like an alien in a foreign land. The cosmic joke was that I believed that life—what is seen and what is touched—was separate, different, and not as sacred as the unseen mysteries of the Divine. I created a battleground for the Soul of God to be victorious over the consciousness of lies I'd subscribed to instead of remembering that I was an open space for the Divine and my humanity to dance in.

I had this sudden urge to throw up, to beg forgiveness for resisting the Life of the Divine Mother within me. I'd managed to keep Her at arm's length, fearing Her touch—as I had Ma's. That evening, I forgave myself for not fully embodying the sacred Feminine—saying yes to Her as living in my own DNA and cellular memory. I'd done my best, given the beliefs I had to dismantle, given the family I was born into. It was a moment of insight in which I saw how I'd greatly underestimated the profound impact that trauma, mental illness, physical pain, and being un-mothered had on the human psyche.

Maybe this was one of the gifts of a stroke: accepting the truth that, like so many women whose voices are silenced, their bodies keep broadcasting their message.

A few days later, I was standing on the shore of the Sea of Galilee, steps away from the site where Jesus chose Peter to be the Rock of the Church. I loved the feel of the small, glistening wet pebbles under my tired feet, and almost cried as the breeze, soft as a feather, ruffled my silver-white hair. I closed my eyes as the blinding sunlight danced on the ripples in the water, falling into a silent reverie.

I was back in Jesus's time, walking with him on the seashore, happy beyond words to be with the man I so loved. Soon I began swallowing hard, choking back the tears: being at this site opened up an old wound, my lost dream—to be a Catholic priest. I accepted that I was an ordained woman by the fact that I experienced and lived from a mystical union with the Divine. My spirit knew that being Annette was enough—more than enough. The irony of all of this is that the dismissal of the feminine within the Church's foundation was exactly what I'd been doing to myself throughout my life—spirit yes, body no!

There on the shores of the Sea of Galilee, Jesus reminded me: the rules of the institution were irrelevant for my present life. My only path was to be the chalice of the Divine Feminine, to be the divine human I am. It was one of those moments when what I mentally knew became a visceral realization down to the marrow of my bones. I bowed to the sea in reverence.

The next day, we visited Mount Tabor, the site where the disciples Peter, James, and John witnessed the transfiguration of Jesus. On this particular morning, there were no clouds in the sky, no humidity to make us uncomfortable, and no crowds to interrupt our visit. As usual, I was straggling behind the group, not wanting to chitchat. I also felt lightheaded, attributing this to a residual symptom of the stroke. But then I had the oddest sensation as if warm sunlight were being poured into my body. And then I saw Jesus for the second time on the trip—this time more brilliant. He was an oval sphere of radiant Light, descending gently into my body, awakening my cells with unconditional Love. There was nothing dramatic or out of the ordinary—merely the memory of how body and Soul are one, held so tenderly in Divine Love and Peace. I was blessed as a living sacrament, an integrated sacred woman.

It was jarring to be within this sphere of ecstatic connection with the Divine and to pretend to be normal in interacting with the group who were gleefully sharing the photos they'd taken. On the one hand, I wanted to remain in a state of bliss with God, without the noise and incessant talking. And, for a split second, I have to admit I wanted to shout, *All of you—stop talking—God is in our midst—can't you feel it?* On the other hand, I'm glad I kept my mouth shut. *Get real, Annette—the Divine is in all aspects of the ordinary and the extraordinary. To be in communion with life is to remember that everything is connected.* When earth lives within the resonance of the Great Mystery, the outer and the inner are all related. Who was I to judge who was more blessed on Mount Tabor that morning? Joy has many faces, and all is from Source. For me, seeing Jesus was as normal and ordinary for me as my friends delighting in each other's company. What a wondrous revelation to be so at ease with moments of grace in the midst of chattiness and friendship.

Epilogue

I came home from the soaring
in which I lost myself
I was song, and the refrain which is God
is still soaring in my ears.
Now I am still and plain;
no more words.
To the others I was like the wind;
I made them shake.
I'd gone very far, as far as the angels,
And high where light thins into nothing.
But deep in the darkness is God.

—RAINER MARIA RILKE

I have flown the friendly skies with Jesus as my co-pilot, I have plummeted into the muck of my internal demons, and now I am home in the richness, the agony and ecstasy of life, my spirit no longer split apart from my body. And "deep in the darkness is God" is, for me, nothing more, nothing less, than the hidden treasure I never gave up trying to find: the Divine Feminine within human form. This concept of the Divine Feminine, the mystic, is not a separate tradition—it is a collective wisdom that has been suppressed and discarded by traditional religions, culture, and patriarchal institutions, held hostage within the memory of our bodies. Diving into the shadows of my life, into my body's history, has been the path to reclaim Her life and Voice from within me.

I deliberately chose to write my story primarily through a spiritual filter, solidly aware of the psychological underpinnings of my mental and medical issues. I spent years pursuing traditional psychotherapy, Western medical approaches, shamanism, and alternative Eastern healings. Some of these contributed to alleviating various symptoms, some aggravated the endless "why can't I be fixed" syndrome. Each offered their best, but an important missing piece only fell into place during graduate school when a Native American friend led me to another opening for making sense of my issues. My friend teased me unmercifully about my "uniqueness" (meaning, weirdness) and recommended that I have an astrological reading with "the most bizarre and brilliant man you'll ever meet. His reading will turn you upside down and make you land in your truth."

On the day of my appointment, as I walked through the wrought iron gate of his enormous Hollywood-style home, my stomach fluttered as if thousands of butterflies were flapping their wings against each other. He motioned me in and I followed him up an imposing, elegant wooden staircase. Once in his office space, we sat across from each other in silence, separated only by the disheveled stack of papers on his regal mahogany desk. He studied my astrological chart for several minutes, occasionally staring intensely at me with hawk eyes, then looking back down at the chart. He repeated this process several times before he spoke. "Well, honey, you are either fucking evolved or you are fucking nuts. I'm not sure yet." I burst out laughing so hard that I sprinted to the bathroom, but my bladder reached it before I did. I gingerly returned to my seat, careful not to jostle the several layers of toilet paper stuffed in my pants. Keeping a poker face, he then remarked in a monotone voice, "Well, from your reaction, you are definitely not fucking nuts. Okay—we can do business."

As my friend had predicted, he was an astrological wizard: "Get over trying to use your mind to understand the movement of the Universal Soul. Quit trying to get fixed—that is ridiculous. You are one 'rare bird,' and you have one task in this lifetime: Remember who your *real Mother* is, and bring *her* story into the world. Honey—this is not easy, but quit fighting it. You have to surrender and die into the life of the Divine Mother. She has sent you here."

Although I'd not said a word about my personal story, he informed me that all the challenges and obstacles I'd encountered—and would continue to have—were a microcosm of the planetary demise of the feminine. I was part of the healing of the schism between being a good-enough spirit and being a good-enough woman, and also part of a movement to awaken the voice of the sacred feminine. He admonished me more than once for wanting to exit this life due to the relentless pain in my head and body. Mind you, I had not mentioned a word about my inner torment about dying. "Your distress is personal and not personal. The Great Mother is groaning in pain, and she needs every midwife possible to bring her to birth. You are one of these women."

In retrospect, I find it fascinating that, at the time of this astrological reading, I had not yet discovered the astrological reading from my cousin when

I was born. From her perspective, the alignment of the stars on my birth chart meant I would most likely take my own life at an early age. This was the victim/survivor consciousness I was born into, an invisible energy field that resonated with themes of diminishment, not being good enough, being angry for having a body, and feeling insane for being informed and guided directly by the Divine and by Spirit guides.

This was the deck of cards Ma was given and she played her hand by relying on religious values that fortified the patriarchal paradigm: have fierce individuality, follow the rules of the Church, never admit your family has dirty laundry—and for God's sake, never, ever cry in front of anyone. Tears were acceptable only behind a closed bathroom or bedroom door, at night, with a rosary in your hands. But, ironically, Ma was also a rebel against tradition in her conviction that a woman is strong if she verbally dominates those who don't agree with her opinion. To give her credit, although her delivery often stung worse than a hornet, she rose above the silenced lambs of her victimized family, surviving by assuming the persona of a fierce, overprotective lioness.

This second astrology reading, received in my sixties, emphasized the imperative of liberating (yes) myself from the paralyzing and damaging energy fields I'd inherited. More than once I wanted to throw in the towel, overburdened with feelings of defeat. It seemed that no matter how often I switched the channels of my negative thinking to wavelengths of higher vibrations, I'd once again find myself scrambling out of another avalanche of misery. The astrologer's message confirmed that I was on an emotionally charged mental battlefield, caught between the narratives I'd created to survive and the divine blueprint of the Mother's agenda. Looking back on this, I am in awe that, unbeknownst to me, there was the presence of the Divine Feminine within me that cradled this polarizing tension, guiding and nourishing me until I was ready to remember and live the consciousness of being an integrated and embodied Divine Woman.

It is humbling to admit that shamanism satisfied the craving I had for extraordinary experiences with the Spirit. I wanted to be a priest, I wanted to be a priestess, I wanted to be a shaman, I wanted to be God's special woman. While working with the spirit world was second nature to me, I know there are many like me who are "ordinary" shamans—living through transformations and rebirths in our lives for the greater good of all. All I ever desired was to bring the unseen gifts into the world of this reality. The love and guidance I receive from the realms of the Spirit is not something to be described in words but to be experienced within unconditional love. And, despite all my "wants," the Divine Soul wanted a greater experience than just being a spirit. It desired the experience of being a complex, messy, cosmic, ordinary, empowered mystic—in the flesh. I was a great candidate for this task: I was head-over-heels in love with God and the Universe; I had a pudgy, imperfect body; I had a mind and body that baffled many a professional; I added unexpected, improper humor to sacred rituals; I prayed with the intensity of the stars; and I fell prey—all too often—to old patterns of body snobbery. I had always embodied an unusual mixture of spiritual and earthly tensions, and this was the only map I had to navigate the mystical waters I swam in.

In the past, admitting that the Divine needs our bodies, and all their functions, in order to experience life would have sounded arrogant or even heretical. Now it is comforting to realize that the human species and the Divine are in an active, evolving holy partnership. This is a form of mysticism I can embrace: one that affirms an intimate coexistence with God, with Life; one that affirms the wisdom of both the extraordinary and the ordinary as direct experiences with the Divine intelligence; one that simultaneously holds the tension between light and dark, trusting that transformation and renewal come from an energy between opposites. I can hold the tension between two realities: giggling with a child smearing chocolate pudding over a new outfit, and heart-sick over the wrenching stories of molested children and detained immigrants. I can fall on my knees over the rape of our Earth and the grief over senseless gun violence. On a personal level, Ma and I were opposites: she was right, I was wrong, or I was right, she was wrong. Ma's path was to rigidly shut down the tension, and mine was to hold it, albeit with trepidation and imperfection. After decades of this holding, a new energy emerged for me, an energy that opens up a space that allows me and you to dance between the worlds, allowing all situations to flow in and out like the breath of the Universe, connecting us to the Oneness of all.

As a child I heard the Song of the Universe—I literally heard the music of the flowers when I placed my ear next to their petals and heard the stories of the tree roots when I stood on them barefoot. The notes from this cosmic symphony penetrated my existence since birth—keeping me sane. Over the years, emotions and thoughts clogged up this direct connection, leaving layers of debris that needed cleaning out. Now, I sense I can rightfully claim my spiritual name, Windsong.

As I was completing this book, I woke up from a dream in which I was effortlessly riding on the back of a large, ordinary-looking white bird. Together we glided through layers of clouds until we arrived in a space I often see in the dreamtime. It was velvety dark and inviting, and only those with spirit eyes could enter. I stepped forward, without the bird, greeted by several friends who have died. They smiled tenderly at me, quickly disappearing into a soft silvery mist. From behind a magnificent tree that is formed by the breath of the darkness, an elegant, glowing young woman appeared. Her eyes were sparkles of blue light and she hummed a song that was reminiscent of how Mother Mary sang to me as a child. "Who are you?" I asked. She responded: "I am you—before illness." Suddenly, the white bird swooped in, lifted me way up before swiftly sinking back to the earth. My divinity returned to earth both within and all around me. In the dream I understood that the mission of Windsong is relatively simple: to remember that the Divine Feminine is not only the consciousness that *is* me but is also the presence that *carries* me. It is a love that calls forth both humanity and divinity to be partners in singing a new song for the earth.

· · · · ·

I am fully aware of the thread of grief that runs through my story. It began with an original wounding in childhood, and layers were added that perpetuated the pain—a pain that manifested itself in killer migraines and intense physical suffering. And yet, in the words of a dear, soul-sister friend, "Grief didn't annihilate you, and that is the message people need to hear. We can coexist with grief, and it's our choice whether we allow it to crush us or intuitively move us forward even when there are no clear signs." I am convinced that, without the divine impulse of my life force, I would not have made the choice. I have struggled, I have surrendered, I walked hand-in-hand with God. I've been forgiven for the terror I had of life, for judging my body as a curse, for accepting pain as the enemy.

The major blind spot I had was the strength of the misogynistic energy within me, an energy of anger and self-deprecation for not being a good-enough woman. I still have moments when I shudder at how tenaciously I wrestled with myself, my religion, the culture I live in just to survive and not be a victim of outdated paradigms. I tremble thinking of how this collective and personal predator-energy continues to entrap the feminine spirit, silencing the visionaries, the dreamers, and the creative, intuitive souls. For years, I denied how suppression of the feminine results in an aching heart, physical pain, and a dimmed spirit.

Perhaps many of you reading these words have flip-flopped through different pools of insanity and spiritual angst, have judged your bodies as a curse, or have looked to death as an escape. In sharing my story, I am hoping that those who suffer from mysterious illnesses that never get "fixed," or those who are ashamed of mystical and intuitive abilities, or hide the grief of their spiritual yearning, will find solace in my words. My path is but one of many, and my hope is to inspire you to awaken to your unique authenticity, supported in knowing you are not crazy and you are not alone in becoming your own brand of mystic. We all have a different story, yet we all have the collective similarity of unopened seeds waiting to crack open. As the thirteenth-century mystic Meister Eckhart says, "The seed of God is in us . . . Now the seed of a pear tree grows into a pear tree, a hazel seed into a hazel tree, and seed of God into God." How the divine nature manifests within our complex bodies will always be a Mystery, and yet, how awesome to open up and deliver the gift of who we are.

Because I am a dreamer, I hope that, in addition to diagnosing mental and physical illness with traditional/alternative methods, we consider the possibility that the Divine's yearning to be embodied can be a contributing factor in the angst of many spiritual individuals. Wouldn't it be a shift of consciousness if depression, anxiety, and bipolar disorders, along with physical pain, included the possibility that the person is uprooted from the Divine Feminine? I think we have forgotten that often what appears as a symptom of mental illness is actually a person's attempt to grasp a different consciousness than what she/he is living in.

Finally, I'd like to say that I am pain-free—but that isn't true. I am one of those sensitive individuals whose frequency demands a daily spiritual practice to transform and release whatever energies come my way, both internal and external. However, I am at peace with being who I am, a song with the wind, a song housed in my body. That is a gift beyond words. I admit I'm no longer driven by perfection and piety, not as ponderous as I used to be, although I'll always be the philosopher coming up with different perspectives. I have little fear when my bawdy, outrageous sides make their appearance at the most inappropriate moments. While not religious, I still participate in a wonderful faith community where my bereavement skills and musical talent can make a contribution. I'm also a young-at-heart old woman who loves to take vacations and play wild card games with my grandsons and family. I delight in looking for fairies and unicorns in the backyard with a precocious young girl who is a believer, and hanging out with incredibly creative teenagers who read fantasy books and go bonkers over Disney, and for whom dance is a passion.

Finally, if I needed proof that the Divine takes human form, I don't have to look further than the presence of Frank in my life. I never take for granted that, without his constant, unconditional loving support, this story would not have been written, would not have been possible. I've known him for close to forty years and have never heard an unkind word from him. Some people believe this is unhealthy or impossible—but the truth is, Frank is love incarnate. Victor Hugo, in *Les Miserables*, says, "To love another person is to see the face of God." This I know to be true with Frank. My love for him is rooted in the stars, and the Spirit planted us in the same earthly garden. We each bring unique gifts to those we serve, and, with each other, our song is one of love, kindness, and peace, with lots of laughter woven through! May we have many more years being together.

Afterword

By Frank Hulefeld

In a way, there is no need for me to tell you, who have read her book, about Annette. You've seen for yourself. But I am Annette's partner, and we love each other with all of our hearts. We have been married for thirty-seven years. So, as someone who has shared Annette's life so intimately, I'd like to tell you a few of the things that I treasure about her.

To start with, I seldom call her *Annette*. We have other names for each other, names that express our affection. She calls me *Bear*, and I call her *Bunny*. Frequently, when I speak to her, I call her *Beautiful Bunny* or *Beautiful Lady*—because I sense the truth about Annette. She is a wonderful person, and she has lived—and continues to live—a beautiful life.

The deepest truth about Annette is that she and the Divine are one. She didn't know this, of course, for a long time. So much of her life-circumstances taught her the opposite—which was the source of the poor self-image that she has had to struggle against all of her life. But, as her book shows, over the course of a perilous life journey, she came to understand the deep mystical union between herself and Spirit (God, Life, the Universe).

The astonishing vision to which she came is that we are all One. But—and this is one of the reasons that she wrote her book—life requires each of us to make the journey and find ourselves along the way. It is her hope that the story of her own journey might help others on the way to their own truth.

Annette certainly inspires me. I have always loved books like *The Lord of the Rings*, books about an ordinary person called to take on something heroic. Annette's life has been a different kind of hero's journey. It doesn't take place in a faraway land but in everyday life, and the dragons she faced are all too common: childhood abuse and poverty, serious illnesses, living with pain, an abusive marriage, a mental breakdown, losing her children, broken bones, hip replacements, high blood pressure, a stroke, and double vision—and other sufferings that she has chosen to omit from her book. The litany of her challenges would seem too much for one person to face. But the Life Force that is in Annette never gave up. To be sure, she faced that temptation, but her inner strength, her spirituality, and our relationship sustained her. She has lived—albeit, sometimes kicking and screaming—heroically.

You who have read her book know that Annette has lived life intensely. Yes, there have been extraordinary things in Annette's life, but most of what she has dealt with are the life tasks that we all face: finding our way, dealing with what life presents us, listening to our deepest self, living in partnership with Spirit, and—through all of this—becoming who we are and being a blessing to the world.

Annette continues to live a grace-filled life, a beautiful life. For example, she is able to draw on all she has faced and all that life has taught her to help people who come to her for counseling. She has the most amazing gift to be present to people, to listen to them from the depths of her being. She truly is with them in their troubles and sorrows, and celebrates their joys and victories with them. Annette does this even though she lives with constant pain. It amazes me how she can cope with it and yet be there for others.

When you meet Annette, you meet this divine goodness. The Spirit of God is so evident in her. She has a beautiful voice, and when she sings at church, the Spirit is singing in her. As I overheard one person say in amazement, she's bringing God to us!

I want to end by sharing what a loving heart Annette has. Our family, and others who are family to us, feel the depth of her love. And me? Late at night, before we fall asleep, Annette and I talk for a good while, sharing what is on our hearts, often holding hands. And the last thing we say is

"I love you, Beautiful Bunny."
"Oh Bear, I love you so."

Annette, you are the heart of my heart. How blessed I am that you are my companion in life. God willing, I will be your companion forever.

May those who read this book see your beauty and share in your goodness. May their lives be blessed by your presence, as mine has been.

You've fulfilled the dream that you've had since you were a young child—the dream of painting a rainbow in the sky for everyone to see the wonders of God.

You've done it, Beautiful Lady. Your life IS the rainbow! You live as a rainbow among us.

From the depth of my soul, I honor you.

Love you forever,
Your Bear

Acknowledgments

*If the only prayer you ever say in your entire life is
thank you, it will be enough.*

—MEISTER ECKHART

I offer my deepest prayer of thanks to the following:

To Frank: Without your tireless editing and good natured and loving encouragement, including healthy smoothies to shore up my aching body, this book would still be a bound dissertation project, gathering dust on the shelf. You understand this book is the work of my life. All I can say is I love you to the moon and back. And truly, you, too, are rooted in the stars!

To Aleksandra (Ola to me): You are not only a brilliant, insightful editor, but your enthusiastic, unwavering encouragement turned my doctoral thesis into a form I never dreamed was possible. Your expertise and support made the birthing of this "baby" a reality. Because of who you are, this process was both relatively painless and transformational, and thank you for holding my hand through the tedious parts! Your belief in my writing, and in the importance of bringing forth Divine Feminine consciousness, is priceless and deeply appreciated.

To Pat: You are my role model in becoming a "conscious crone," and a major inspiration for me to awaken and live from Divine Feminine consciousness. You are a living, spiritual art form, and I still get teary-eyed remembering the day the shut paint box from my childhood opened up in your art studio—a gesture that also opened up my love for writing. Your friendship and astute direction are treasures.

To Fred: Your blessing of my work, three weeks prior to your untimely death in July 2018, is forever imprinted in my heart. We had a mutual connection in our search for the Dark Madonna, and you were one of those humble, rare individuals with whom I shared raucous, deep belly humor alongside profound spiritual ceremonies and conversations. I miss you, Fred. I am grateful you breathed your spirit into the pages of this manuscript.

Acknowledgments

To everyone who read and offered feedback as this manuscript was in various stages of development: Pat, Chuck, Steve, Shay, Ruth, Carol, Marsha, Annie, Jenna, Myron, Connie, and Tom. I am overwhelmed by the generosity of your time, the depth of your responses, and stunning acknowledgments. And thank you to Natalie, for your behind-the-scenes support. The honor for me—and it is humbling—is that you have all seen the divine in me, named my gifts, and blessed my work. Each of you is a guide, friend, and reflecting mirror of ordinary holiness and mastery. You assisted me in bringing closure to the "not good enough" mentality that haunted me for years.

To the staff at Round Table Companies: I never imagined I'd be published by such an outstanding, skilled, compassionate, and authentic group. Every phone call and discussion offered wonderful options for change while respecting, always, what was important to me. Your collaborative style is remarkable!

To Bridget: You surrendered to the Spirit of the Feminine in interpreting my story through your stunning art. What flowed onto the canvas is nothing short of breath-taking. And how amazing that you named it "Rooted in the Stars"!

To my sons, John and Tom, their wives, Lenore and Dianna, and grandsons, Nick and Ben. I hope my story inspires you to always follow the path of your soulful heart, to live authentically, even if that means making difficult choices. You are incredibly important to me, and I'm deeply grateful that you've been there when I needed you. Thank you for celebrating my life and teasing me with love when I became so immersed in my writing that I forgot correct birthday dates! Love is the glue that has bonded us for sure, and, like with Frank, I love you to the moon and back!

To all my teachers, mentors, and healers: Male, female, Christian, Jew, shaman—you affirmed the mystic, the shaman, the ordinary in me. You opened windows to my Spirit that brought me far beyond the limitations of my past, and I have soared, I have crashed, and I now I live mystically alive in this human form.

Thank you to the members of my intentional faith community, SGFMC. Since Frank and I married, you've embraced us as part of your family. So many connections, so many interweavings in each other's lives—how blessed we are.

Thank you to Abby, Emma, and Sammie: Your love of life, dance, music, books, adventure, and so much more have reawakened joy in my life! You are to me what Disney is to you: pure magic, wonder, and endless possibility.

About the Author

Annette M. Hulefeld, DMin, LCSW, certified grief support specialist, has worked as a licensed clinical social worker and psychotherapist for over thirty-five years. She specializes in the treatment of depression and anxiety directly related to various forms of abuse, diminishment, and loss. She works with women, men, teens, and families.

After receiving her doctorate in ministry, she expanded her practice, working as a psycho-spiritual advisor, integrating psychological growth with native and mystical traditions, including intuitive tarot readings and dreamwork. Annette's background in shamanism and initiations into indigenous healing rituals allow her to adeptly travel between the seen and unseen worlds, weaving Spirit and ancestral wisdom into every facet of ordinary life.

Annette has presented at dozens of conferences and workshops for over thirty years on topics ranging from near-death experience, shamanism, and the sacred feminine to dealing with grief and end-of-life. She has led local drum circles and healing rituals in the US, Egypt, Peru, and France.

She has dedicated herself to nearly fifty years of volunteer service in music and bereavement ministries, as well as ten years as a pastoral minister in her faith community.

Annette loves to sing, create inspiring cards, hang out with her beloved Frank, play card games filled with side-splitting laughter with her awesome family, and travel on vacations with her grandsons. Her heart smiles when walking by the ocean on a windy day.

· · · · ·

www.annettehulefeld.com